NON-STATE THREATS AND FUTURE WARS

Editor

ROBERT J. BUNKER

FRANK CASS
LONDON • PORTLAND, OR

First published in 2003 in Great Britain by
FRANK CASS AND COMPANY LIMITED
Crown House, 47 Chase Side
Southgate, London N14 5BP

and in the United States of America by
FRANK CASS
c/o ISBS, 5824 N.E. Hassalo Street,
Portland, Oregon 97213-3644

Website: *www.frankcass.com*

British Library Cataloguing in Publication Data

Non-state threats and future wars
1.National security 2.Military policy 3.Subversive activities 4.Crime prevention 5.Terrorism – Prevention
I.Bunker, Robert J.
355′.03

ISBN 07146 5374 8 (cloth)
ISBN 07146 8308 6 (paper)

Library of Congress Cataloging-in-Publication Data

Non-state threats and future wars / editor, Robert J. Bunker.
p. cm.
"First appeared in a special issue … of Small wars & insurgencies ISSN 0959-2318) 13/2 (Summer 2002) published by Frank Cass" –Verso t.p.

Includes bibliographical references and index.
ISBN 0-7146-5374-8 – ISBN 0-7146-8308-6 (pbk.)
1. National security. 2. Non-governmental organizations 3. Military art and science – History – 20th century. 4. Military art and science – History – 21st century. 5. Terrorism – Prevention. 6. Subversive activities. 7. Crime prevention. 8. World politics – 1989-
I. Bunker, Robert J. II. Small wars & insurgencies.
UA10.5 .N65 2002
355′.033 – dc21 2002015229

This group of studies first appeared in a Special Issue on 'Non-State Threats and Future Wars' of *Small Wars & Insurgencies* (ISSN 0959-2318) 13/2 (Summer 2002) published by Frank Cass

Printed in Great Britain by
Anthony Rowe Ltd., Chippenham, Wiltshire

Contents

Preface:
New Context, Smart Enemies

PHIL WILLIAMS

The decade after the end of the Cold War and the collapse of the Soviet Union was marked by prosperity and optimism, especially in the United States. A contagious economic crisis in Asia was contained and United States hegemony was seen (in the United States at least) as providing the basis for a new peaceful and stable international order. Global governance mechanisms, underpinned by United States military and economic dominance, appeared to provide appropriate responses to new international challenges. The United States military worried about an emergent China and a resurgent Russia, but these were essentially long term challenges that did little to disturb the existing harmony. Terrorism and organized crime were regarded as nuisances, part of a new security agenda that was far less challenging and dangerous than the threat that had been posed by Soviet military power and ideological ambitions.

The optimism of the 1990s was based in many respects on illusion: the Clinton administration defined United States security largely in terms of maintaining prosperity. The impact of organized crime and corruption on states in transition was understood conceptually, but was largely ignored in the formulation and implementation of United States policy towards Russia while the challenge posed by Al-Qaeda and international terrorism more generally was treated as a sideshow requiring some attention but no sustained effort or resources. Yet the illusion continued in the first eight months of the Bush administration. While ballistic missile defense was elevated in importance, for the most part, continuity of assumption and policy was the order of the day. Asymmetrical threats were regarded as something to be concerned about but, implicitly at least, were deemed preferable to symmetrical threats.

These illusions were shattered on 11 September 2001. The Al-Qaeda attacks on the World Trade Center and the Pentagon were a prime example of asymmetrical warfare – 19 men, (albeit with support from a larger network) were able to cause the deaths of around 3,000 people as well as enormous economic and psychological damage. In effect, the attacks marked the end of a period of optimism and the beginning of a recognition that the world of the twenty-first century was not as readily amenable to

American power and influence as had been assumed.

Against that background, this work takes on particular importance. It reflects the fact that the world has changed fundamentally and that there is a new security environment populated by smart enemies. The United States can no longer take security for granted let alone reduce it to economic prosperity. Indeed, the challenge of this new century is one that transcends Al-Qaeda, even though the network, in spite of US military success in Afghanistan, is likely to remain for some time the most immediate and serious threat to United States national security. The challenge is to establish a degree of governance in a world of growing disorder. It is a formidable challenge, reflecting new complexities in global politics that call many of the existing assumptions into question, and demanding innovative and imaginative responses based on new organizational structures as well as new security mechanisms and instruments. Perhaps, most of all, it requires a sensitivity to enemies who make up for their lack of raw power in their capacity to fight smart – and sometimes to avoid fighting at all, preferring corruption and co-option to confrontation and conflict.

There are several characteristics of this new environment that need to be taken into account as policy-makers struggle to establish order out of disorder. These are not ephemeral or temporary characteristics, but emergent realities that first have to be understood and appreciated fully and then incorporated into a new framework for policy and strategy.

The first of the new realities is that international security has become much more complex than in the past. Attention can no longer be focused solely on states; it is also necessary to contend with a wide range of what James Rosenau termed 'sovereignty free' actors.[1] Many of these can not only mobilize considerable resources and exercise major influence on political and economic processes but also have what Thomas Schelling, in a different context, described as the power to hurt.[2] Rosenau has argued very persuasively that one of the key issues for the future of global politics is the interplay between the state-centric world (the traditional world of high policy, geopolitics) and the multi-centric world (the host of non-state or, using his term, sovereignty-free actors that increasingly loom large in international relations). This interplay is perhaps best exemplified in the notion of the Al-Qaeda network as an anti-hegemonic force – a role traditionally played by states. Al-Qaeda seeks to eliminate United States military and cultural presence from Saudi Arabia in particular and the Middle East more generally and has taken the lead in challenging an hegemonic power that it regards as malevolent rather than benevolent.

It is also necessary to bear in mind, however, that the notion of the state-centric versus the multi-centric system is not a simple dichotomy. Although alliances will vary from issue to issue, one very real possibility is that some states will defect from multilateral governance efforts. Rogue states that tacitly support terrorist networks are the most obvious defectors. As well as overt defection, there is also the problem of covert defection as some states cosmetically conform with international norms and standards (as in the effort, for example, to combat money laundering) or formally participate in multilateral initiatives but then do little or nothing in terms of implementation. If this complicates the response, it should not obscure the need to think beyond the box of inter-state relations. The difficulty is that governments, including the United States, have developed diplomatic and military systems and institutions that are based almost exclusively on the state-centric paradigm. Governments are prepared and equipped to deal with threats from other governments. They are familiar with a struggle of like versus like in which the actor with most resources comes out ahead.

The second new reality is that the old distinction between foreign and domestic is no longer simply under siege; it has broken down finally and irrevocably. States can no longer remain insulated from undesirable transnational forces whether it is Middle Eastern terrorists operating in the United States or Chinese criminal networks operating in Japan, challenging the traditional dominance of indigenous Yakuza organizations in Japan's criminal markets. Such developments require a comprehensive reappraisal of the old dichotomy between intelligence (foreign) and law enforcement (domestic) and a merging of skills and capabilities that have hitherto been kept separate.

The third reality is that states are not what they were – or at least are not what we thought they were. This does not mean that the Westphalian system is at an end; it does mean, however, that we can no longer think of states as we did through the twentieth century, when the problem was essentially one of power and ambition. The traditional focus on the balance of power cannot be jettisoned; great power rivalry and the dangers of large-scale military conflict are not going to go away. Yet they are only one of the threats that have to be faced – and are not as pervasive as in the past.

The real challenge is that the world has entered the era of the qualified state. The problem is not strong states flexing their military muscles, but weak states that are unable to maintain authority and legitimacy or make appropriate provision for their citizens; states that are unable to eliminate no-go zones in their territory and thereby become safe havens for transnational criminal or terrorist networks. Moreover, state-building is a far more difficult enterprise than is often assumed. In Bosnia, for example, the Dayton accords envisaged the emergence of a centralized state which would increase the resource base and pave for the way for the gradual integration of different ethnic communities.

What has happened in fact is that the separatist national parties working in close cooperation with organized crime have obtained control over criminal markets as well as of corruption and rent-seeking opportunities, using these to enrich themselves at the expense of the over-arching state apparatus. The state, in effect, has been ripped off and organized crime has become a spoiler not only in a peacekeeping contingency but also in the state-building endeavor. Important as these cases are, the problems are not confined to weak states. Even modern efficient, legitimate, democratic states can be described as sovereignty-challenged in the sense that they cannot control who or what crosses their borders. Most states in the world are unwitting transshipment states for illegal, regulated, or stolen products on their way to the national markets in which they have the highest return.

The fourth new reality is that the United States has to confront a new breed of smart enemies that are: network-based; transnational in scope; highly flexible and adaptable in their operations; learn from their mistakes; have an ability to both exploit and embed themselves in social and financial institutions in ways that are virtually undetectable; and possess a capacity for regeneration even when they have suffered considerable degradation.[3]

The network dimension is discussed fully and brilliantly in the foreword to this work by David Ronfeldt. Along with this, however, goes the fact that both terrorist and criminal networks are smart organizations. They possess a real capacity to reduce, manage and mitigate the risks they confront from enemy states. After the Medellin and Cali drug trafficking organizations were destroyed, for example, Colombian drug trafficking networks truncated their activities, passing cocaine to Mexican and Dominican groups for transshipment to the United States. Although this reduced the profits, it also reduced the risk of bringing the Colombians into direct contact with United States law enforcement agencies and being targeted by them, as the Medellin and Cali enterprises had been.

Even the loss of profit from wholesaling in United States markets was offset to some extent by expansion and diversification of markets in Western Europe and the former Soviet Union and by the diversification into heroin. Criminal enterprises and terrorist networks also have to be understood in terms of what Michael Kenney has described as 'learning organizations'.[4] Recognizing the capacity of criminal and terrorist networks to learn, to adapt, and to improve what they are doing whether it is targeting enemies or exploiting markets is the beginning of wisdom in combating them.

The fifth reality is that globalization – which was seen implicitly at least as the spread of liberal democratic values and free market – has a down side and a dark side. Although legitimate businesses have benefited from opportunities to exploit global markets, the major beneficiaries of globalization have been transnational criminal networks that use the global trade system to embed illegal products in legal commodity flows, the global financial system to move and hide their money, the global telecommunications system to transmit directives and messages, and the global transportation system to move people and products. In addition, both criminals and terrorist have used global diasporas and transnational ethnic networks as cover and recruitment for their activities. As a result, combating criminal and terrorist activity has become very difficult without impeding the rapid flows of money, goods, and services on which modern commerce and finance depends.

Globalization is also related to the sixth new reality that is shaping a very different security environment – the diffusion of technology and expertise from traditional great powers to other states and to sovereignty free actors. Moreover, this technological diffusion acts as a 'great equalizer' especially in relation to societies like the United States where sophistication has become a source of vulnerability. Perhaps nowhere is this diffusion more significant than in the area of computers and information technology. The United States has become so reliant on computer systems for the effective functioning of the economy and society that this has become a major vulnerability. United States infrastructure, for example, presents a tempting target set to terrorist organizations. Moreover, this is an area where – as Roger Molander and the other authors of a RAND study on information warfare published in the mid-1990s, pointed out – the entry costs for acquiring offensive capabilities are very modest.[5]

This is linked, of course, to the notion of asymmetric warfare in which enemies are able to exploit aspects of modern societies and economies that have traditionally been seen as strengths not vulnerabilities. On 11 September the terrorists did more than hijack planes – they turned part of the United States transportation system into an extremely effective weapon system. Similarly, whoever was responsible for the anthrax letters in the fall of 2001 transformed the United States mail delivery system into an efficient, cheap, and readily available weapons diffusion network.

The implications of all this are extremely sobering. The new security environment is far more formidable than the straightforward military threat to which the United States and its allies became so accustomed during the Cold War. If the United States, in particular, is to respond successfully to these new security challenges then it has to do three things.

The first is to meet Sun Tzu's very old imperative: to know the enemy. This requires far better intelligence than ever before. Much of this can be collected only through multilateral efforts – and United States intelligence agencies should collaborate much more fully with foreign agencies that can infiltrate Al-Qaeda and similar networks with greater ease and lower risk of detection than can United States intelligence personnel. Knowing the new enemy also requires extremely effective techniques for fusion of highly classified and open source material, traditional intelligence and law enforcement intelligence, foreign intelligence and domestic intelligence, and strategic warning and tactical indicators. Indeed, for the new challenges intelligence superiority is far more important than the weapons superiority which the United States so obviously enjoys but which, in so many ways, is meaningless.

Second, it is essential to adopt new ways of thinking that go well beyond the conventional wisdom. It is possible, for example, that a major nuclear weapon delivery system in the future will be an inter-modal container that is brought into a busy United States port as part of a legitimate shipment of goods. In the new security environment, container defense might be more important than ballistic missile defense – especially in relation to homeland security. Although such arguments have had little impact on an administration so fully committed to ballistic missile defense, in other areas there are positive signs.

Certainly the Bush administration, immediately after 11 September adopted the rhetoric of network warfare. Yet, even here it is not clear that in Afghanistan the United States military undertook serious network damage assessment, or began to anticipate the ways in which the Al-Qaeda network could adapt to the new security environment it now faces. For United States military planners, the challenge is to think in very different ways from wars in which industrial or technological superiority was the key to victory. Indeed, the United States has to confront enemies for whom traditional notions of victory and defeat mean very little so long as they can continue to inflict pain on America.

Finally, the United States needs to reassess the institutions and procedures through which national security policy is made and implemented. It is essential that it break down much of the institutional stove-piping that characterizes not only intelligence collection and analysis but also strategic and policy planning and task implementation. It is difficult to create new structures that are immediately effective. Yet it is important that institutional innovation be encouraged at all levels, that traditional bureaucratic distinctions and demarcations be overcome and that a premium be placed on the creation of smart institutions to combat smart enemies. Anything less is unlikely to succeed.

In other words, just as the United States faces a new strategic environment, it needs to develop new methods and procedures for responding to it. The enemy is flexible, nimble and innovative; government is laboriously slow, wedded to established methods and restricted by standard operational procedures. It needs to overcome these deficiencies if it is to meet the challenges that Robert J. Bunker and the galaxy of experts that he has assembled lay out so effectively in this volume. This book contributes significantly to an understanding of the new enemies and the new kinds of threats characteristic of a world in which disorder is no longer on the margins of global politics but a central feature of the global environment. For those with the responsibility for making and implementing national security policy, the analysis of the new threats provided by the editor and authors could hardly be more compelling The difficulty is in developing institutional responses that are appropriate to these new threats; the frightening thing is that failure to do so is likely to be so costly.

NOTES

1. On sovereignty free actors see James Rosenau, *Turbulence in World Politics* (Princeton UP, 1990).
2. Thomas C. Schelling, *Arms and Influence* (New Haven, CT: Yale UP 1967) is a brilliant exposition of how the 'power to hurt' can be used for bargaining purposes.
3. See the author's 'Transnational Criminal Networks' in Johan Arquilla and David Ronfeldt, (eds.) *Networks and Netwars* (Santa Monica, CA: RAND 2001) pp.61–98
4. Michael Kenney, 'When Criminals Outsmart the State: Understanding the Learning Capacity of Colombian Drug Trafficking Organizations', *Transnational Organized Crime* 5/1 (Spring 1999) pp.97–119.
5. This is one of the themes in Roger Molander et al., *Strategic Information Warfare* (Santa Monica, CA: RAND 1996).

Foreword: Netwar Observations

DAVID F. RONFELDT

It has been evident for years, thanks in part to thinkers like those writing in this work, that the nature of conflict is changing across the spectrum. Sadly, the terrorist attacks on New York and Washington, and thus on America, brought this home with a vengeance in September 2001, making this book more timely and significant than ever. The small-unit nature of those attackers, their innovative use of network forms of organization, strategy and tactics, and the mix of non-state (and possibly state) forces behind them are precisely what many contributors to this book have been writing and warning about for years.

Networked adversaries, not only the cutting-edge terrorists of Al-Qaeda and related groups, but also ethno-nationalist fighters in places like Chechnya and Sri Lanka, criminal enterprises in Colombia and Russia, and street gangs and anarchists from Los Angeles to London, draw strength from what they can accomplish across five levels of theory and practice:

- Organizational level – their networked organizational design;
- Doctrinal level – collaborative strategies and methods, like swarming;
- Technological level – in particular, their information systems;
- Social level – the personal ties that assure loyalty and trust;
- Narrative level – the story they tell, to themselves and to others.

The strength of such protagonists depends on their functioning well across all five levels. The strongest networks will be those in which the organizational design is sustained by a winning story and a well-defined doctrine, and all this is layered atop suitable communications systems and strong personal and social ties at the base. This applies as well to state actors who may have to organize their own, unusual networks, and hybrids of networks and hierarchies, in order to fight back resoundingly.

Each of these levels deserves more comment than I can provide here (for extended discussion, see the co-authored paper titled 'Networks, Netwars, and the Fight for the Future' posted at http://firstmonday.org/issues/issue6_10/index.html). What should be noted, nonetheless, is that analysts and practitioners, especially in the United States, tend to emphasize the technological level. But the other levels are equally important. Analyzing all five levels in skilled detail is necessary for providing 'net assessments' of networked adversaries, and of state capacities to respond and fight back. In particular, it is a step forward to find that an adversary is organized as a flat, relatively leaderless, non-hierarchical network, but it is only an initial step. Exactly what kind of network is it? Hub, multi-hub, all-channel, core/periphery, or what? And where are the bridges and holes that may connect to other actors? Such questions must be addressed, for each design has different strengths, weaknesses, and implications. Some may be more vulnerable to leadership or key-node targeting than others, though networks may be generally less vulnerable than hierarchies in this respect. Interesting ideas and observations have been circulating lately about how to disrupt, destabilize, and dismantle networks, but so far, much less is understood about how to analyze the capacity of networks for recovery and re-assembly, possibly into a different design.

The network appears to be the next major form of organization, long after tribes, hierarchies, and markets, to come into its own to redefine societies, and in so doing, the nature of conflict and cooperation. Power continues to migrate to non-state actors who can organize into sprawling multiorganizational networks more readily than can traditional, hierarchical, state actors. This implies that conflicts will be increasingly waged by 'networks', perhaps more than by 'hierarchies'. Thus, as John Arquilla and I have written elsewhere, most recently, in *Networks and Netwars: The Future of Terror, Crime, and Militancy* (RAND, 2001), U.S. policymakers and strategists who deal with information-age conflict should heed three overarching propositions.

1. *Hierarchies have a difficult time fighting networks.* There are examples of this across the conflict spectrum. Note in particular the difficulties that many governments have in trying to defeat transnationally networked criminal organizations engaged in drug smuggling, as in Colombia. But this deep dynamic is not all to the bad. For example, in the early 1990s the Zapatista movement in Mexico, with its legions of supporters and sympathizers among local and transnational NGOs, all of them quite well networked and determined to use swarming strategies, put a democratizing autocracy on the defensive and helped pressure it to continue adopting political reforms.

2. *It takes networks to fight networks.* Governments that want to improve their own defensive and offensive capabilities may have to adopt organizational designs and strategies like those of their adversaries. This does not mean mirroring the adversary, but rather learning to draw on the same design principles that he has already learned about the rise of network forms in the information age. To some extent, this means adopting ever

more advanced information systems. But emphasizing technology will not, by itself, produce optimal results; even more important is a willingness to innovate organizationally and doctrinally, notably by building new mechanisms for interagency, inter-service, multi-jurisdictional, and transnational cooperation.

Of course, it is not necessary or even feasible for governments to replace their hierarchies with networks. The challenge is to blend these two forms effectively, creating hybrids that allow governments to retain central authority and accountability while also fielding newly effective networks for intelligence-gathering, information-sharing, and operational agility to pursue information-age threats and challenges, whether generated by terrorists, ethnonationalists, militias, criminals, anarchists, strategic hackers, or other actors.

3. *Whoever masters the network form first and best gains advantages.* In these early decades of the information age, non-state adversaries who are advanced at networking and swarming – be they criminals, terrorists, or militant social anarchists – are enjoying an increase in their power relative to state agencies. Networking and swarming enable them to compete better with states and other centrally organized actors. The histories of Al-Qaeda, Hamas and the Cali cartel illustrate this, as, on the bright side, does the International Campaign to Ban Landmines.

Most people might hope for the emergence of a new form of organization to be led by 'good guys' who do 'the right thing' and grow stronger because of it. But history does not support this contention. The cutting edge in the early rise of a new form is just as often found among malcontents, ne'er-do-wells, and clever opportunists, all eager to take advantage of new ways to maneuver, exploit, and dominate. Many centuries ago, for example, the rise of hierarchical forms of organization, which displaced traditional, consultative, tribal forms, was initially attended, in parts of the world, by the rise of ferocious chieftains bent on military conquest, and of violent secret societies run according to rank. This was long before the hierarchical form matured through the institutionalization of states, empires, and professional administrative and bureaucratic systems. In like manner, the early spread of the market form, only a few centuries ago, was accompanied by a spawn of usurers, pirates, smugglers, and monopolists who sought to elude state controls over their earnings and enterprises.

Why should this pattern not be repeated in the emerging age of networks? There appears to be a subtle, dialectical interplay between the bright and dark sides in the rise of a new form of organization. The agencies of democratic governments may be so deeply embedded in and constrained by a society's established forms of organization that many have difficulty becoming the early innovators and adopters of a new form. In contrast, nimble, opportunistic, bad guys may have a freer, easier time acting as the cutting edge. Responding belatedly to them, with hindsight and aforethought, may be what finally ends up spurring the good guys to innovate. In the most difficult areas, crime and terrorism, steps to improve intra- and international networking are moving in the right direction. But far more remains to be done. The writers in this book know this, and are set to offer many insights for aiding the process.

Introduction and Strategic Overview: Epochal Change

ROBERT J. BUNKER

The intent behind this special book project was to bring together a world-class team of defense and national security scholars and real-world military and law enforcement operators to focus on the topic of 'Non-State Threats and Future Conflict and Wars'. Many of the contributors have been writing and speaking about this topic for years but have never had a chance to come together in one work and provide a united front concerning the growing threat non-state entities represent to the security interests of nation-states.

The project started in Summer 2001 and finished toward the end of February 2002. The tragic events of 11 September 2001 have left an indelible mark upon this issue and strengthened the conviction of the contributors as to its timely nature and the critical need that it fills. Our world forever changed halfway through the project and with that change the first of the new wars of the twenty-first century began. In retrospect, this project is both proactive and reactive in nature – we knew where the security environment was heading but thought (or hoped) the post-Cold War honeymoon period would last longer. The night before the attack, I spoke about this very topic with my friend and colleague, John Sullivan. We were to speak at a Jane's security conference in Salt Lake City, Utah, the next day. That following morning and ensuing days were a difficult period for all of us. I, for one, went into my conference session with two trade towers aflame and came out with both of them nothing more than fallen heaps of concrete and twisted metal entombing thousands. That memory will forever haunt me.

As these words are being written, the United States of America and her coalition nation-states have engaged the Al-Qaeda terrorist network and their criminal Taliban allies on Afghani soil.[1] Dislodging the Taliban from power proved to be far easier than expected.[2] In hindsight, it can be said that a weak nation-state, one which had long ago 'failed' and been captured by criminal-soldiers, is no match against a determined US and her allies. Defeating Al-Qaeda is, however, a different matter. This shadowy networked entity is transnational in character and operates in over 60 countries. While the loss of an allied Afghanistan is a blow to that network, it continues to function and appears, unfortunately, to flourish.

Al-Qaeda will be much studied by scholars for years to come. Initial perceptions suggest that this network is what we would term 'an early nation-state killer'. It could thus be viewed as a first-generation organization. Our concern should be somewhat less about the Al-Qaeda itself and more about its evolutionary spin-offs leading eventually to second- and even third-generation networked OPFOR (opposition forces) organizational forms. This moves us from the operational level of thinking into the strategic. Radical Islamic documents have shown that the end state desired by this network is the return of the Khilafat (Caliphate) and with it the establishment of a transnational radical Islamic order. For descendent forms of the Al-Qaeda to achieve that vision using chemical, biological, radiological or nuclear (CBRN) weapons of mass destruction (WMD)-based 'Martyrdom (Suicide) Operations' is a serious likelihood and therefore must be included in our future strategic planning.

It is best to place the events of 11 September, and the subject matter of this special issue, in broad strategic context. First, it is necessary to provide some background. My association with this emergent security environment dates back to 1987. While a doctoral student, an independent study on Strategic Theory I undertook with one of my professors, T. Lindsay Moore, lead to the creation of what is known as 'Fourth Epoch War' theory. This theory focuses on cyclical periods of non-state (criminal) soldier/mercenary ascendancy on the Western battlefield. These periods correlate with eras of dominant organizational-form (city- and feudal-state) breakdown.

Drawing upon my earlier research on Soviet linkages to terrorist and guerrilla groups, I immediately became concerned that history might once again be repeating itself. If this were the case, it would represent a direct threat to the future integrity of the United States. From the beginning, research concerning 'fourth epoch war' was thus meant eventually to be used in an applied manner by the US military; it was later that law enforcement applications also became evident. It was not until after the completion of my doctoral program that my publication of 'The Transition to Fourth Epoch War' in the *Marine Corps Gazette* (1994) marked the first public appearance of this theory.

Two figures will be provided to help place this special issue in context. While they may not be 'right' about the future security environment, they tend to be 'less wrong' than most figures. In the war against non-state entities, we do not need to strive for perfection – all we have to do is get the future less wrong than our opponents. The first figure concerns the 'not crime-not war' operational environment. It dates back to the mid-1990s, but was really drawn up for National Law Enforcement and Corrections Technology Center-West briefings only within the last few years. Basically, we are in an operational environment for which traditional nation-state military and police forces are ill-suited to function. This operational

FIGURE 1
BLURRING OF CRIME AND WAR

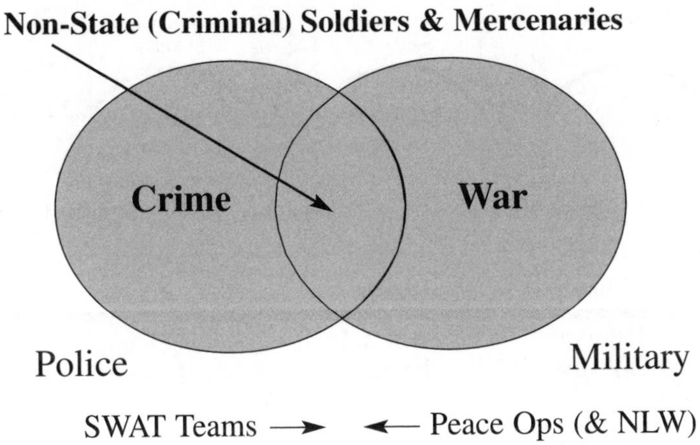

Non-State (Criminal) Soldiers & Mercenaries

Crime

War

Police

Military

SWAT Teams ⟶ ⟵ Peace Ops (& NLW)

Source: Courtesy of NLECTC-West ©

environment is expanding and the networked threats within it appear to be evolving at a rapid pace. It represents a literal playground for criminal-soldiers and mercenaries.

The second figure is that of the Fourth Epoch War historical model. It has been in existence since 1987. The only real change to this figure concerns non-lethal weapons (NLW) being listed during the post-modern epochal transition. Initially, directed energy weapons (DEW) were listed. These are basically the same weapons, however; NLW seem to be more inclusive so developments such as nanotechnology can be brought in. Just as the firearm and cannon revolutionized warfare during the last great epochal shift into the modern world, so will NLW revolutionize warfare into the post-modern world. Unfortunately, if historical patterns hold true (although our intent is for them not to), criminal-soldiers fighting for networked OPFORs are even more likely to use NLW against us than nation-states are to use them against the bad guys.

This strategic view of the emergent security environment based on the revolution in political and military affairs (RPMA) thus has a technological dimension, as does the revolution in military affairs (RMA). The difference is that the RMA is a historically inaccurate 'operational level' theory based on change equivalent to that which occurred in the 1920s/1930s. The US

FIGURE 2
EPOCHAL SHIFTS IN WESTERN CIVILIZATION

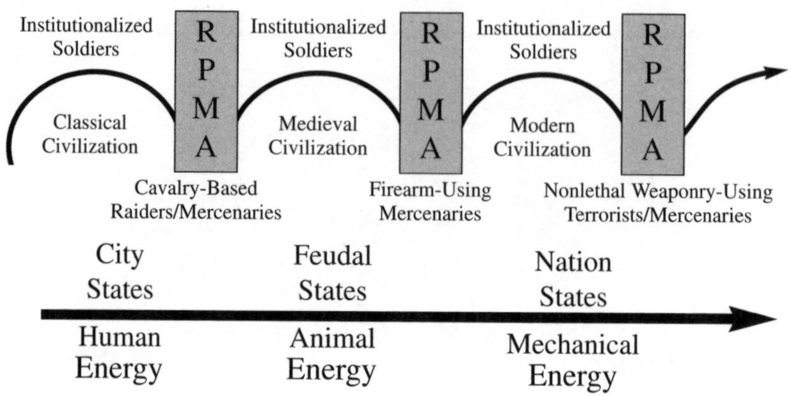

Source: Courtesy of NLECTC-West ©

Department of Defense-promoted RMA theory ignores the social and political context of the change now taking place. The RMA traces its lineage back to faulty Soviet 'historical modeling' of their military technical revolution (MTR) as derived from sixth-generation warfare theory (Slipchenko).

I do not claim, by any means, to be the first to recognize where the future security environment was heading. Terrorism expert Brian Jenkins in his masterful yet often overlooked *New Modes of Conflict* (1983) may have even been the first to do so. Rather, my perceptions are in line with the growing body of 'non-state threat' and 'counter-RMA' works.

One of the dominant terms used for this growing body of 'non-state threat' work is 'fourth-generation warfare'. William S. Lind *et al.*'s initial 1989 *Marine Corps Gazette* article begins by reviewing three modern generations of warfare: warfare of line and column, French *bataille conduite* (attrition warfare), and German maneuver warfare.[3] It proposes the emergence of two future generations driven by ideas and technology, respectively. Over time, it became apparent to those authors that the idea-driven terrorist low intensity conflict (LIC) viewpoint represented where the fourth generation was heading. This thinking has since become intermingled with concepts of 'non-trinitarian war' (Martin van Creveld), 'transnational organized crime' (Phil Williams, Mark Galeotti, and others), 'the new warrior class' (Ralph Peters), 'netwar' (John Arquilla and David

Ronfeldt), and 'fourth epoch war/RPMA' (Robert Bunker, T. Lindsay Moore, and others).

The perceptions of the various authors predate the publication of their works by years as did mine. Those writers, and others not listed, were seeing much of what I was seeing and many things I was, in fact, not seeing. We all hold critical pieces to the mosaic which is unfolding. Hence, I have found that our thinking is better when fused together, just as are our operational military and responder (law, fire, health) assets when formed into joint (and tailored) forces. This book should be considered an initial joint force product – one of our networks, a good guy network, wrote it and, in it, we have attempted to assemble the mosaic pieces together. This may help us avoid the modern pitfall of 'informational seams' where information is hoarded and not shared among allied agencies and groups.

The book is divided into four major sections. The first concerns theory. The first contribution is an update of the seminal work, *The Transformation of War*, and the second represents an update of the important essay concerning 'The New Warrior Class'. Both of these works have had a significant impact on non-state threat perceptions.

The second section concerns non-state threats and case studies. It provides an overview of various non-state threats ranging from organized crime networks to cartels, gangs, and warlords. The emergence and relationship of mercenary and private security corporations to nation-states is also discussed.

In addition, case studies concerning Colombia and Pakistan and the Kashmir are presented. The third section is based on counter-OPFOR strategies which detail advanced concepts, urban battlespace environmental percepons, weaponry, intelligence preparation, networked force structure, and C4I. The fourth section contains two items. The first contribution is an archival document from the late 1987 period. It is an unpublished manuscript concerning early fourth epoch war theory. The second contribution is never before published interviews with Chechen commanders and key staff officers who participated in combat operations against Russian forces in the 1994–1996 conflict. The book also benefits from a preface and a foreword by transnational organized crime and netwar scholars, respectively.

I wish to thank the contributors to this issue for their professionalism and dedication to the vision which it represents – the defense of the nation-state against non-state threat entities. A majority of the contributors went operational after 9-11 and have had to work long hours at their military, law enforcement, and governmental-support jobs in addition to finding the time to complete their assigned writing tasks. I also wish to thank the *SW&I* editors Thomas-Durell Young and Paul B. Rich for initially approaching me to undertake the editorship of a special issue of their journal. It has been a great privilege working with them and the esteemed team of contributors assembled together for this project. While I cannot thank every contributor by name, and I thank you all, I would like to single out Martin van Creveld and Ralph Peters for supporting me early on in this endeavor. Once I obtained the green light from them, I knew the project would be a successful endeavor.

ROBERT J. BUNKER
Los Angeles, CA
February 2002

NOTES

1. Concurrent with our reaction to the 9-11 attacks, the nation suffered from the disruptive effects of WMD terrorism based upon a relatively small number of anthrax letters sent to various locations in the Eastern United States. The perpetrator(s) may be foreign or domestic (or blurred), fully networked, a renegade node, a lone wolf operator, or even the agent of a hostile state entity. We currently know little about this new opponent, but certainly they too will someday feel the full weight of our retribution.
2. For background on the conflict in Afghanistan see Ali A. Jalali, 'Afghanistan: The Anatomy of an Ongoing Conflict', *Parameters* 31/1 (Spring 2001) pp.85–98.
3. William S. Lind *et al.*, 'The Changing Face of War: Into the Fourth Generation', *Marine Corps Gazette* (Oct. 1989) pp.22–6. See also William S. Lind, Maj. John Schmitt, USMCR, and Col. Gary I. Wilson, USMCR, 'Fourth Generation Warfare: Another Look', *Marine Corps Gazette* (Dec. 1994) pp.34–7.

Part One

Theory

The Transformation of War Revisited

MARTIN VAN CREVELD

To write a book is one thing, to criticize it another. For an author to criticize his own book is almost unheard of and may seem hubristic;[1] however, in view of the central place which *The Transformation of War* now occupies in the strategic debate, it is a task that cannot be avoided. In terms of world history, the ten years that have passed since the book first saw the light of day have been enormously eventful. In terms of military and strategic theory, those same ten years have witnessed a vast number of interesting contributions made by an equally vast number of capable people.

If only to clear my own mind concerning the nature of those theoretical and historical developments, asking what in *The Transformation of War*, was correct, what was wrong, and why seems a worth-while exercise. In doing so, I can only hope that the exercise will benefit a few people other than myself.

The Demise of Interstate War

At the time when *The Transformation of War* was written in 1988–89, the Soviet Union was still a functioning superpower. The Cold War was still raging, and the arms race – which had been fueled by President Reagan's vast increases to the defense budget – was assuming dimensions almost unprecedented in history until then. From the Arctic to the northern shores of the Adriatic Sea, on both sides of the Iron Curtain many hundreds of thousands of troops belonging to the mightiest armed forces in history stood guard and watched each other. Thousands of miles away in Korea a similar situation prevailed; and, at times, appeared even more menacing as border incidents led to war scares and war scares were accompanied by border incidents. In Washington DC, in London, in Paris, in Bonn, in Moscow, in Pyong Yang and Seoul and Taipei – to say nothing of Beijing – politicians, strategists and commanders spent sleepless nights asking themselves how those forces were going to fight each other, if they ever did.

A mere decade later, almost all of this has disappeared like snow under the sun. The Warsaw Pact no longer exists. With it went the Cold War and the fears that it inspired. For a time it looked as if large-scale conventional warfare might enjoy a revival in the Persian Gulf. In preparation for

Operation 'Desert Storm' large ground, air and sea forces belonging to many nations were assembled and put under a single command. The signal having been given, cruise missiles were launched and struck their targets deep inside Iraq. Fighter-bombers and bombers took off from their bases and flew thousands of missions. Finally, armored divisions broke loose and chased each other across the desert; engaging in maneuvers that pretended, though they did not quite succeed, to revive the kind of war that Guderian and Patton had waged in 1939–45.

In the event, it only took a few days to realize that Iraq had been greatly overrated. Far from possessing the world's fifth-largest armed forces as had been feared at the time, in reality it was a third rate opponent. Quantitatively as well as qualitatively, 17 million Iraqis, three million of whom were not even Iraqis, proved incapable of putting up a serious resistance to the mighty Coalition that confronted them. One result of this was that the total number of killed in action (KIA) suffered by the Coalition forces was under 200. Given that Iraqi dead were estimated at 35,000,[2] it could almost be said that this was not so much war as slaughter.

Above all, Iraq was a third rate opponent because, unlike several members of the Coalition by which it was faced, it did not have nuclear weapons in its arsenal. As a result, once the forces had been put into position and the Saudi oilfields secured against a possible attack, there was practically no way in which Saddam Hussein was capable of inflicting serious damage on any member of the Coalition. Those members, on their part, had it within their power to turn Iraq into a radioactive desert within a matter of hours; and do so, moreover, while using such a small fraction of their real military potential that it would have been difficult to express in percentage points.

What would have happened if Iraq *had* possessed nuclear weapons as well as the appropriate delivery vehicles is anything but easy to say. Almost certainly, though, the existence of even a small number of nuclear-tipped Scuds would have made Saudi Arabia and Turkey much more reluctant to let the Allies use their territories as a staging ground for the attack; if, indeed, they would have allowed them to do so at all. Had Iraq possessed missiles capable, say, of reaching Paris, then almost certainly the war would never have been started at all. Had it possessed missiles capable, say, of reaching London, then it is almost impossible to imagine the heavy bombers being allowed to use British airfields on their way to Iraqi targets. Nor did these facts escape the attention of those involved. It was the Indian chief of staff who said the war's main lesson was that one should not fight the US without nuclear weapons; in refusing to abandon his nuclear weapons program,[3] Saddam too shows he understands that lesson.

Skipping over the Kosovo campaign of 1999, what was true in 1990–91 was even more true in the autumn of 2001. This time the opponent was not a state – by most criteria, Afghanistan simply *is* not a state – but two extremely loose organizations, the Taliban and Al-Qaeda. The most sophisticated weapons available to the Taliban were some 25-year-old Soviet tanks, aircraft, and anti-aircraft batteries left over from before the invasion of 1979 or else captured from the Red Army. Had it occurred to anyone to rank Afghanistan among the military powers of the world, surely it would have figured near the very bottom of the list; Afghanistan, moreover, was devastated by over two decades of near-continuous warfare the number of whose victims reached into the millions. Once again, cruise missiles were fired and the world's most advanced bombers and fighter-bombers took off. In the air alone the ratio of forces was perhaps a thousand to one, satellites not included. Suppose, though, the Taliban had somehow come into possession even of a single nuclear weapon and a delivery vehicle capable of reaching, say, Islamabad or the capital of Tajikistan? In that case, once again, no doubt the war would never have been started.

To generalize, the main thesis of *The Transformation of War*, namely that major armed conflict between major powers is on its way out, seems to have been borne out during the ten years since the book's publication. One would not want to completely rule out other factors that contributed to this: changing attitudes to war, the identification of nationality and territory which has made conquest unacceptable, growing international interdependence, and so on. Still, the main reason for the process is perfectly clear. It is the fact that any state capable of building even moderately sized, more or less modern, conventional armed forces is also capable of building nuclear weapons and will surely do so if it feels its vital interests, let alone existence, are threatened.

Judging by several examples, indeed, building nuclear weapons is actually easier than building conventional ones. Thus China exploded its first atomic bomb in 1964 and its first hydrogen device in 1967, years before it even considered building a modern fighter-bomber. Israel, at that time an underdeveloped and desperately poor country in the Middle East, also assembled its first nuclear weapon years before it set out to build sophisticated conventional ones. In the case of India and Pakistan the gap between nuclear and conventional capability is even larger. In terms of GNP per capita both countries are among the least developed on earth, to the point that most of their peoples do not even have access to clean running water. Both only have a very limited military-industrial infrastructure. What conventional weapons they possess are approaching obsolescence; some, indeed, were purchased precisely because they were obsolescent and, therefore, cheap. Nevertheless, both have possessed nuclear weapons for years and are steadily working to improve them and to develop new delivery vehicles for them.

As predicted in *The Transformation of War*, the world's conventional forces have been shrinking fast. Those of the US are down from 2,118,000 to 1,366,000, a decline of 35 per cent; of the remainder, only a small fraction are engaged against the Taliban or are likely to become so in the future. Those of the former Soviet Union are down from 4,000,000 to 1,004,000 Russian ones, plus whatever doubtful forces can be fielded by some of the successor states from the Baltic Sea to Central Asia.

Shifting our gaze to the West, there are now fewer than one quarter as many German troops left as, counting both Germanies, there were in 1989. The situation of the French, British, Italian and Spanish forces is scarcely any better. Some of NATO's smaller members, including not least its new former Eastern bloc members, are approaching the point where they scarcely any more have armed forces. Whereas those that they do have are capable of being used, if at all, only in conjunction with their larger neighbors.

As to qualitative improvements, in many cases they only exist on paper as procurement programs are cancelled, cut, or postponed and as the weapons that are available are so few in number and so expensive that their loss cannot be contemplated. Even in the Middle East, which for decades used to be the region with the most conventional wars, during the decade before the outbreak of the Second Palestinian Uprising, Israel was able to cut defense-spending from 14 to 9 per cent of GNP.[4] That region apart, only a few countries are still building or purchasing arms on any scale. Even if they do, the objective is usually not to expand their forces but to 'modernize' them, a sort of military way of keeping up with the Joneses and proving one is not yet moribund.

Some would argue that the death-knell of the armored knight was sounded at Crécy in 1346, yet it was only in the middle of the sixteenth century that the day of the fully armored cavalryman was finally over. A mere ten years after the end of the Cold War, it may be too early to announce the final demise of conventional wars and of the conventional armed forces that have been designed to fight them. As usual, the most dangerous flashpoint appears to be the Middle East and indeed it is not difficult to think of scenarios which will set the entire region aflame. One may, however, assume that the continuing proliferation of nuclear weapons and their delivery vehicles will sooner or later lead to a nuclear Iran, a nuclear Iraq, a nuclear Egypt, and possibly a nuclear Libya and Syria as well.[5] So long as this does not happen, then any war that may break out in the region will be comparatively harmless to anybody except the parties directly involved. If it does happen, then hopefully major warfare between major regional states will come to an end as it already has in most other places. On the other hand, the outcome may be a nuclear holocaust; the latter possibility was clearly alluded to by the head of SHAVAK, General (res.) Ami Ayalon, when he said that, in case of attack, Israel might resort to an 'irrational' response.[6] Either way, we seem to have passed a point of no return. May thou rest in peace, major conventional war.

The Rise of Non-Trinitarian War

Whereas, during the last decade, major conventional wars between major states have been few and far between, wars against or between organizations other than states have proliferated and are proliferating. Among those which have proliferated but were brought to an end (sometimes more, sometimes less) are the ones in Algeria, Angola, East Timor, Egypt, Lebanon, Mozambique, Northern Ireland, Rwanda, Somalia, Turkish Kurdistan, and most of the regions comprising the former Yugoslavia.

Among those that have proliferated but do not seem to be under control are the ones in Afghanistan, Chechnya, Colombia, the Congo, Kashmir, Liberia, the Land of Israel, Macedonia, the Philippines, Sierra Leone, Spain, the Spanish Sahara, Sri Lanka, and the Sudan. From Indonesia to Pakistan, quite a number of countries seem to be on the brink of civil war if they have not crossed it already. To all this must be added what are surely the most spectacular acts of terrorism ever carried out by any organization at any time and place: those of Al-Qaeda against the Twin Towers in New York City and on the Pentagon across the Potomac from Washington DC.

In places where the tanks are still rolling and/or aircraft flying, perhaps the most outstanding fact is their inability to bring such wars under control. To use the example of my own country, the Lebanese border has been a focus of tension since the first katyusha rockets came howling across the border in 1968.[7] Between that date and the spring of 2000 scarcely a week passed without Israel Defense Forces (IDF) aircraft overflying the country; later they were joined by some of the most advanced attack helicopters in existence. Over the years they dropped hundreds of thousands of bombs and fired hundreds of thousands of missiles. Not content with this, several times they were joined by more or less massive ground forces.

The latter either invaded Lebanon (at one time they even occupied its capital) or else deployed such accurate firepower as has scarcely been seen in history until then. In point of sophistication, if not of scale, the Israeli effort could compare with that of the current American one in Afghanistan. Given the small area over which the IDF operated, in point of intensity it may well have been similar; all, as became clear when Israel finally withdrew, to no avail.

The wars in question are, of course, not all of the same kind. Some were much more intensive than others, involving hundreds of thousands and even millions of casualties. Some could best be described as terrorism, others as guerrilla war, others still as more or less open struggles between competing militias, and others still as genocide pure and simple. While these categories are important as well as useful, they do not really go down to the bottom of the matter. In my view, that bottom consists of the fact that, unlike conventional wars, the conflicts in question were not trinitarian.

To Clausewitz, from whom I took the notion,[8] a trinitarian war is based on a clear division of labor between the government that wages and directs it, the armed forces that fight and die, and the people who pay and/or suffer; indeed so important were these distinctions that he used them even to analyze what he called 'popular war' (*Volkskrieg*). At the risk of committing sacrilege, I would like to suggest that he was wrong and that the most characteristic fact about the great majority of armed conflicts during the last decade or so is precisely that these distinctions did not exist in the same form. Sometimes they only applied to one side, and sometimes, as in Somalia and (before the current US intervention) Afghanistan, they did not apply at all. Which of course is one reason why some of these conflicts have been incomparably more bloody than the belligerents' military capabilities would lead us to expect.

Returning to the *Transformation of War*, the prediction that history is witnessing a major shift from trinitarian to non-trinitarian war seems to have fulfilled itself and is still fulfilling itself on an almost daily basis. Judging by the performance of the Israelis in Lebanon as well as many others, moreover, the regular armed forces of most states are hardly any closer to getting a grip on this kind of war than they were a decade ago.

Some are throwing everything they have at the country most suspected of harboring terrorism, to what avail remains to be seen. Many, particularly in Western Europe, seem to be putting their heads in the sand, pretending non-trinitarian war does not exist or does not concern them and trying to preserve their structure even as the economic resources at their disposal as well as their order of battle continue to shrink. Others simply pray that it will go away so they can heave a sigh of relief and return to 'real soldiering'. Others simply get angry, as once happened to this author when, as he was addressing the Israeli General Staff, one of the generals present started thumping the table and shouting that none of the above is true.

Information Warfare: A Joker in the Pack?

Since *The Transformation of War* first appeared, many other attempts have been made to guess what future war might be like. Very numerous new concepts have appeared out of nowhere and are being bandied about as in a game of squash with multiple players; everywhere one looks there are balls being hit, returned, or else bouncing of walls in all kinds of expected and unexpected directions. One of the most brightly colored balls has the label the revolution in military affairs (RMA) attached to it. Others represent the system of systems, population war, environmental war, asymmetrical war, infrastructure war, non-lethal war, gray area war, informal war, information war (strategic and tactical), netwar, cyberwar, mediawar, neocortical war and postmodern war.

All these and many others have been jostling with each other while trying to gain acceptance both on the printed page – which, in spite of the Internet, remains the main medium where the debate is carried – on and in the offices where decisions are made and resources allocated. Just to prepare a list of them, let alone explain the significance of each, would require an entire volume.

As their names suggest, most of the new forms of war either seek to come to terms with the unprecedented rapid developments that are taking place in the field of computers and data processing or else to take advantage of those developments.[9] Sometimes it is merely a question of designing better means to identify targets and destroy them;[10] in other cases the talk is of information itself being used as a weapon either by ourselves or by our adversaries.

The former course is usually known as the revolution in military affairs and, its name notwithstanding, is clearly evolutionary as better communications, improved data processors, more stealthy weapon systems, and more precisely guided munitions take over. The latter is usually known as information warfare and may indeed have revolutionary potential. An observer looking back at *The Transformation of War* from the vantage point of 2001 might well argue that its greatest single shortcoming is the absence of any reference to information warfare. Taking the opportunity, it is a shortcoming which I would like to correct.

As just said, information war is the attempt to use information not just in order to better direct other weapons but as a weapon in itself. Conversely, the feasibility of information warfare – assuming, for the moment, that it is indeed feasible – arises from the fact that modern societies and their armed forces are extraordinarily dependent on information and becoming more so with each passing day.

Since the invention of the microprocessor in 1979 these devices have been incorporated in practically every technical, logistic, and administrative system underlying modern life; from those that regulate our water supply to those that make sure that taxes are paid and aircraft do not collide. Should any number of these devices cease to function then the resulting chaos is unimaginable. Some commentators have painted gruesome scenarios as faulty chips cause passenger aircraft to fall out of the sky, ATM machines to start spewing out money indiscriminately, and telephone networks to either shut down or start misdirecting calls at random.[11] Others believe that stock markets could be made to crash or else that the electricity supplies of entire countries could be cut off for long periods of time, perhaps leading to the death of millions as the economies in question grind to a halt.

What makes defense against information warfare so extraordinarily difficult is, of course, the fact that so many of the computers in question have long ceased being isolated. With every passing day more of them are linked to each other; and in the vast majority of cases the medium that links them is the ordinary civilian telephone network. Though billions have been sunk and are still being sunk into the erection of firewalls whose purpose is to isolate any part of the net from any other, everyday experience shows that they are not perfect; in theory, and perhaps in practice as well, the only way to render a computer or group of computers hacker-proof is to take it or them off the net.

This solution is akin to setting up a railway line that only enables trains to run from point A to point B but which does not have any links with the remaining system. Clearly there are some circumstances in which the construction of such a line is warranted and where, indeed, it may be the only solution to certain problems. Clearly, too, the vast majority of lines will have to be linked with each other if they are to be cost effective and if, indeed, their technical potential is to be realized to the full.

Whether or not the worst scenarios that have been painted in regard to information warfare are capable of being realized is not at issue here and, if humanity is lucky, may never be known. Proceeding on the understanding it has *some* potential, however, the question is who stands to lose and who stands to gain. Our first assumption must be that the experts who try to protect the system and those who try to penetrate it are equally available, equally capable, and equally honest or corruptible.

Now it is a well known fact that computer experts, especially the younger ones among them, are among the most mobile of all professional groups. Perhaps starting as isolated hackers, they seldom have any strong feelings of loyalty towards any particular employer and very often they can be hired and fired at the drop of a hat. At different points in his career the same expert, using the same tools or very similar ones, may well be working now to penetrate a system, now to defend it, and now to manage systems that are charged with *both* offense and defense.[12] Hence the assumption that people on both sides are equally capable does not appear unwarranted.

In conventional warfare, the fact that an advance has to be made, supplies brought forward, ground occupied, and garrisons left behind tends to work against the attack and in favor of the defense; in so far as traversing territory takes time, the same is true of that factor.[13] In information warfare, both geographical space and time are irrelevant. Attacks scarcely require a base. They do not demand that supplies be gathered first, and can be directed at any point from any other point regardless of distance. If properly executed, they may also erase their own traces even as they are carried out or shortly thereafter; indeed one of the main problems facing the defense is to distinguish deliberate attacks from technical problems of every kind. For all these reasons, such warfare would appear to be a leveler. Especially when compared with conventional war as it has developed between 1830 – what I have called, in another context, the 'Age of Systems'[14] – and 1945, it favors the small against the large.

The advantages that information warfare provides to the attacker would be even greater if he or she, (this field being one of the few where gender truly makes no difference) does not strike roots at any particular place but retains his mobility instead.[15] Rather than waiting for the government-sent SWAT team to find him and strike at him, he should be capable of easily packing up his equipment and going somewhere else. In theory if not in practice all he needs to take with him is a laptop. Sometimes even a laptop may be superfluous; arriving at the new location, our hacker may simply buy another one and feed it with programs that are kept on a disk or downloaded from the Internet. In reality all that is needed is access to a telephone link. As computer technology converges with that of cellular phones, soon he will not need even that.

Next, the question of cost. At the beginning of the twenty-first century, building up first rate conventional armed forces will take years, involve many tens if not hundreds of thousands of people, and cost tens if not hundreds of billions of dollars. At the beginning of the twenty-first century, penetrating the information system of such forces and rendering those forces wholly or partly inoperable can be achieved – assuming it can be achieved at all – at a very small fraction of that cost. To be sure, scenarios that tell of a lonely Indian hacker working for Mr Putin, sitting at the North Pole and using a laptop in order to single handedly bring down the strategic information infrastructure of a big power are wildly exaggerated. Still, as experience has shown, in the absence of adequate defenses even the damage that a lonely hacker working his laptop through a telephone link located at the North Pole can do may be enormous. Provided it is aimed at the right target and in the right manner, it could even be catastrophic.

Thus, whichever way one looks at it, information warfare seems to act as an equalizer.[16] To be sure, imagining scenarios under which it may be directed by one state against another is not impossible and such scenarios have already been realized on some occasions. For example, mainland Chinese hackers are said to have caused a flag on Taiwan's parliament to be lowered. During the 1999 Kosovo campaign their Serb colleagues apparently tried to disrupt the operations of Munich international airport. On the whole, however, it is much more likely to be used by non-state organizations, even if some of those organizations themselves work on behalf of states.

In resorting to information warfare, such organizations have the advantage of being more mobile and less strongly bound to one place. Unlike states they do not have an extensive infrastructure to protect; instead they make use of whatever is available at the place where they happen to be located at the moment. In this way, the advent of information warfare is probably one more reason behind the ongoing historical shift away form major war between major states towards the non-trinitarian world of future conflict.

Clausewitz Revisited

Though critics may blame *The Transformation of War* for not having dealt with information warfare as perhaps it should have, on the other hand the term information warfare itself is only a few years old. What was born yesterday may well die tomorrow; in other words, whether information warfare is really as important as has been claimed remains to be seen. Meanwhile, very few critics have taken up the book's second major theme as, in my view, they should have.[17] That theme is that the nature of war is widely misunderstood. And that this misunderstanding, far from being superficial or accidental, goes back directly to no less a person than Carl von Clausewitz.[18]

To some, inquiries concerning the nature of war may well appear academic, even superfluous. In fact it is the most important question of all; given that the nature of a thing goes very far to dictate what we can or can not do in, to, and with it. According to the most famous sentence that Clausewitz, himself a Prussian staff officer sworn to carry out his superiors' orders, ever wrote, war is the continuation of policy by other means. As a prescription of the way things should be the truth of the dictum is undeniable. As a description of the way things are it is very often anything but correct. The lower down the war-making hierarchy we proceed, the less true it becomes.

Undoubtedly, the World War I French and German soldiers described by Ilya Ehrenburg in *Thirteen Pipes* were not the only ones who fought 'for iron, or coal, or honor, or the devil knows what'. Consider also the example of *The Good Soldier Schweik*. Though Schweik believed that Austria was going to fight with the French against the Germans ('low scum') this did not prevent him from cheering the outbreak of World War I as loudly as anyone else; when it turned out he had been wrong and the alliances were reversed, he *still* cheered. At Schweik's level, to speak of war as the continuation of policy may be so false as to be almost comic. Yet it is at this level that war is very often decided by the readiness, or lack of it, of people to fight and risk their lives.

In *The Transformation of War* I argued that war is not so much a continuation of policy as a form of sport such as football or chess. Like football, it is very often not a means to an end but an end in itself. Much more than football, it is an activity in which players very often *surrender* their tiny share of 'policy', that is, their personal interests. Rather than let themselves be guided by interest they lay down their lives for something they feel is greater, or more important, or more valuable, than themselves, be it king or country or freedom or anything else; currently the most successful candidate seems to be Allah, who considering the way He can inspire people to commit suicide for him must be Akhbar indeed. This is true even to the point where war becomes the most sublime human activity of all. As poets from Homer to Nietzsche knew, real freedom can only exist where people fear nothing and expect nothing.

Still proceeding with the same analogy: like football, war is a two-sided activity where opposing teams clash. As in football, each of the teams is constrained by circumstances but is nevertheless to a large extent free to do as it sees fit. As in football, the objective is to inflict as much damage (score goals) on the enemy as possible while suffering as little damage as possible oneself. As in football, the way to achieve this goal is by means of teamwork relying on a practiced combination of skill, force and guile. As in football, high motivation is absolutely essential although, admittedly, not so powerful as to render all other factors irrelevant. Finally, as in football, a match is only possible where it does not consist of a single blow; in case a single blow suffices (e.g. Iraq over-running Kuwait in 1990) war is neither necessary nor possible.

Finally, as in football, the question arises what will happen if the strength of the opposing teams is skewed; in other words, in a situation where one side is *much* stronger than the other yet obliged by circumstances to play against the other repeatedly and for a long time. In Chapter 6.3 of *The Transformation of War* I dealt with this question at length. My conclusion was that the logic of football will operate and that, both in point of skill and in point of motivation, war is a mutual learning process. This means that the stronger side, by the very process of 'fighting' the weak, will almost certainly end up by becoming weak himself; whereas the weaker side, provided only he can gain sufficient time, will almost certainly end up by becoming strong.

At the theoretical level, *The Transformation of War* used the analogy of sport in order to try and provide a non-Clausewitzian, non-strategic, understanding of war and the logic on which it operates. At the practical level, this dynamic is almost certainly *the* best explanation as to why, over the last decades, so many of the most powerful, best organized, best equipped, forces that ever existed have been defeated by groups of men and women who, as is currently the case in Afghanistan, literally went barefoot and could not even read. I would suggest that, to the extent that critics have not taken up this theme in *The Transformation of War* and are still clinging to a view of armed conflict as a rational activity directed towards rational ends, they do so at their peril; let those who have ears to listen, listen!

Conclusions

Ten years after *The Transformation of War* was published, and in spite of the momentous changes in the geo-strategic environment that have taken place since, it is becoming only all too clear that the picture it painted of future war was broadly correct. So, notwithstanding all attempts to blow new life into them and modernize them, was its vision of the way the conventional forces which are designed for it would develop, or rather implode; watching America's most powerful and most advanced bombers and fighters pound Afghanistan, sometimes one does not know whether to laugh or to cry. Ten years after the book was published, it is also easier to see some of the things which it did *not* mention. Probably the most important one is information warfare. Even though, if truth to be said, the real significance of that concept remains to be seen.

Above all, ten years after the book was published most people have not yet taken a fresh look at the real nature of war and the logic on which it operates. Instead of returning to the basics and asking what makes men fight, they continue to parrot Clausewitz on war being the continuation of politics by other means. Instead of coming to terms with war as a messy, bloody clash in which people are bound to be injured and killed, they send in bombers and cruise missiles in the hope that technology may obviate the deaths and make the injuries unnecessary. As the attack on the Twin Towers and the Pentagon showed, today more than ever those who stick their heads in the sand may very well end up by being kicked in the butt.

NOTES

1. I can call, however, on the example of Aldous Huxley in *Brave New World Revisited* (New York, NY: Bantam 1958); also on that of Friedrich Nietzsche, *Ecce Homo* (Harmondsworth, Middlesex: Penguin 1988) [1888].
2. L. Freedman and E. Karsh, *The Gulf Conflict* (London: Faber 1993) p.408.
3. See Testimony of Paul Leventahl, Nuclear Control Institute, before the senate Foreign Relations Subcommittee on near Eastern and South Asian Affairs, 22 March 2000,

<www.nci.org/iraq322.htm>.

4. Data from International Institute of Strategic Studies, *The Military Balance, 1990–91* (London: IISS 1990) pp.17, 33, 49, 83, 63, 71, 78, 106; International Institute of Strategic Studies, *The Military Balance, 2000–1* (London: IISS 2000) pp.25, 20, 61, 80–1, 58, 67, 75, 142.
5. See, most recently, Gerald Steinberg, 'Israel Looks over the Horizon: Responding to the Threats of Weapons Proliferation', 1 July 2001, <www.jcpa.org/jl/vp457.htm>.
6. Israel Radio, news bulletin, 1400 hours, 4 Dec. 2001.
7. An overview of the war may be found in M. van Creveld, *The Sword and the Olive; a Critical History of the Israel Defense Force* (New York, NY: Public Affairs 1998) pp.285–306.
8. Carl von Clausewitz, *On War* (Princeton UP 1976) p.89.
9. One of the most recent attempts is Ralph Peters, 'The Plague of Ideas', *Parameters* 30/4 (Winter 2000–1) pp.4–20.
10. See on this for example B. Owens, *Lifting the Fog of War* (New York, NY: Farrar, Strauss & Giroux 2000).
11. See e.g. R. G. Molander and others, *Strategic Information Warfare* (Santa Monica, CA: RAND 1996) pp.xiii, 6–9.
12. See on this Gregory J. Rattray, 'The Cyberterrorism Threat', in James E. Smith and William C. Thomas (eds.), *The Terrorism Threat and U.S Government Response: Operational and Organizational Factors* (Colorado Springs: USAF Academy 2001) pp.98–9.
13. Carl von Clausewitz, *On War* (note 8) pp.357–69.
14. Martin van Creveld, *Technology and War, 2000 B.C to the Present* (New York, NY: Free Press 1989) pp.156–73.
15. See on this for example William Schwartau, *Cyber Terrorism: Protecting Your Personal Security in the Electronic Age* (New York, NY: Thunder Mouth 1996) especially pp.543–4.
16. See on this James E. Smith and William C. Thomas, 'The Terrorist Threat in Strategic Context', in idem (eds.), *The Terrorism Threat and US Government Response: Operational and Organizational Factors* (Colorado Springs: USAF Academy 2001) pp.27–8.
17. One of the few exceptions is T. von Trotha, 'Zur Typologie Kriegeriescher Aktionsmacht', in S. Neckel and M. Schwab-Trapp (eds.), *Ordnungen der Gewalt* (Opladen, Leske: 1999) pp.71–96.
18. See on this Martin van Creveld, *The Transformation of War* (New York, NY: The Free Press 1991) pp.335, 124–6.

The New Warrior Class Revisited

RALPH PETERS

History has a wicked sense of humor. On the morning of September 11th, 2001, I sat down to write an essay reconsidering, after a decade's interval, 'The New Warrior Class,' a piece that had suggested the US military pay just a bit more attention to irregular and unconventional threats such as ethnic bullies, terrorists, religious extremists, tribal warriors, narco-guerrillas, and the all-others category that interests adventurers and special operations soldiers, but unnerves diplomats, defense contractors and generals yearning to fight massive tank battles against any armored patsy they might be lucky enough to conjure. The phone rang. It was my mother, whose appetite for disaster is insatiable. She recommended that I turn on the television.

It took four months for me to get back to the essay.

In the wake of 9-11-01, there is nothing I would delete from the original piece. I believe the intervening years have proven the accuracy of my observations (for such they were – observations – not ideas by any means, but simply a reporting of things noted on journeys through the world's backwaters). Lest anyone find the preceding statement arrogant, I hasten to declare, with all the penitence of an old Bolshevik placed before the tribunal of the workers and peasants, what I got wrong, my clumsy sin of omission: Although the essay spoke of the threat from terrorists, and I maintained a long concern thereafter with our unwillingness to respond effectively to terrorist attacks against us, I still underestimated the enemy. That was unforgivable – especially for a former intelligence officer who spent much of his career warning others that they must never do precisely that.

Another essay of mine from the mid-nineties made the specific point that even a nuclear attack on lower Manhattan would not stop the stock market for very long, since we could quickly reconstruct the data from brokerage offices around the nation. Yet, I simply assumed, without much thought, that we had to beware one big strike. In my mind, I did not credit Islamic terrorists, especially, with the ability to mount such a brilliant, elegant and well-coordinated assault on multiple targets. I had preached, with great zeal, that every culture on earth produced geniuses, and that a proportion of those geniuses might be hostile to us and lethal. But, like many a preacher before me, I ignored my own homily. I said the words, but did not live them. Nor did I foresee the complex ramifications of such a successful and theatrical terrorist strike. I considered only the physical, not the psychological, consequences, another whopping mistake for an old intel hand (old, clearly, does not necessarily mean wise).

Because of my interest in irregular combatants (and plain old killers, those fundamentalists of human behavior), I was asked to participate in a number of discussions about the terrorist threat over the years. My consistent position was that our enemies were deadly and serious, but not a threat to the survival of our nation. Despite the hullabaloo about weapons of mass destruction, I still believe I was right about that. The great weakness of God-clutching terrorist movements, especially, is that, having sighted or even imagined a glimmer of success, they rush to overreach, and by the extremity of their deeds mobilize their enemies to an annihilating response. This was as true of Jewish zealots two millennia ago and of German anarcho-Protestant insurgents during the 'Peasants War' of the 1520s as it is of apocalyptic Islamic terrorists at the beginning of the twenty-first century.

I consistently stressed that our culture, society and economy were so robust that, for the terrorists, our ultimate invincibility must be terribly frustrating. And it is. The overwhelming majority of American lives, if not spirits, returned to normal by September 12th. And in the following weeks and months, the spirits recovered, too. The paradoxical results of the attacks on the World Trade Center Towers and the Pentagon were to bring Americans together in a profound wave of patriotism, to excite a furious desire for vengeance – which we are taking – and to draw together a surprisingly broad, if unevenly committed, alliance against terrorism. Determination will fade, old squabbles will re-erupt, and other priorities will re-emerge. Yet, though we may see still more spectacular terrorist attacks in the future, in a deeper sense the high watermark of terrorism may have been reached and passed. Its seriousness is now reckoned. In the end, the terrorists appear to have done an even worse job of misunderstanding and underestimating us than we did in our misjudgment of them. And they are paying the price.

I would not alter the words I wrote, but I would add to them, putting in a bit more that I think I have learned about terrorism since 'The New Warrior Class' went to press. Those interested in the subject break down terrorists in a number of ways. I divide them into two basic groups: *practical terrorists*, with relatively rational (if sometimes highly ambitious) political goals, and *apocalyptic terrorists*, men driven by religious, often messianic, visions – men who yearn toward Armageddon, and for whom no victory could be sufficient (the practical terrorist may one day sit in his country's parliament, if he is not killed in his youth, but the apocalyptic terrorist wants to expedite the Day of Judgment; the first fights for changes in 'the system,' while the second wants only to destroy it, no matter his rhetoric about earthly concerns). Our guard was down because we were accustomed to dealing with practical terrorists – even Timothy McVeigh had a finite, earthly end in mind, despite his warped perspective on the possible. Terrorists were expected to land hijacked airplanes and make demands. Instead, we faced terrorists cast from an ancient mold, men frustrated with the things of the earth and impatient with their god's tempo, men who flew airplanes into skyscrapers full of the innocent in the belief that their deeds served divine ends and who hoped to jumpstart a kingdom of god on earth. While the practical terrorist may be a man (or woman) of great and conscious courage, the apocalyptic terrorist is always a man terrified of life's demands – more afraid of living than of dying. For the practical terrorist, death is a sometimes-necessary misfortune, while for the apocalyptic terrorist it is an answer – which does tend to complicate the negotiated settlements that have become the pornography of choice for Western diplomats. Above all, the apocalyptic terrorist is an egotist, convinced that his god has chosen him as an instrument. He cannot be rehabilitated, and must be killed or forever locked away. And killing him is better.

But I have written elsewhere of that, too, and a writer who repeats himself is simply a plagiarist with poor taste (if you're going to lift something, lift something better than your own stuff, for God's sake). So let me turn again to that new warrior class, while striving to minimize the inevitable repetition. I believe the categories of warriors I described in that now-dusty essay then expanded by one more (to five) in a subsequent piece still hold solidly and describe the acolytes of terror and their supporters as well as they did Balkan thugs and Somali tribesmen. These archetypes are anthropological, or even Jungian, not an original concept of mine. Again, I only picked up the pieces lying about and slapped them together. The warriors had been out there killing, simply waiting for someone to call them by name.

In summary, I see these irregular combatants as drawn from five socio-psychological pools. The proportions of each type of warrior in any hostile group may vary widely, depending on the duration and environment of a given conflict, but each sort of enemy is always there, be it in a greater or lesser degree.

First, there are the warriors from the underclass, men without prospects in time of peace, who become 'somebodies' through the exercise of violence and the totems of power. Whether social misfits who become Serb butchers, or Hitler's Brownshirts, or simply the gritty bastards who enjoy a good pogrom anywhere in the world, these men usually form the initial 'infantry' around which a much larger organization may coalesce over time.

Most will quit when the tides of conflict turn decisively against them, but others must be killed, unwilling to give up the only satisfying life they have ever known.

Second, we find 'course-of-conflict' joiners, young men who only sign up for a program of violence when other options are closed off. Over time, they may provide the largest number of recruits to the cause, swelling the ranks to impressive, but ultimately hollow numbers. Although some may acquire a taste for killing and destruction, most of these What-choice-did-I-have? fighters will gladly attempt to reintegrate into a society upon which peace has been imposed. Unless they evolve into a different category of warrior (and these categories are not fixed or exclusive), these men are not natural born killers and do not particularly want to die for their cause. But they will pull the trigger while their side is winning.

Third come the opportunists, the entrepreneurs of conflict, a group my analysis initially slighted. These are the What's-in-it-for-me? actors who, given their lack of scruples, can be viciously cruel when winning, but who will generally look for a way to jump from a losing side. Often highly intelligent, they can also be charismatic, inspiring a loyalty-to-the-death they never feel themselves.

Fourth, come the hardcore believers, whether convinced nationalists, religious fanatics, or simply men who have succumbed entirely to a leader (and the leader is often more important than the cause – human bonds matter and routinely transcend logic). They will die for what they believe in, and the more exclusive, restrictive and harsh the system of allegiance to which they have committed themselves, the more deadly – or, at least, the readier to die – they will be.

Fifth are the mercenaries, the demobilized or deserted soldiers, the men who know the formal trade of killing in combat. They polish the destructive power of the collective. Some of them will fight to the last from sheer pride, but others would rather live to fight another day. Many can be bought.

During the recent, innovative campaign in Afghanistan, all five types were in evidence. Although Al-Qaeda, given its rigorous screening, appears to have had a higher proportion of genuine believers in its ranks, ongoing analysis of prisoners may show a more complex picture. And the Taliban's swift collapse as a governing power demonstrates how, given the absence of choices, a movement's ranks may be swelled by many lacking a commitment unto death – the Taliban fielded tens of thousands of young men who simply found no better choice. As I write, in January, 2002, we have seen the warrior patterns borne out. The men whose trade is war, the mercenaries or lifelong fighters, switched sides when the time was ripe, either for money, or for survival, or because the opportunities had shifted. Many a warlord proved to be no more than an entrepreneur of conflict and, as soon as the Taliban had fallen, went back to collecting tolls along roads (or to outright banditry), to stealing food aid and extorting money from journalists (not necessarily an evil pursuit), and to grasping any advantages they could. The boys and men who had been drawn or forced into the Taliban's ranks gladly faded away, while the unskilled bully-boys shifted effortlessly into the role of providing muscle for the more promising warlords. Only the true believers fought to the last, or fled in hopes of fighting on a more promising future battlefield, or hid themselves in the hope that the storm would pass – or continue, even now, to fight on. But the sheer numbers tell a great deal about the importance of responding to warrior threats with resolve and overwhelming force. Initially, the Taliban was believed to number between 40,000 and 50,000 rifles, five times the estimated strength of the Northern Alliance, America's temporary proxies. But those committed unto death were only a small fraction of that force, and the numbers shifted from one side to the other as easily as mercury spills down an upended surface.

When dealing with warriors, whether Islamic extremists, or Latin American narcos and paramilitaries, or pirates in Malay or Indonesian waters, the critical factor is strength of will. Western states invariably have the raw power to defeat warriors, although conventional forces may not be the ideal choice to combat them (in Afghanistan, we used our own 'irregulars,' special operations forces, to tremendous effect – but, lacking proxies or in a bigger conflict, conventional forces would have to augment the effort). Our soldiers are very well-trained for conventional conflicts and, over the past decade, a great deal more training has been devoted to irregular threats and 'peace operations.' But regular infantry – especially their leaders – are trained and expected to stop killing too soon. Special operations forces, far from reporters and cameras, can behave far more ruthlessly – and judicious savagery is essential in cracking apart warrior organizations and spinning off the rank and file who lack a mortal commitment to their cause. You cannot defeat warriors gently. And the hardcore believers must always be killed or imprisoned (again, killed is always better, no exceptions). You must kill them both to eliminate them as a threat and as an example. The worst advice that can be given is 'Don't make them into martyrs.' Better a dead martyr than a living inspiration. Even after the events of September 11th, 2001, some readers may judge this advice cruel, or wanton, or gratuitous. But there always have been, and always will be, some of our fellow human beings who need killing for the common good of the rest.

But whether we speak of commandos or conventional infantrymen, strength of will is not lacking in our soldiers (I'm smug about my position in September, 2001, when pundits who had never laced up a combat boot warned us that all the Afghan tribesmen were ten feet tall and had never been conquered – anyone who knew history or had been to the region knew otherwise – and my own position was that we could win handily, if only we made up our minds to do it right). The difficulty lies in exciting and sustaining the requisite commitment to destroy warriors on the part of democratic governments. Now, I am proud of the deliberate and effective response of our government to the terror attacks of 9-11-01 (the same pundits who said it couldn't be done, now find fault with the way the campaign in Afghanistan was run; doubtless, these lions of the green room would have savaged Hannibal's reputation for negligence after Cannae). I believe much has changed – overnight – since the awful decade of Clintonian cowardice and the previous administration's willful ignorance of global reality. President Bush has continued to stress that the war against terror will be a long struggle and that the campaign in Afghanistan was only a beginning. The months between the writing and the publication of the collection for which this piece has been promised will have taught us all a great deal. But, be it in a year, or in five years, some of our strength of will, alacrity and single-mindedness will diminish. That is a law of human physics. We must hope that sufficient will remains to do that which is needful, and that we will never again wallow in the fecklessness of the Clinton years, when terrorists had carte blanche and dead American servicemen and -women were merely annoyances to be forgotten at their President's convenience, not victims to be avenged. Of course, the terrorists themselves will do their part to re-excite us when our energies flag. But we have done a very impressive job so far of relearning the brutality necessary to deal with terrorists and other forms of warriors.

A great advantage, of course, was our enhanced ability to attack our enemies from the air – especially after special operations forces hit the ground and began focusing our attacks, which had been largely ineffective until then, despite hundreds of billions of dollars worth of strategic sensors available to us. It long has been a curiosity to me that Westerners in general will tolerate tremendous damage inflicted by technology, at a psychological remove, while they will take to the streets in protest when lesser harm is inflicted by soldiers on the ground (I speak primarily of Europeans, since Americans have a healthier tolerance for slaughtering their enemies than outraged academics would allow). Attempts by the Taliban and their supporters to convince the world that America was targeting civilians just did not work this time (the claims were not true, but that has never bothered Europeans, with their love of complaint, to say nothing of the Muslim world, with its addiction to delusion). The terrorist attacks shocked even German undergraduates and French intellectuals into a new appreciation of strategic reality. And when American airpower killed Taliban frontline troops by the hundreds and did its best to exterminate some thousands of Al-Qaeda activists, there was no audible criticism from any source that mattered. My point is that 'sterile killing' has long been acceptable to us – a pilot's bombs may kill civilians, but the pilot is not judged a criminal, while the soldier on the ground is always suspect. Soldiers are expected to show mercy and moderation, and to take prisoners. Machines are not. The pilot gets a superlative efficiency report for the same results that get an infantryman court-martialed. Yet, the system works, and that is the soul of the matter.

I remain convinced, nonetheless, that ground forces will have an enduring, major role to play against warriors, especially in urban areas and on other complex terrain (as I write, our special operators are rooting through cave complexes and Marines are helicoptering about in pursuit of fugitives in the Afghan wastes, and we see again the need for balanced forces). But if we are to allow ground troops to be as effective as we need them to be, we have to recognize that we dare not compromise with warriors, or attempt to impress them with military demonstrations, or wage a war measured out by teaspoons. You must fight them with overwhelming power and ceaseless effort, not with modulated attacks that seek to avoid giving offense to third parties. Our only weakness in Afghanistan – understandable, given the legacy of the last decade and all the myths that had to be cast aside – was that we did not hit hard enough early enough, using an even greater range of forces. But military operations are rarely perfect, and this was a 'recovery' campaign for a government – our own – that had been sick with illusions, both about the role of the military and about the nature of our enemies. But I believe we have now learned the right lessons. The trick will be to avoid forgetting them.

And will there be more warriors? I wrote above that I believe terrorism may have reached and passed a high-watermark. But that means only that, in the words of an old Irish rebel tune, 'The West's awake.' The world's discontents and dislocations will supply more than adequate numbers of warriors, whether terrorists, genocidal tribesmen, ethnic bullies, international criminals, or 'near-armies,' those formations that fall between rude guerrilla movements and fully-organized military establishments. Warriors were here long before the first soldier – that disciplined, organized, legally-bound representative of state power – and, if we are unlucky, warriors will be here after the last soldiers have gone. The warrior, the man who profits from violence, who is drawn to it and sometimes even loves it, is a basic human archetype. As long as there are men and women upon this earth, there will be men who kill and think their killing good.

During the next decades, the greatest number of warriors who annoy the West will continue to come from the Islamic world. We face a situation unique in human history: A vast, old civilization, reaching literally from the Atlantic to the Pacific in its home dominions, and with outposts virtually everywhere, is failing on every front that matters. An entire world-view, with its encompassing culture and insistent tradition, has proved non-competitive not only for post-modern, but even for modern times. As the dynamic states and peoples of the West and in East Asia fuse informational creativity, startling human efficiency, and adaptive industrialism into (recessions notwithstanding) systems of wealth generation and power unthinkable even a generation ago (remember the 1970s anybody?), Islam has yet to display the industrial-age competence of Britain in the mid-nineteenth century. And there is absolutely no formula for the core Muslim states to catch up, nor will there be any such program. So much that allows late-modern and post-modern economies and societies to triumph is anathema (in the true sense of that word) to the Muslim world: Human equality that transcends birth status, gender and race; free flows of information and a populace able to tell fact from fiction; the rule of law; protection from corruption; recognition of the popular will (democracy being its most evolved form); reliable governments; self-criticism; accurate accounting; liberal education; civic responsibility; the ability to operate socially and economically across family and ethnic lines; religious pluralism....

Islam's collapse as a socio-economic and organizational system is hardly reason for gloating, since it portends continuing difficulties for the rest of us. Of course, it would be better for all were the Muslim world competitive in the production of goods and services, in social effervescence, and in the quality of life provided to the citizens of Islamic states. But it simply is not going to happen on a significant scale. As Bernard Lewis, the greatest scholar of the Arab world in our time, has pointed out, Muslims faced a fundamental choice when confronted with Western successes and their own failures: They could either ask what went wrong and how it might be fixed, or they could ask who they might blame. They chose the wonderful comfort of blaming others for their own failings. And now it is frankly too late for them to recover. They lag so far behind, while the accelerated progress of successful states and cultures races ahead at an ever-increasing velocity, that it is a mathematical, as well as a practical, impossibility for them ever to reach developmental parity or to even approach it.

What will happen? None of us can say with satisfactory precision. Some regions or individual cities, and certainly plenty of individuals, in the Islamic world may do very well indeed. But the majority of Islamic states between the Pillars of Hercules and the Hindu Kush – if not still farther afield – are going to continue to grow relatively (and some absolutely) poorer, as prospects falter and populations increase. This need not lead to a

Malthusian cataclysm, and the likeliest scenario is for the realms of Islam to muddle on through in shabby mediocrity, never satisfied, but surviving on the cast-offs of the West. But it is certainly a guarantee of an ample supply of discontented young males (like those 19 'martyrs' of 9-11-01) with no satisfying vision of worldly success before them.

This situation – and the propensity for violence – is compounded by the psychological dysfunction that pervades the Islamic world. Although it is impermissible to mention such matters in 'serious' strategic discussions, Muslim males, individually and collectively, are terrified of female sexuality, and the simultaneously seductive and horrifying images of women they glean from their distorted views of the West drive them into a madness for which we lack the specific vocabulary. There is perhaps no creature – not even the unicorn – rarer than a sexually-contented terrorist, and many another warrior has never developed into any form of manhood a psychologist would recognize as healthy and mature. But this, too, has been discussed elsewhere and at length, so I will simply offer that, among the many factors we foolishly exclude from strategic analysis (religion only belatedly made it into the club of 'discussables') is sexual neurosis, individual and collective. Of course, superficially puritanical (and, thus, hypocritical) societies always suffer such disorders, but never in the annals of humanity has it posed so massive a threat. If a single factor unified the terrorists of 9-11-01, it was not a strict adherence to Islam – given the lap dances and booze that pleased at least some of the hijackers. Rather, it was that, to a man, they were simply afraid of the girls. I would put it still more bluntly, were it not for the inevitability of censorship.

Certainly, threats will appear elsewhere, although they will nowhere prove as consistent, as inchoate, or as implacable as those emerging from the Muslim world. Warriors have despoiled much of Africa and likely will continue to do so. But African violence remains, at least for now, introverted and fratricidal. We need have no quarrel with Africa – although human ingenuity may yet invent one. But we likely will need to intervene occasionally, when local violence becomes intolerable. In Asia, the security situation is complex and mutable, with China as the great unknown. Asia, too, has produced its share of warriors down the centuries – as has every people and culture we might examine. Latin America has been a congenial home to *caudillos* and killers, from the Rio Grande to Patagonia, since at least the Spanish conquest – and perhaps longer still. But that hybrid civilization may have begun to turn a corner. It will not rival today's most successful states in wealth or social fairness, but, despite some current disappointments and turmoil, the region may emerge as a halfway success, with satisfactory lives on offer for an increasing number of its people, if never for all of them. Even Europe, civilized almost to inanity, harbors its ineradicable warriors, from Basque terrorists, to Corsican separatists, to the gunmen of Northern Ireland (who have proven, so graphically, that neither Catholics nor Protestants have an advantage of virtue). Until all of mankind reaches a true, impossible utopia, the warrior will be with us.

I am inexpressibly optimistic about the future of the United States, and expect positive tomorrows for most of the countries that share at least our practical, if not always our moral, values. Granted a few more decades of life, I expect to see a continued expansion of wealth, opportunity and convenience (a quality too often underestimated in its importance – can't all of human progress really be measured as the march of convenience?). I expect our power to grow exponentially, in every sphere, from cultural and linguistic hegemony to an even-now-unthinkable military superiority. And I hope to delight in yet-unimaginable technological innovations and creations. But I do not expect the darkness to leave the heart of man. Whether from the countless mutant forms of jealousy, from real or perceived need, from the fury of belief, or from the collective madness that haunts the long human experience, I know that we will face violent threats, from heartless, ruthless men, and that we will need to kill them.

The key to winning against warriors is strength of will, supported by valor, conviction and physical power. I do not worry about the determination or courage of our soldiers. But our leaders will remain a cause for concern over the years and decades. It is usually easy – and briefly pleasant – to do less than necessary, then declare victory. But the warrior of implacable belief is deterred only by death, and early intervention is the only way to minimize his appeal and affect. If we truly wish to increase our domestic security and global safety, we would do well to cast aside a lovely, but utterly-false Western myth: That human life is precious. Human life is incalculably cheap. And we must always make certain that the warrior's life is priced far lower than our own, since, though we may value the lives of our countrymen, he does not share our prejudice – as we have learned, again, so very painfully. Our security can never be bought solely with money or even with the most skilled diplomacy, and it certainly cannot be secured with good intentions. A healthy state must cultivate a discriminating appetite for killing.

Part Two

Non-State Threats and Case Studies

Transnational Organized Crime: Law Enforcement as a Global Battlespace

MARK GALEOTTI

Karl Marx may have got something right, after all. His concept of thesis and antithesis rests upon the belief that, until history has played itself out and reached some stage of utopian perfection, each phase of social and economic evolution – the thesis – embodies within it its own nemesis – the antithesis. In this respect, transnational organized crime is the internal enemy, the cancer within modern transnational society. The more any society becomes complex, organized and inter-connected, so too does its crime. Similarly, the more any economic system operates across regional and national boundaries, the more its criminals will adopt a similarly broad perspective. After all, they have been active and eager surfers on this new wave.

Indeed, in many ways they have adapted much more quickly than governments, with all the enthusiasm of any other entrepreneur offered vast new markets and opportunities. The turnover of the global criminal economy is now very roughly estimated at one trillion dollars, of which narcotics may account for about half. Up to half a trillion dollars are laundered through the world's financial systems every year. Furthermore, organized crime is evolving, not just embracing new markets and new technologies but moving from traditional hierarchies towards more flexible, network-based structures.

However, this is not just an expansion of existing organized criminal activities, it is part of a step-change, a process of globalization and inter-penetration which is reshaping the planet's underworld. The smallest street gang may now be part of a global network, pushing drugs grown or manufactured on the other side of the world, which were smuggled along multifunctional cross-border routes which also move illegal migrants and stolen or counterfeit goods, paying their suppliers with cash soon to be laundered through the virtual economy of international financial transfers. In this respect, almost all forms of organized crime are by now at the very least implicitly transnational.

Of course, it is too soon to announce the passing of the nation-state, which has proven a stubborn and resilient beast, unprepared to surrender to transnational political organisations and the tyranny of universal economic forces. However, the global underworld is witnessing the rise of explicitly transnational and multicultural criminal networks, as the old 'empires' – largely defined by their ethnic identity or territorial influence – willingly evolve into new forms. As a result, one of the defining security issues of the twenty-first century will be the struggle between an 'upperworld' defined by increasingly open economic systems and democratic politics and an underworld willing and able to use and distort these trends for its own ends.

Furthermore, this struggle will be played out within a battlespace that is as indefinite as it is ubiquitous, ranging from the virtual expanse of cyberspace, through the campaign to shape the ideals and habits of generations, to the overt struggles between states and criminals. If the battlespace is defined by concentric areas of operations, influence and interest, defined as an actor's core 'battlefield', the adjacent areas subject to some degree of affect and those further reaches where events will have an influence on the combat but are essentially beyond the actor's immediate control, then a whole new set of definitions will be required to cope with this new style of conflict.

Influence or control over marginalized communities will be as important as physical control of national borders and a badly-drafted law may prove a greater source of vulnerability as a badly-guarded arsenal. Furthermore, the nature of 'combat assets' and even the definition of success against this kind of non-state threat must be reviewed. A million dollars devoted to drug rehabilitation may prove more cost-effective than the same amount spent interdicting smugglers' routes, as so long as there is a market, the smugglers can find new routes and simply roll increased business costs into the prices they charge addicts. A police operation which captures ten criminals but at the price of disrupting the work of a hundred businesses and alienating a thousand people may be counted a defeat.

Evolution in Action

One of the key problems in defining and countering this threat is the fact that the underworld of the twenty-first century will be transnational, dynamic, fragmentary, networked and inclusive. It is evolving at least as rapidly as its legal, 'upperworld' counterpart – and to a large extent in response to the same pressures and opportunities.[1] A whole range of factors are having an impact, but broadly speaking they can be broken down into five main categories:

Technological Drivers

Technology is reshaping the underworld as comprehensively as the upperworld, whether increasing the ease and speed of travel or introducing new illicit commodities to be sold, from counterfeit medicines to synthetic narcotics.

For example, the use of controlled, hydroponic cultivation methods has allowed drugs to be raised in inappropriate climates; cannabis is reportedly now, for example, the single biggest cash crop in the US state of Oregon. However, it is the rapid expansion in telecommunications and the consequent expansion of cyberspace which is proving a particular source of new opportunities, from rapid and secure communication to laundering funds through Internet banks. This even raises the prospect of, in the future, 'virtual gangs' – if transnational organized crime is moving towards a structure dominated by the flexible, non-ethnic network, then it would be entirely possible not just to use the Internet to carry out crimes but as the 'turf' of a group. This would be a development of the existing groups of hackers and crackers, as they organized and regularized their operations, to form criminal gangs whose members need never meet or be in the same city or country.

Political Drivers

At its most basic, crime is defined by laws, and laws are defined by states. More broadly, organized and transnational crime must and does respond to a whole range of political changes, from the ebb and flow of state power to wars and natural disasters. The collapse of the USSR was a seismic event, which unleashed a new and fast-moving form of organized crime onto the world, but the return of Hong Kong and Macao to Chinese control, war in the Balkans and many other geopolitical upsets have all had serious implications for the global underworld.

The Balkan wars, for example, made it even harder to block heroin-trafficking routes into Europe from the south-west. The spread of migrants and refugees into the European Union also created new criminal networks, most especially the Albanians who now handle much of the wholesale heroin trafficking for Turkish gangs. As for the return of Hong Kong to Chinese rule this did not, as some observers expected, lead to an exodus of the locally-based Triad groupings. They rightly assumed that the People's Republic would offer every bit as congenial an environment for their operations. Indeed, it has allowed them to extend their activities onto the mainland, developing links with corrupt local and national officials and investing in and preying on the new Chinese economy. In the longer term, there may be a shift in power towards the Big Circle Boys (*Dai Huen Jai*), the only major criminal organization still based on the mainland, but this will probably take the form of a more-or-less amicable fusion of mainland, Hong Kong and Macao-based structures.

Economic Drivers

Organized crime is similarly responsive to its economic environment as markets open and close. Even physical and environmental changes can have an impact on what is and is not economic to produce or sell. Global warming, for example, will play its part in changing the geography of drug production, and is already permitting the production of opium and marijuana in new parts of southern and east-central Russia. As with all markets, there are balances to be struck between profit and risk. One reason why transnational organized crime has not on the whole involved itself in the trade of weapons of mass destruction or their technologies and components is precisely because of the costs associated with the business, including tougher law enforcement, which would affect all the network's operations.

Enforcement Drivers

This emphasizes an important but often neglected point: amid all the understandable concerns about the threat it is worth remembering that law enforcement can work. However, successful police operations and the introduction and enforcement of new laws can also have surprising and counter-productive effects. US-backed victories against drug cartels in Peru and Bolivia, for example, drove the *narcotraficantes* closer to the USA and Mexico, and also broke the large cartels down into smaller, but also more flexible, so-called *cartelitos*. On the other hand, pressure on both the Italian and US mafias has weakened them both and forced them to be more cautious.

In Japan, by contrast, an end to decades of acceptance of the *boryokudan* (or Yakuza) has had a major impact on their more overt activities. However, the more powerful Yakuza – most notably the Yamaguchi-gumi – have assembled the necessary 'critical mass' of economic and political power largely to ride these waves. Like the Mafia, they are increasingly leaving street operations to local clients and franchisees, while instead concentrating on the strategic level of operations.

Internal Drivers

The global underworld is also not purely a product of its context, it is also shaped by internal and often contingent factors. Alliances between organizations can avoid conflict and maximize efficiency, just as feuds and competition may shatter an organization or alternatively elevate a stronger, more effective new organization in an exercise in social Darwinism. Structural changes within the underworld are also of great importance as, reflecting new challenges and opportunities, even the old, monolithic gangs are going 'post-modern', and instead are becoming loose networks of semi-autonomous criminal entrepreneurs. In this respect, the rise of a new organizational paradigm is not just a product of other factors, it is a force in and of itself.

This new paradigm is thus the criminal structure which is not a disciplined gang or clearly defined conspiratorial hierarchy. Indeed, it is a very disorganized form of organized crime, one characterized by networks of semiautonomous individuals and small groups. They may pay some form of 'tribute' to a patron or into communal funds in return for mutual support and access to communal services, but otherwise they generally operate independently, coming together in *ad hoc* teams to exploit particular opportunities or resist a common threat. Such a structure is flexible and entrepreneurial, able very quickly to respond to its market, political and law-enforcement environment. Where the old model for organized crime was pyramidal, these networks have relatively flat hierarchies. There are senior figures, with greater resources, contacts or moral authority, but they do not give orders so much as have greater assets with which to purchase or compel the assistance of others within the network.

This is a structure emphasizing linkages based on deals and mutual advantage rather than discipline or traditional authority. It is also one especially well suited to crossing the old boundaries of nation and community. After all, one by-product of globalization and the shift from rigidly structured gangs to looser, network-style ones, is an ethnic diversification of organized crime. Where once a gang might be based on a single ethnic group (or even home region or village), be identified as such, and rely on this to provide everything from the internal language to operational culture, now there is little reason for such an exclusive approach. Instead, organized crime is becoming increasingly inclusive: people and groups with the right skills, contacts or territory can be accepted into the network so long as they simply prove able to operate within the dominant culture. This is not in essence new: the Cosa Nostra in the USA brought in such non-Italians as 'Dutch' Schultz – actually of German origin – as long as they were able to operate 'Sicilian-style'. What is new is the scale at which this is being practised. Even such hitherto exclusive structures as the Yakuza are beginning to bring in outsiders, as Korean gangs begin, in effect, to operate Yakuza 'franchises' on particular territories.

A further reflection of the criminals' eager exploitation of new opportunities is their adaptation not just to new technologies in general but weapons in particular. Obviously their main tools of the trade are the conventional knife, gun and bomb. Even so, their linkages with terrorism and their resources have ensured that, if they choose, the criminals can obtain leading-edge weapons and training. Where it is appropriate or advantageous, though, the criminals also acquire, deal and use even more esoteric weapons with which to threaten and attack human and material targets. Consider, for example, Russian banker Ivan Kivelidi. Once it became clear how difficult it would be to penetrate his security with a conventional assassination, his enemies murdered him in 1995 by secreting a secret chemical poison designed for military use in his office.

In many cases, though, the main targets of unconventional attacks are systems and information. Although transnational crime tends to use computers and the Internet for financial traffic and communications rather than as a weapon, there have been cases of their offensive use against prey or law-enforcement agencies which have been almost invariably transnational in nature. However, in some cases, a mere credible threat suffices. 'EMP bombs', suitcase-sized devices which release an electromagnetic pulse capable of scrambling electronic systems within a 200-meter radius, can have a catastrophic impact on computer systems. Several financial institutions have quietly paid blackmail money to organized criminal groups rather than take the risk of being targeted with such weapons – even without proof that they are in the criminals' arsenals.

Conquest?

In many ways, the traditional demarcations between national security and law enforcement concerns are becoming increasingly less meaningful. Admittedly, cases in which criminals come to dominate countries are rare, and they tend not to be directly transnational in origin. Where this has happened, it usually reflects a fusion of domestic criminal and political interests – often within authoritarian states – with an eye to exploiting transnational opportunities. In such operations, the 'battlefield' tends to be defined by the nation's political and economic systems, either by penetration or by the violent imposition of new paradigms by coup or plot.

The best examples are 'narcocracies' such as Bolivia under General Luis Garcia Meza (1980–81) and Myanmar (Burma), but, if anything, such overt 'captured states' will be even less a feature of the future. The networks of modern transnational crime are well able to penetrate modern states and find useful allies, contacts and clients within them so that they have little need or interest in so crude a tactic.

'Captured states' are, after all, obvious criminal havens and will be treated as such – their banking systems will be regarded as compromised, cargoes coming from them are subject to extra scrutiny and their citizens are treated as potential fifth-columnists. Far better to subvert and operate within countries which maintain a suitable appearance of order and respectability: rent your politicians and administrators when you need them, do not become them.

Of course, organized crime is often powerful enough to create its own 'states-within-states', usually with an explicitly transnational context, such as the poppy fields of the Chu Valley, which stretches between Kazakstan and Kyrgyzstan. These undermine the integrity of their host states and of national borders alike. In many cases this takes the form of outright insurgency, but it can just as easily operate by subversion and subterfuge.

The Mohawk territory of Akwesasne straddles the US and Canadian borders, for example, and many Mohawks reject the legitimacy of the border that divides them. This has helped make it the most important contraband smuggling route on the US/Canadian border. Such criminal successes, though, tend to reflect problems within states and societies or even general or localized collapse. The main threat is not from some direct struggle of a specific organized criminal group against a specific state because, ultimately, the criminals can only triumph against states which have lost the disposition or ability to resist – what Lenin called the 'critical absence of will' on the part of a ruling elite which was a precondition for revolution.

The Arsenal of Chaos

The presence of powerful, flexible transnational criminals networks is less of a direct threat to the nation state so much as an eager and useful ally for others who would challenge or destroy it. In the aftermath of the 11 September 2001 attacks on New York and Washington, the spotlight has inevitably been turned on international terrorism. Transnational crime and terrorism have often been useful to each other in the past and will probably be all the more so in the future.

There is now increasing evidence of a growing symbiosis in the relationship between certain terrorist factions and transnational organized crime, not least as the former look for new ways to finance themselves now that such traditional supporters as the USSR, China and Libya either do not exist or have scaled down their activities. Such groups as Peru's remaining *Sendero Luminoso* and elements of the Northern Irish paramilitaries have in many ways lost their political rationale – organized crime, which began as a means to an end, has become an end in itself. However, while these groups are essentially national, they work with and thus link into transnational networks and this trend thus has transnational implications.

For example, the willingness of the Kosovo Liberation Army to turn a blind eye to major shipments of heroin through areas under their control, in return for funds and weapons for their war against Serbia, helped keep open a route through which 80–90 per cent of the heroin reaching Europe was moved, while also contributing to the rise of Albanian organized crime across the Continent. In many cases, the links are even more direct, with organisations such as Al-Qaeda in Afghanistan and Hizballah in Lebanon, which produce narcotics for sale to criminal trafficking networks.

Less visible is the way transnational criminal networks can provide valuable goods and services to terrorists and insurgents. In the past, this has especially been in the form of weaponry. Indeed, the very existence of substantial stocks of weapons and channels through which more can be imported is often a cause of regional instability in itself. However, as, when and if the US-led 'war on international terrorism' begins to succeed in its aims of cutting the terrorists' traditional routes for moving and laundering their funds – especially the *hawala* underground banking network – then they will be forced to seek alternative channels. Just as transnational organized crime has broken international sanctions (smuggling, for example, embargoed computers to the USSR or Iraq), so too it can service terrorism. It already has such financial networks in place, and although it charges a rather higher rate for its services, if this is the price for continuing secure and effective operations, then terrorist movements will almost certainly pay it.

Covert Threats: Penetration, Debilitation and Re-socialization

The most insidious challenge is not so much one posed by specific groups so much as the deeper, cultural struggle of the legitimate 'upperworld' – however imperfect and compromised – with an alternative world and ideology of global criminal entrepreneurship. In the most extreme cases, criminals can acquire, sometimes as a result of a definite 'public relations' strategy, a degree of public legitimacy, whether this is through fostering a myth of community spirit (as witnessed by the Yakuza's prompt dispatch of aid to the survivors of the 1995 Kobe earthquake) or by posing as champions of national or cultural identity (whether in Kosovo, Chechnya or Kurdistan).[2]

If criminal groupings can subvert or suborn a sizeable fraction of a national, regional or ethnic community, then they become far more powerful and harder to combat. This will also affect wider security considerations. Endemic corruption has, for example, led to the widespread use of moonlighting Russian Spetsnaz special forces soldiers as *mafiya* hitmen and has also helped arm Chechen rebels from military arsenals. The threats posed to the nation-state are even greater when these criminal groupings operate transnationally, or else are linked into cross-border networks.

The prevalence of gangs linked with the Russian *mafiya* groupings in East/Central Europe is a serious security concern at a time when many of these countries are seeking NATO membership. Conversely, Moscow has become increasingly alarmed at the evidence that illegal Chinese migration into its sparsely-populated Far East has been accompanied by the intrusion of Chinese organized crime, especially linked to the Big Circle Boys. One

Federal Security Service officer even went so far as to characterize this rather hysterically as 'invasion by crime, perhaps to prepare the ground for a more conventional campaign'.[3]

This cultural subversion does not only operate at the grassroots level. Given that the working estimate for the annual turnover of global criminal activity is equivalent to some 5 per cent of total global economic activity, it is not surprising that transnational criminal activities, particularly drug trafficking and money-laundering, can be vital mainstays of a regional or even national economy. Even if much of the proceeds of crime then moves on to some other country, some remains, providing employment and 'trickle down' re-investment.

Indeed, from offshore banking centres whose secrecy laws are clearly there to be used by criminals to drugs-producing parts of the Developing World many countries are all but 'hooked' on their involvement in transnational crime. By 1999, for example, Mexico's narcotics industry was worth an estimated $30 billion in profits – four times the revenue from the country's largest legal export, oil. Similarly, marginalised and pariah states have also turned to state-sponsored crime to bypass sanctions and raise revenue. Most notably, North Korea raises perhaps $200 million annually through such criminal activities, most notably the production and distribution of opiates and methamphetamines.

The Law Enforcement Battlespace

Modern crime has developed within modern economic and political structures. There is no 'other' against which to focus national efforts: organized crime thrives and survives precisely because it meets internal demands, unmet by the state, whether for commodities, for opportunities for advancement or for security. Nation-states will find themselves operating on a variety of levels in this battlespace. Their areas of operations will be defined not only by their sovereignty but also forms of conflict, ranging from socialization to control of financial flows. However, legal sovereignty does not necessarily mean genuine control, so in some areas and locations, the battlespace will not merely be contested, but the role of the state may be limited to exerting influence. Furthermore, as nations also operate transnationally, in some ways the areas of operation will expand (for example, through direct intervention abroad or the use of bilateral agreements to compel local law enforcers to act in their name) but also contract (as international obligations may limit the freedom of maneuver even in domestic affairs). In this context, the dividing line between areas of operation and influence may be indefinite and very changeable.

In this struggle, a nation-state's area of interest will be global and holistic. What happens anywhere on the globe can impact on the struggle against transnational crime, whether famine in Africa (which may trigger new waves of illegal migrants) or freedom of information legislation in Europe (which could restrict the use of eavesdropping and communications intercepts by the police). Nor is this merely geographic: a technological innovation may have a direct impact on operations within the battlespace. The creation and dissemination of PGP internet encryption technology was a great boon for the communications security of transnational organized crime, for example, while advances in printing processes made counterfeiting older-style banknotes without the latest safeguards relatively easy. Yet so too may cultural or even philosophical trends. The flood of Japanese gangster films emphasizing the power and honour of the Yakuza undoubtedly had an impact on Asian street gangs along the West Coast of the USA and also led to several actively seeking linkages with the Japanese-based networks.

It is thus impossible to define the forces and weapons with which this war will be fought, as the battlespace is defined by a whole variety of different environments and contexts. An efficient Customs Service will do little directly to combat violent crime on the streets, but can help interdict flows of drugs and weapons, which would otherwise help arm and fund gangs which the police would have to combat on the streets. If meanwhile the state itself is discriminating against minorities and denying them legal opportunities, though, there will be a steady stream of alienated clients and eager recruits for the criminals, such that the Customs and police are doing no more than holding the line.

Of course, it is also true that the evolution of modern society has provided the nation-state with a formidable arsenal of its own, from working international police cooperation to flexible military forces as able to fight a war in Kuwait as keep the peace in Kosovo. Furthermore, as transnational crime moves from a hierarchical structure to a loose network, the gains it makes in flexibility and survivability are at least in part offset by new limitations. These networks cannot focus their efforts to the same degree as a hierarchy. Furthermore, as they broaden their membership and lose their original cultural and ethnic identities, they also lose the old sense of primal loyalty and become vulnerable to infiltration, internal dissent and defection.

The late twentieth century saw an extraordinary development in the transnational, even global, inter-connectivity of political, social and economic systems, and, as Phil Williams put it, 'transnational organized crime can be understood as the dark side of interdependence and globalization'.[4] Transnational crime will never be able to mount the kind of overt, lethal strike to the nation-state as conventional enemies or even insurgent movements – nor would it probably want to. However, as 'old' and 'new' security worlds merge, it will represent a threat on a variety of levels. It can act as a powerful 'force multiplier' to terrorists and insurgents and even a covert weapon in inter-state conflicts. It can degrade security assets. It can undermine and subvert national morale, identity and financial and political structures. In this respect, transnational organised crime poses a distinctive challenge both to the nation-state and to this new 'interdependent and globalized' world system.

NOTES

1. I develop this theme in more depth in two linked articles which launched the 'Global Crime Watch' section in *Jane's Intelligence Review*: 'Crimes of the new millennium' 12/8 (Aug. 2000) and 'The new world of organized crime' 12/9 (Sept. 2000).
2. Eric Hobsbawm, for example, developed the concept of the 'Social Bandit' in his book *Bandits* (orig. pub. 1969; rev. ed.: London: Weidenfeld 2000). While his Marxist views led to an idealized notion of the revolutionary and egalitarian nature of the phenomenon, if anything the basic idea is increasingly relevant in the twenty-first century, as globalization spreads a feeling of disempowerment among many communities and modern media can be used to create suitable myths of popular resistance through crime.
3. Personal conversation, Jan. 2000.
4. P. Williams, 'Transnational criminal organizations and international security', in M. Klare and Y. Chandrani (eds.) *World Security: challenges for a new century*, 3rd edition (New York, NY: St Martin's Press 1998) p.250.

Drug Cartels, Street Gangs, and Warlords

JOHN P. SULLIVAN and ROBERT J. BUNKER

The societal changes associated with the accessibility of information technology that stimulate networked organizational forms are changing the nature of conflict and crime. New, often non-state, entities and organizational structures are adapting to these circumstances and altering the global political landscape. In this frontier, non-state actors are asserting their ability to influence global civil society, while at times challenging states and state institutions to gain social, political, or economic influence.

Netwar, the now and future war waged by irregular adversaries including terrorists, drugs cartels, criminal gangs, and ethnonationalist extremists, is a new mode of irregular conflict that blends war, terrorism, and crime. RAND analysts John Arquilla and David Rondfelt were early observers of this trend where technological and organizational changes that benefit relatively small actors can fuel asymmetric threats. They succinctly note that networks can prevail over hierarchies in this emerging post-modern operational or battle space: 'Power is migrating to small, non-state actors who can organize into sprawling networks more readily than can traditionally hierarchical nation-state actors.'[1]

This essay reviews the actual and potential evolution of drug cartels, street gangs, and warlords from hierarchical organizations to Internetted transnational criminal actors that may further evolve into new war-making entities capable of challenging the legitimacy and even the solvency of nation-states. This potential was recognized by eminent military historian Martin van Creveld in his prescient observation that, 'In the future, war will not be waged by armies but by groups whom today we call terrorists, guerrillas, bandits and robbers, but who will undoubtedly hit upon more formal titles to describe themselves.'[2]

Drug Cartels: Toward Criminal Free-States?

Transnational crime is now widely recognized as a threat to political, economic, environmental and social systems worldwide.[3] This threat goes beyond the substantial illegal drug trade and its attendant violence to include major fraud, corruption and manipulation of both political and financial systems. Transnational criminal organizations (TCOs) potentially undermine not only civil society, but also political systems and state sovereignty by normalizing violence, legitimizing corruption, distorting market mechanisms through the disruption of equitable commercial transactions, and degrading the environment by sidelining environmental regulation and safeguards.

A range of TCOs (e.g., Chinese Triads, Russian Mafiya, Colombian cartels, the Japanese Yakuza, Sicilian Mafia and others) have engaged in global activities challenging state institutions and stability. While most, like Colombia's Cali cartel, avoided politics to pursue profit, their mixture of competition and cooperation with each other, governments and commercial entities can foster instability with corruption, co-option and political manipulation emerging as primary tools once criminal groups become embedded within a society.

TCOs are especially suited to network forms of organization. They often cooperate to maximize profits and circumvent interdiction by police, law enforcement agencies (LEAs) and governments. The networks established by these groups display a remarkable capacity to transcend borders and flow around legal or geographic boundaries. These networks based on risk reduction (joining with locals to exploit local conditions or access corrupt officials), market extension (new products or outlets), or product exchange (such as guns for drugs) expand the capabilities of individual criminal entities, often minimizing competition and conflict. Often transnational in character, these organized drug or crime networks are essentially borderless and difficult to combat since opposing LEAs are generally constrained by sub-national and national boundaries.

Extending their reach and influence by co-opting individuals and organizations through bribery, coercion and intimidation to sustain their activities, these groups are emerging as a serious impediment to democratic governance and a free market economy. At sub-national levels, such corruption can also have profound effects. At a neighborhood level, political and operational corruption can diminish public safety, placing residents at risk to endemic violence and inter-gang conflict, essentially resulting in a 'failed community', a virtual analog of a 'failed state'.

These consequences of rapid social change place the centuries-old idea of 'a struggle between nation-states or their coalitions over the preservation and extension of national sovereignty' in danger of becoming irrelevant. Long-standing assumptions about war-fighting (and policing for that matter), that include definitions of victory and defeat, threat entities, and battles and conflict itself, are being challenged.[4] At national levels the adversary will not necessarily be an emerging peer competitor. At sub-national levels, organized criminals and gangs will not necessarily be the usual suspects.

This threat could involve new half-political, half-criminal powers as a dominant threat, flourishing in a growing failed-state operational environment where a condition of 'not war-not crime' prevails. In 1998, Bunker postulated a 'new war-making entity' (Black and BlackFor, its military arm) with intertwined criminal and war-making functions and a networked, vice hierarchical decision-making structure.[5] In that formulation, Black's geographic boundaries may or may not have been contiguous, not all of its territories were delineated, and it was recognized that some of its territories could occupy areas within zones currently occupied by failed states.

In the scenario, BlackFor was comprised of 'non-state soldiers,' a cheap light force comprised of disenfranchised 'outsiders' who embrace criminal behavior. Mercenaries, ranging from terrorists to private security and intelligence firms, augment BlackFor's non-state soldiers. Finally, Black embraced advanced technology weaponry including weapons of mass destruction (WMD), radio frequency weapons (RFWs) and cybotage. BlueFor (a classic modern military) would have had to counter terrorists, narco-groups, and gangs in a 'police'-type setting for which its forces were not suited. Furthermore, victory in a conventional sense may not be achievable in such conflicts. This is the type of conflict we are currently engaged in against terrorists such as Osama bin Laden and the networked Al-Qaeda. Cartels are another example of this type competitor. Now we will summarize the evolution of cartels through three phases along the path toward becoming potential challengers to the Westphalian state.

First-Phase Cartel (Aggressive Competitor)

The first-phase cartel form originated in Colombia during the 1980s and arose as an outcome of increasing US demand for cocaine (see Table 1). This type of cartel, characterized by the Medellín model, realized economies of scale not known to the individual cocaine entrepreneurs of the mid-1970s. This early cartel is an aggressive competitor to the Westphalian state because of its propensity for extreme violence, uncompromising nature, and willingness to directly challenge the authority of the state.

This group possessed very limited transnational and inter-enterprise links. Structurally, while emerging Internetted channels were apparent, this cartel form was dominated by a small cadre of leaders at the top of its organizational chart. In the countryside and jungles, criminal armies were established to protect trafficker personnel and assets, both laboratories and estates, from threats of guerrilla 'taxation' and kidnapping attempts. Technology use and acquisition by this cartel was conventional in nature. Seizure manifests of weapons and equipment list predominantly small arms and ammunition, grenades and explosives, radios, and various forms of

TABLE 1
PHASES OF CARTEL EVOLUTION

First-phase cartel aggressive competitor	Second-phase cartel subtle co-opter	Third phase cartel criminal state successor
Medellín model	Cali model	Ciudad del Este/ Netwarrior model
Hierarchical/Limited Transnational and inter-enterprise links/Emerging Internetted organization	Local (domestic) Internetted organization/ Emerging transnational and inter-enterprise links	Global Internetted organization/Evolved transnational and inter-enterprise links
Indiscriminate violence	Symbolic violence Corruption	Discriminate violence Entrenched corruption (legitimized)
Criminal use and provision	Transitional (both criminal and mercenary) use	Mercenary use and provision
Conventional technology use and acquisition	Transitional technology use and acquisition	Full spectrum technology use, acquisition and targeting
Entrepreneurial/Limited economic reach	Semi-institutionalized/ Widening economic reach	Institutionalized/ Global economic reach
Small scale public profiting	Regional public profiting	Mass public profiting
Limited 'product' focus	Expanding 'product' focus	Broad range of products/activities
Criminal entity emerging (netwarrior)	Transitional entity (nascent netwarrior)	New war-making entity (evolved netwarrior)

vehicles that are common to paramilitary groups.

Economic and product limitations on this phase of cartel development also handicapped it. The profits it generated specifically enriched the cartel bosses and their families and retainers, those private contractors associated with them, and some of the local populace in the cartel's immediate sphere of influence. In retrospect, the Medellín model was a new and very successful, albeit short lived, form of criminal entity. Its leadership, while tactically and operationally brilliant, was strategically ignorant. Their attempt at directly taking on a Westphalian state politically and militarily was both organizationally and individually suicidal as witnessed by the successful decapitation of the top Medellín leadership ranks by governmental forces in the early 1990s.

Against the vast resources and legitimacy of the Colombian government, this emerging netwarrior was ultimately no match and was crushed. Still, the lessons learned for the cartel evolutionary form were not lost and many of the mistakes made would not be repeated by the more advanced manifestation that was developing in Cali.

Second-Phase Cartel (Subtle Co-Opter)

The second-phase cartel form also originally developed in Colombia but, in this instance, is centered in the city of Cali. Unlike their Medellín counterparts, the Cali group, which emerged in the early 1980s, is a shadowy organization devoid of an actual kingpin. Its organization is more distributed and network-like, rather than hierarchical, in nature. Many of its characteristics and activities are stealth-masked and dispersed, which provide it with many operational capabilities not possessed by the first-phase cartel form. Specifically, it possesses leadership clusters that are more difficult to identify and target with a decapitation attack. The Cali group is also more sophisticated in its criminal pursuits and far more likely to rely upon corruption, rather than violence or overt political gambits, to achieve its organizational ends.

This cartel form has also spread to Mexico with the rise of the Mexican Federation, an alliance of the 'big four' mafias based in Tijuana, Sonora, Juárez, and the Gulf. One of the true dangers of the Cali model for the Westphalian state is its Internetted organization. In Colombia, a two-tiered network developed based upon a core group of members bonded by trust, which was very hard to penetrate, and an expendable peripheral membership which could be coupled and decoupled as needed, much like a tinker toy set.

This organizational structure possessed numerous advantages. In the city of Cali, for example, an information web was established based upon street vendors and taxi drivers to monitor law enforcement movements. Such networks also enjoy quicker reaction cycles because of increased multi-channel information flow, the aforementioned stealthing of key nodal members/leadership clusters, and the ability to sustain increased levels of structural damage because of redundant communication paths.

A major noticeable difference between the Medellín and Cali models is their respective orientation towards the use of violence. The Cali model is far less prone to violence than the Medellín group and when utilized, it is far more discriminate. Violence thus takes on a more symbolic nature and on the surface makes this cartel form appear to be less of a threat to the Westphalian state than a first phase cartel. However, this is far from the case. With an emphasis upon silver over lead, the threat becomes more sophisticated and relies upon a subtle-co-opting approach. Such premeditated narco-corruption literally eats away at the institutions of the state and destroys its social and political bonds and relationships. This pattern of narco-corruption is also becoming increasingly advanced in Mexico where most of the state institutions have been compromised and, in numerous cases, rely upon a 'corruption tax' on the cartels for part of their operating budget. These events suggest that this cartel form is beginning to graft itself onto the pre-existing state structures.

The second-phase cartel form is also transitional in its reliance upon enforcer and operational personnel, with a shift away from criminals toward true mercenaries who are more specialized in nature. For example, US and Mexican street gang members, as well as Mexican police officers and soldiers have contracted out to the cartels. An incident illustrative for its brazenness is the May 1993 shooting of Cardinal Juan Jesus Posadas Ocampo by Logan Heights gang members who had been hired by the Tijuana cartel out of their San Diego neighborhood.[6]

Technology use and acquisition is also in a transitional state with more common forms of weaponry being gradually supplanted by more specialized military and advanced devices. Use of advanced intelligence-gathering equipment, such as night vision devices, by drug smugglers attempting to penetrate the US border has also been reported to have taken place.

The Cali model represents a far more successful and robust organizational form than the earlier Medellín mafia. This transitional entity is still a nascent netwarrior, however, and is not immune to disruption. Arrests of key figures have lowered their public posture and many of the individuals and groups owing allegiance to the Cali group have gone deeper underground and may be connected to the dozens of so-called 'baby cartels' which have since emerged.

Third-Phase Cartel (Criminal State Successor)

Third-phase cartels, if and when they emerge, have the potential to pose a significant challenge to the modern nation-state and its institutions. A third-phase cartel is a consequence of unremitting corruption and co-option of state institutions. While this 'criminal state successor' has yet to emerge, warning signs of its eventual arrival are present in many states worldwide.

Of immediate importance in the United States are conditions favoring narco- or criminal-state evolution in Mexico. Thus far, Mexico has not developed into a kleptocracy, but the potential is there. This echoes the pattern seen in Colombia. For example, the Cali cartel infiltrated Colombia's society by using complicity, intimidation, and fear of narco-terrorism, corruption and indifference. These factors are increasingly evident in Mexico. Consider Mexico's near-endemic pattern of assassinations, which have even rocked *Partido Revolucionario Institucional* (Institutional Revolutionary Party or PRI). The 23 March 1994 assassination of presidential candidate Luis Donaldo Colosio and the 28 September 1994 daylight execution of PRI secretary-general Francisco Ruiz Massieu are extreme examples. These events symbolize the lawlessness, corruption and fratricidal rivalry among gangs and politicians aligned with competing narco gangs that are eroding social and civic institutions.

Such endemic corruption and violence – frequently referred to as the 'Colombianization of Mexico' – result not from mere infiltration of government, but from permeation of the government where the authorities and drug traffickers are the same people. Drug warfare, corruption and the co-option of the Mexican military are particularly alarming if one considers that illicit drugs are among the most dynamic sectors of Mexico's ailing economy, with the result that the Mexican economy has been largely propped up with narco-dollars.

The majority of Mexican cartels (Gulf, Tijuana, and so on) are seizing political control through co-option rather than emerging as competitors to the state (as in the example of Colombia's Medellín cartel). This allows the cartels to exert greater influence within segments of the 'government'. Rather than being a competitor for political-economic dominance, the cartels seek avenues for enabling their activities. Co-option and corruption are thus aimed at removing the cartels from the limits of state sovereignty.

Such corruption and distortion of the state, where criminal organizations are fused to the existing state hierarchy like a parasite or gain local dominance within an exiting state, can potentially lead to the emergence of the third-phase cartel acting as a criminal free state or enclave. This trend is evident in some parts of Mexico – notably Sinaloa and Quintana Roo.

Over 200 well-armed gangs operate in Sinaloa. These criminal enterprises transcend drug running, embracing highway robbery, murder-for-hire and kidnapping. Sinaloan drug cartels emerged in the 1970s and 1980s to stabilize and control the drug trade, minimizing the impact of violence on the community. This tacit agreement is now unraveling as new traffickers are emerging to replace their defunct predecessors. (Sinaloan drug lords Joaquin 'El Chapo' Guzman and Hector 'El Guero' Palma are in prison, and Amado Carillo Fuentes is dead.) Their replacements, a new breed of trafficker, are more callous, less willing to accept control or moderation, and criminally ambitious.

Mexican traffickers are expanding their reach to less patrolled areas, using corruption to virtually take over states such as Quintana Roo (which includes Cancun). Quintana Roo is not only viewed as a hotbed of co-opted government and corruption but, in the eyes of some, 'has become a narco-state.'[7] A network of government protection supports Quintana Roo's cartels. Police protect drug shipments, and corruption allegations linking Quintana Roo's government to drug trafficking have appeared in *Reforma* and *Processo*. These charges have been supported by US and Mexican intelligence.[8]

Catalysts favoring the emergence of the third phase cartel are poor economic performance, conflict between (and within) traditional oligarchies (such as in Mexico within the PRI or between federal and state governments) and social, economic and ethnic disparities. Indicators of transition include increased conflict, political turmoil, increased 'symbolic' violence (assassinations of politicians, judicial and police officials, journalists, and human rights workers), increased violence/engagements between co-opted factions of the police, enhanced employment of mercenaries, devaluation of currency, and increased migration.

These issues are also present in Haiti, a failing state a few hundred miles off the US coast. Efforts toward building a democratic government have been thwarted by endemic corruption. International drug cartels are infiltrating Haiti's impoverished society, co-opting politicians, corrupting police and fueling disorder. The drug trade is filling the void in government stability and international monetary aid, undermining US nation-building efforts contingent upon fostering an effective, corruption free modern police force. Corruption and political stalemate contribute to the existence of a virtual narco-state.

The fullest development of a criminal enclave exists in the South American jungle at the intersection of three nations. Ciudad del Este, Paraguay, is the center of this criminal near free state. Paraguay, Brazil and Argentina converge at this riverfront outpost. A jungle hub for the world's outlaws, a global village of outlaws, the triple border zone serves as a free enclave for significant criminal activity, including people who are dedicated to supporting and sustaining acts of terrorism. Denizens of the enclave include Lebanese terrorists, Colombian drug smugglers, Nigerian gangsters and, emphasizing its role as a beachhead for Asian mafias, Japanese Yakuza, Tai Chen (Cantonese mafia), Fuk Ching, the Big Circle Boys, and the Flying Dragons. Within the enclave, a polyglot mix of thugs demonstrates the potential of criminal netwarriors to exploit the globalization of organized crime.

The blurring of borders – a symbol of the post-modern, information age – is clearly demonstrated here, where the mafias exploit interconnected economies. With the ability to overwhelm governments weakened by corruption and jurisdictional obstacles, the mafias of Ciudad del Este and its Brazilian twin city of Foz do Iguacu demonstrate remarkable power and reach. Terrorism interlocks with organized crime in the enclave, a post-modern free city that is a haven to Middle Eastern terrorists, a hub for the European and US drug trade, a center for compact disc, video and software piracy, and base for gunrunners diverting US weapons to the violent and heavily armed drug gangs in the *favelas* of Rio de Janeiro and Sao Paulo.

The convergence of cartel evolution and manifestation of Internetted criminal enterprises is so pronounced in this enclave, that we call the third phase cartel the Ciudad del Este model. The transnational criminal organizations here demonstrate the potential for criminal networks to challenge state sovereignty and gain local dominance. These networked 'enclaves' or a third phase cartel embracing similar characteristics could become a dominant actor within a network of transnational criminal organizations, and potentially gain legitimacy or at least political influence within the network of state actors.

Street Gangs: Three Generations on the Road to Netwar

A close analysis of urban street gangs shows that some of these criminal enterprises have evolved through three generations[9] – transitioning from traditional turf gangs, to market-oriented drug gangs, to a new generation that mixes political and mercenary elements. As gangs negotiate this generational shift, their voyage is influenced by three factors: politicization, internationalization, and sophistication. This 'third-generation' gang entails many of the organizational and operational attributes found with net-based triads, cartels and terrorist entities. The characteristics of these three generations of gangs are summarized in Figure 1.

FIGURE 1
CHARACTERISTICS OF STREET GANG GENERATIONS

Limited	**Politicization**	Evolved
←		→
Local	**Internationalization**	Global
←		→
First generation	Second generation	Third generation
Turf gang Turf protection	Drug gang Market protection	Mercenary gang Power/financial acquisition
Proto-netwarrior	Emerging netwarrior	Netwarrior
←		→
Less sophisticated	**Sophistication**	More sophisticated

First-Generation Gangs

Traditional street gangs are primarily turf-oriented. Operating at the lower end of extreme societal violence, they have loose leadership and focus their attention on turf protection and gang loyalty within their immediate environs (often a few blocks or a neighborhood). When they engage in criminal enterprise, it is largely opportunistic and individual in scope. These turf gangs are limited in political scope, and lack sophistication. When they engage in inter-gang rivalry, it is localized (often by city blocks). Despite their limited spatial influence, these gangs due to their informal network-like attributes can be viewed as proto-netwarriors since local criminal organizations can evolve into armed bands of non-state soldiers should they gain in sophistication within failed communities with disintegrating social structure. While most gangs will stay firmly in the first generation, a few (such as some 'Crip' and 'Blood' sets and some Hispanic gangs like '18th Street') span both the first and second (nascent organized crime groups with a drug focus).

Second-Generation Gangs

Second generation gangs are organized for business. They are entrepreneurial and drug-centered. They protect their markets and use violence to control their competition. They have a broader, market-focused, sometimes overtly political, agenda and operate in a broader spatial or geographic area. Their operations sometimes involve multi-state and even international areas. Their tendency for centralized leadership and sophisticated operations for market protection places them in the center of the range of politicization, internationalization and sophistication.

Second-generation gangs, like other more sophisticated criminal enterprises, sometimes use violence as political interference to incapacitate enforcement efforts by police and security organs. Generally, this instrumental violence occurs in failed states, but clearly occurs when gangs dominate community life within 'failed communities'. Further evolution of these gangs is a danger when they link with and provide services to TCOs and participate within narcotics trafficking and distribution networks and other criminal ventures. Because of their attributes, second generation gangs can be considered emerging netwarriors.

Third-Generation Gangs

Most – in fact the overwhelming majority – of street gangs remain firmly in the first or second generations; however a small number in the United States and South Africa have acquired third-generation attributes. A third-generation street gang has evolved political aims, operates, or aspires to operate at the global end of the spectrum, and uses its sophistication to garner power, financial acquisition and engage in mercenary-type activities. Thus far, these gangs have been largely mercenary in orientation; yet, in some cases they seek political and social objectives. Examples of third-generation gangs can be seen in Chicago, San Diego, Los Angeles, and Cape Town, South Africa. Chicago witnessed the first third-generation incursion when in 1986 the 'El Rukn' gang (later known as the 'Black P Stone Nation'), under the leadership of Jeff Fort, sought to carry out terrorist attacks on behalf of Libyan President Gaddafi.

The political dimension of the third generation has also emerged in Chicago, where gang 'empowerment' and political objectives manifest themselves in '21st-Century Vote' and 'United Concerned Voters' League', the political arms of the 'Gangster Disciples' and 'Unknown Conservative Vice Lords' respectively. These gangs have evolved from turf-based entities, to drug-oriented enterprises operating in up to 35 states, to complex organizations controlling entire housing projects, schools and blocks, that conduct overt political activity while actively seeking to infiltrate and co-opt local police and contract security forces.

South Africa also experiences third-generation activity, with Cape area gangs – such as 'Hard Livings' – engaged in both political action and a long-standing terrorist or quasi-terrorist near-war with the vigilante group Pagad (People Against Gangsterism and Drugs). This shift from simple market protection to power acquisition is characteristic of third-generation activity.

Internationalization is the final indicator of gang evolution. Gangs in Los Angeles and San Diego have been notable in this regard, with Los Angeles gangs having outposts in Tijuana, Mexico, Nicaragua, El Salvador, and Belize, and San Diego gangs linking with Baja cartels. The mercenary foray of San Diego's 'Calle Treinta' ('30th St.'/'Logan Heights') gang into the binational orbit of the Arellano-Felix (Tijuana) cartel is notable for assassinations, drive-by shootings and other enforcement slayings, including the 1993 slaying of Cardinal Juan Jesus Posadas Ocampo in Guadalajara. Because of their attributes, third-generation gangs can be considered netwarriors.

Warlords Filling the Vacuum

Warlords are important to our discussion, since they are the embodiment of the rule of the criminal gang, cartel and criminal free-state. As experience has aptly demonstrated, warlords are a challenge and obstacle to the stable structures of liberal democracy and the modern state. In the typical formulation, warlordism is the province of failed or near-failed states, yet as a discussion of gang or cartel controlled areas of urban 'failed communities' readily demonstrates, proto- or virtual warlords can occupy similar niches in more stable polities. Generally, however, it is in the failed state context where warlords are of most concern.

Warlords depend upon armed force to exert their will, they are facilitated by the usurption of the rule of law, and often, if not always, rely upon criminal support (arms and drugs trafficking, extortion, the black market) to ensure their reach. As such, warlords occupy the vacuum of weak states and corrupt regimes. Sometimes they are firmly linked to clans or criminal organizations; at others, they negotiate their existence with such actors. It should be noted, however, that not all warlords are the same and not all exercise total control over their areas of operations or interest. Rival warlords can contest each other for control of a zone, and can differ considerably in their level of power, authority, reach and military prowess.

As actors exploiting vacuums of power and state control, warlords are frequently linked to the diverse varieties of political (and criminal) violence: ethnic riots, genocide, gang assaults, ethnic feuds and terrorism. For example, consider the Senas (Armies) of India and Pakistan. These paramilitary groups are often dedicated to regional ethnic causes and involved in sectarian violence of all stripes throughout the subcontinent. Senas, with their varying mixes of gangsterism, violence, and party contacts, entertain political aspirations in their areas. Some have formed State governments, and most are ethically based proto-parties.'[10]

Recent experience has reaffirmed the threat of warlords, and indeed the link between warlords and other networked threats. For example, warlords are seeking to exploit the vacuum left in the wake of the fall of the Taliban, itself a variation of a warlord regime. Terrorist networks such as Osama bin Laden's Al-Qaeda have supported or exploited relationships with warlords in Somalia and Afghanistan to anchor their global terrorist actions. Similarly, warlords have stymied the progress of the rule of law throughout Africa, Asia and South America at various times. Coalescing in the milieu of criminal gangs, these rogue regimes frequently stimulate recurrent riots, punctuated by terrorism, along the transition to warfare.

Clearly not all warlords are the same, nor occupy the same niche in the continuum of instability.[11] Some occupy that niche of endemic low-intensity conflict (LIC) dominated by gangsterism and brigandage. Others are aspiring nationalists or proto-nationalists driving regional/secessionst movements devoid of overt criminal motivations. A third variety, warlords who engage in netwar, also appears at the center of the continuum. This center position is the province of transnational warlordism. That is the threat seen with bin Laden, Al-Qaeda and the Taliban in Afganistan and elsewhere. Figure 2, developed by Sullivan, depicts the warlord continuum.

FIGURE 2
WARLORD CONTINUUM (OF INSTABILITY)

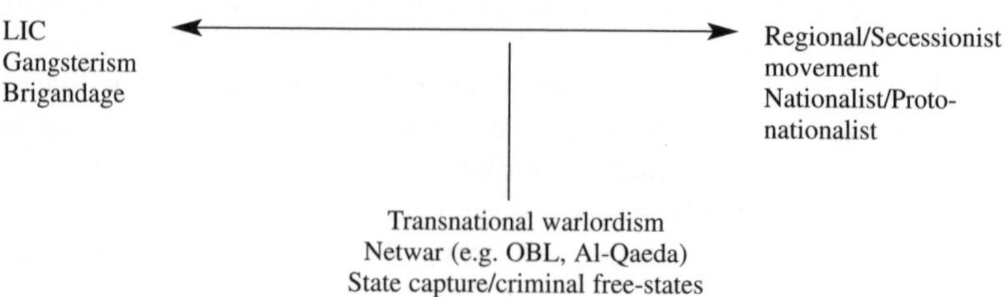

In these instances, the networked warlords engage in state capture (or establishment of a criminal free-zone in failed regions) to solidify a node to export networked transnational conflict.

Conclusion

The groups discussed here all share a common tendency toward becoming violent, pernicious threats to domestic and international security and global civil society. Those at the lower range (street gangs of the first and second generation) and those at the middle to higher range (third-generation gangs, first- and second-phase cartels and warlords) are particularly worrisome. All share networked organizational features and are difficult to counter. These groups have the potential to refine network designs and new technological tools to challenge the dominance of nation-states and carve out new realms of activity for the non-state soldier.

Criminal organizations, particularly drug cartels and other transnational groups, and even warlords, are becoming increasingly networked in terms of organization and influence. Due to increased sophistication and access to technology, but more likely due to a social Darwinism, they have honed their ability to co-opt, corrupt and challenge state institutions. In doing so they have refined their use of violence. We believe they have become a more insidious threat than their more outwardly brutal ancestors.

As these groups evolve, they challenge notions of the state and political organization. States are, at least in the current scheme of things, entities that possess a legitimate monopoly on the use of violence within a specified territory. A third-phase cartel, criminal free state or free enclave would essentially be a para-state, that is, an entity that challenges that monopoly, much the same as warlords within failed states.

It is clear that a para-state on the scope of a third phase cartel or criminal free state could become a new war-making entity, and a challenger to the nation-state. Such an entity could be a narco- or criminal state, be a dominant actor within a network of transnational organizations, engage in mercenary use or provision, dominate portions of a local state, region or trade bloc, and eventually gain legitimacy and influence in the network of political actors. Clearly, such a non-trinitarian entity challenges our current institutions and, at least during a transitional period, can be expected to exploit corruption, co-option, terrorism, crime and violence toward its ends.

NOTES

1. John Arquilla and David Ronfeldt, 'A New Epoch – And Spectrum – Of conflict,' in idem (eds.) *In Athena's Camp: Preparing for Conflict in the Information Age* (Santa Monica CA: RAND 1997) p.5. For a more recent exploration of netwar and its darker consequences, see also John Arquilla and David Ronfeldt (eds.) *Networks and Netwars: The Future of Terror, Crime, and Militancy* (Santa Monica, CA: RAND 2001).
2. Martin van Creveld, *The Transformation of War* (New York, NY: The Free Press 1991) p.197.
3. See Robert J. Bunker and John P. Sullivan, 'Cartel Evolution: Potentials and Consequences,' *Transnational Organized Crime* 4/2 (Summer 1998) pp.55–74 for a comprehensive treatment of cartel evolution underlying this analysis.
4. Robert J. Bunker, 'Epochal Change: War Over Social and Political Organization', *Parameters* 27/2 (Summer 1997) pp.15–24.
5. Robert J. Bunker, *Five-Dimensional (Cyber) Warfighting: Can the Army After Next be Defeated Through Complex Concepts and Technologies?* (Carlisle, PA: US Army War College, Strategic Studies Institute, March 1998).
6. See Valerie Alvord, 'Gang members tied to drug cartel indicted', *The San Diego Union-Tribune* (Wednesday, 11 Feb. 1998) p.B-3 and John P. Sullivan, 'Third Generation Street Gangs: Turf, Cartels and Net Warriors', *Transnational Organized Crime* 3/3 (Autumn 1997) p.106.
7. Mary Beth Sheridan, 'Traffickers Move Into Yucatan Peninsula', *Los Angeles Times*, Column One (27 Aug. 1998).
8. Ibid.
9. See Sullivan, 'Third Generation Street Gangs (note 6) pp.95–108, and 'Urban Gangs Evolving as Criminal Netwar Actors', *Small Wars and Insurgencies* 11/1 (Spring 2000) pp.82–96 for a discussion of the analysis underlying this section.
10. David L. Horowitz, *The Deadly Ethnic Riot* (Berkeley: Univ. of California Press 2001) p.246.
11. This analysis of a continuum of warlords draws upon the observations found in Paul B. Rich, 'Warlordism, Complex Emergencies and the Search for a Doctrine of Humanitarian Intervention', in D.S. Gordon and F.H. Toase (eds.) *Aspects of Peacekeeping* (London and Portland, OR: Frank Cass 2001) pp.253–73.

Private Military Companies: Mercenaries for the 21st Century

THOMAS K. ADAMS

Mercenaries and auxiliaries are useless and dangerous.
Niccolò Machiavelli, *The Prince*, Chapter XII
[orig. published 1513]

Machiavelli's comment reflected the long standing consensus on mercenaries, but early 21st-century governments are finding them to be quite useful. How dangerous they are remains to be seen.

The subject of mercenaries captured the headlines in September 2001 following the tragic terrorist attacks on the World Trade Center and the Pentagon. Almost immediately, reports began to surface that British 'mercenaries', usually former Special Air Services (SAS), were hunting terrorist suspect Osama bin Laden in pursuit of the multimillion dollar reward offered by the United States. Less publicly, it was also heard that official inquiries had been made through a UK-based private military company (PMC) called Sandline. Reportedly, the hope was that some of Sandline's highly unofficial sources could assist in the search for bin Laden and his Al-Qaeda terrorist network.

PMCs had already gained considerable press attention shortly before September 11 – in the summer and early fall of 2001. A spate of newspaper reports appeared then, accusing President George W. Bush of planning to deploy a 'private army' of former US servicemen to South America as part of the war against drugs.[1]

In fact, by the summer of 2001, there were already American civilian contractors in Colombia involved in activities ranging from administering judicial reform programs to helping internal refugees. But the news media ignored them in favor of the far more interesting efforts of those firms training Colombian police and counterinsurgency forces. The media did occasionally note that the rise of civilian paramilitary companies was by no means isolated to United States contractors; dozens of similar firms from various countries had been quietly springing up around the world for more than a decade.

The rise of these firms has not been well received. At about the same time President Bush was being pummeled in the newspapers, the United

Nations Commission on Human Rights (UNHCHR) and various public interest groups were busily condemning the so-called mercenaries. In June 2001, a conference of international civil society organizations released a scathing joint report entitled 'Private Military Intervention & Arms Proliferation in Conflicts in Africa'. The group was 'appalled by the role of private military companies and their associated mining companies, rogue airlines and arms brokers in illicit arms transfers, illegitimate resource appropriation and reproduction of violence and poverty'.[2]

Meanwhile, DynCorp of Reston, Virginia, a military contractor, announced that it had more than $1.8 billion in annual revenues for 2000, a $6.1 billion-dollar contract backlog and more than 20,000 employees in more than 550 locations worldwide.[3] Its 2001 revenue was projected at more than $2 billion. If nothing else, the announcement illustrated that 'mercenaries' or private military companies were alive and well in the new century.

Defining 'Mercenaries'

Now, it must be recognized that civilian contractors of various sorts have been providing non-combat services to the military since Roman times and probably before. When the German battleship *Bismarck* engaged the British battleship HMS *Prince of Wales* in the Denmark Strait early in World War II, civilian contractors died in the British ship. But those contractors were strictly concerned with a newly installed turret mechanism. They did not load, aim or fire the guns and did not train anyone else to do so. A number of firms such as BDM International Inc., Brown & Root, and Pacific Architects and Engineering have long provided less dramatic logistical support to US and foreign militaries. But, like the contractors in the *Prince of Wales*, these companies did not provide direct military assistance. The significant point here is that the new class of military corporations does provide this kind of direct military service. Analysts and officials became interested in this phenomenon in the early 1990s, when they noticed that private firms, loosely characterized as 'mercenaries', were taking a noticeably greater role in various armed conflicts, a phenomenon that troubled some of them greatly.

The mere existence of mercenaries in the twentieth century was certainly not news. During the 1950s and 1960s mercenary units and individuals had been active in Africa, notably in the Congo. In the 1970s and 1980s they figured in coup attempts in Guinea, Equatorial Guinea, Benin, Togo, the Comoros Islands and the Seychelles. By the 1980s, movies like *The Wild Geese* (1978) and *Dogs of War* (1980) had made swashbuckling 'mercs' a part of popular culture.

But the 'old' mercenaries were usually regarded as colorful adventurers

– interesting, though of marginal importance. The new mercenaries are something else. The traditional mercs were more or less *ad hoc* collections of former soldiers who provided experience, leadership, small arms and an occasional armored car. Their organizations were as ephemeral as the causes they fought for.

On the other hand, the new ones are first and foremost *businesses*. Their members are as likely to wear gray flannel as camouflage and to present themselves as free-market businessmen rather than soldiers of fortune. The have a distinct business nature with a permanent core staff and on-going marketing, and their operations emphasize private enterprise, efficiency and expertise. They are also unlike ordinary security firms that provide private guards, buildings watchmen and the like.

Some of the long-standing guard services and security companies have international connections but they differ from the new 'mercenaries' in that their functions do not involve training in military methods, leadership, or equipment. The new international security firms embody all those features. Often organized by retired senior military officers, some of the new firms offer a narrow selection of very specialized services while others can provide a full range of military-related functions. Since the term 'mercenaries' is loaded with negative connotations, they often call themselves 'private military companies' (PMCs) or, sometimes, private security companies (PSCs).

Not only do these companies reject the term 'mercenaries', but there is also some doubt as to how well they fit the traditional conception of hired soldiers. Upon examination, 'mercenary' turns out to be a somewhat slippery term.

The common-language sense of the term usually indicates adventurers of the sort depicted in popular books and movies, and certainly not upstanding international business firms. In popular usage it is often simply an insult, applied to any police, military, or paramilitary that the user dislikes.

The 1977 Protocol to the Geneva Convention states that a 'mercenary' is 'one who is motivated essentially by the desire for private gain and is promised material compensation substantially in excess of that promised or paid to combatants in the armed forces of that party'.[4] This rule originally applied only to international conflicts, but equally, it is rather general and could be interpreted to apply to anyone providing any form of direct paid service to a military establishment, no matter how benign.

Furthermore, most of the larger PMCs make certain that they operate with the explicit consent of the national governments concerned, not only the receiving state, but also the one where the PMC is headquartered. In some cases, such as the Vinnell Corporation contract with Saudi Arabia and Military Professional Resources Incorporated (MPRI)'s contract in former

Yugoslavia, the contract is 'brokered' (formally or informally) by the national government within whose domain the PMC is based. It may actually be part of a bilateral agreement between the states involved.[5] Some firms have reportedly turned down contracts because they did not accord with the policies of their host governments.[6]

PMCs came to popular attention in the 1990s thanks to a series of high-profile contracts. In March 1994, the Croatian Ministry of Defense arranged with MPRI, a private US firm, to professionalize its army. That same year, the Angolan government hired a South African firm, Executive Outcomes (EO), to help fight the rebel forces of UNITA (União Nacional para a Independência Total de Angola). The following year the government of Sierra Leone contracted with EO to quell a rebellion, and establish internal order. Then, in 1997, another firm, called Sandline International, was hired to quell a nine-year armed independence movement in Bougainville, Papua New Guinea. Meanwhile, the London-based Saladin company reportedly organized counterinsurgency work in Sri Lanka and security training in the Middle East.[7]

Unlike 'old-fashioned' mercenaries, PMC activity is not limited to security, light forces and basic infantry skills. The year 1999 saw Russia's Sukhoi Design Bureau provide modern Su-27 aircraft to Ethiopia for its war with Eritrea. Since Ethiopia could not support the high-tech planes, Sukhoi reportedly included former Russian military pilots, mechanics, and ground personnel on contract, in effect delivering a small, but complete, air force.[8] The Vinnell Corporation of California trains light armored brigades (including artillery and air defense) for the Saudi Arabian military. Another US military firm working in Saudi Arabia, Booz-Allen & Hamilton, drills the Saudi Marine Corps and maintains the Saudi Armed Forces Staff College. Science Applications International Corp. (SAIC) assists the Saudi Navy and O'Gara Protective Services provides security for the Saudi royal family.

Another large but less well-known firm, UK-based Defense Systems Limited (DSL), is reportedly one of the world's largest suppliers of specialist security services. DSL describes its core business as devising and implementing solutions to complex security problems in high-risk areas that include Algeria, Angola, and Colombia. Allegedly, it has also provided counterinsurgency training for security forces in Sri Lanka, Papua New Guinea and Mozambique. Its client list includes De Beers, Texaco, Chevron Schlumberger, British Gas, British Petroleum, Bechtel, BHP Mineral, American Airlines, CARE (Cooperative for Assistance and Relief Everywhere), Caritas and USAID. At least seven United Nations organizations utilize DSL in security roles.[9]

Furthermore, these are only highlights. The private Center for Defense

Information lists dozens of similar organizations with international operations including Combat Force, Investments Surveys, Honey Badger Arms and Ammunition, Shield Security, Kas Enterprises, Saracen International and Longreach Security (all in South Africa). International military firms based in other parts of the world include Alpha Five, Corporate Trading International, Omega Support Ltd., Parasec Strategic Concept, Jardine Securicor Gurkha Services (Hong Kong), Gurkha Security Guards (Isle of Man, UK), and Special Project Service Ltd (UK).[10]

If some of these firms are secretive, still others court publicity and many maintain public websites on the Internet. An October 2001 scan of the Internet revealed numerous suppliers of military and paramilitary services including Grupo Golan (Israel), Global Studies Group (US), and Sakina Security Services (Russia). They offered just about every kind of specialty from training military dogs (Close Quarter Battle K-9 [US]) to providing anti-piracy protection. Alpha-A (Russia), for example, provides security for goods in transport across the former Soviet Union. Other PMC services include security analyses, audits, and training as well as anti-industrial espionage, sniping, and 'getaway' driving.

For some observers, the proliferation and rapid growth of these firms strongly suggested that nation-states might be losing their monopoly over military means. If true this was indeed serious since one of the defining characteristics of the modern state (and one of the most cherished) is the right to employ force, especially deadly force; particularly through military means. Any compromise of that monopoly would be very significant indeed.[11]

The 21st Century is Not a Safe Place

Actually, the blossoming of private military companies is not very surprising. Like most social phenomena, PMCs appeared in response to a change in conditions. With the end of the Cold War the rationale for much of the century's military activity was gone. Without that threat to galvanize public opinion, the great powers became much more sensitive to the domestic political consequences of military casualties, especially for causes not directly tied to the national interest. The bad experience of early 1990s operations such as Bosnia and Somalia combined with this fear to lead most powerful states away from peripheral involvements. As Stephen Kinloch points out, this is not necessarily a bad thing: 'fear of casualties on the part of states can be considered a healthy phenomenon, reflecting governments' responsibility and their accountability for the lives of their citizens'. After all, he goes on, 'national armed forces are primarily for the defense and protection of the interests and citizens of the country they serve'.[12] The downside, of course, is that the most powerful states perform much less policing on the periphery than had been the case.

Additionally, the last half of the twentieth century produced many marginally viable states and exposed the weakness of some older ones. Governments in Ethiopia, Liberia, Somalia, and Zaire lost significant support when their Cold War sponsors cut military assistance. The result has been a large number of intrastate conflicts: revolutions, irredentism, independence and separatist movements. Nearly all of these are barely on the fringes of major power interests and no longer of great concern to the former adversaries of the now-defunct bipolar world. This may be sensible and even prudent of the great powers but it creates a self-help environment for those individuals, states, corporations and other entities that must live and operate in these borderlands of the developed world.

Part of the problem is that some of these weaker states simply cannot meet the financial and political costs of maintaining an effective security establishment even at the level of local police and border guards. For them, assistance from a private military company may be very attractive, not least because it is relatively cheap.

An effective standing professional military is a very expensive proposition. This is especially true when such a force must be maintained over long periods when there is no serious need for it. Furthermore, sad experience has shown that, for many developing countries, a permanent military establishment can be a threat to internal stability and worst of all, ineffective when finally needed. Nevertheless, military forces are usually considered an indispensable part of the trappings of sovereignty – the result being many poorly paid, ill-trained and ineffective forces. It is all very well to criticize African governments for purchasing security in return for a stake in their mineral resources. However, the only realistic choices for such governments may be to obtain outside military assistance in the form of mercenaries or forfeit power.

For such governments, private military corporations can be a very attractive alternative; they can be employed and dismissed on the basis of performance and need, rather than political timetables. They are available quickly when required and without political strings attached.

Further, PMCs are by definition 'outside' elements. This is one of the popular arguments against them. However, by the same token, their 'outsideness' can also mean that they are not part of the political, tribal and factional struggles that are often an important cause for intrastate conflict. Nor are weak states the only customers of private military services. Even relief and humanitarian organizations may become a market thanks to the incidence of hostage takings, threats of violence, and killings. Insurgencies have been increasingly likely to rob or coerce aid organizations for their foreign exchange, communications, and logistics (this kind of activity was a major reason for US and UN military intervention in Somalia in the early 1990s). UNHCHR has lost personnel in Rwanda, delegates for the International Committee of the Red Cross (ICRC) were murdered in Chechnya, and CARE USA workers have been killed in Somalia and Sudan.[13]

A 1998 study observed that more Red Cross workers have been killed in action in recent times than US Army personnel.[14] As expressed by Christopher Spearin of the Canadian Center for Foreign Policy Development, 'In the weak state environment, gone is the assumption that host governments are willing or able to provide security for the populace, let alone ensure that humanitarian operations are able to proceed relatively unmolested.'[15]

The security situation for these organizations is serious enough for CARE Canada and the University of Toronto to issue a joint report, 'Mean Times: Humanitarian Action in Complex Emergencies – Stark Choices, Cruel Dilemmas' (1999). The report proposes that humanitarian organizations should consider relying on the growing private security industry.

Seen in these terms, the proliferation of PMCs is an accommodation to reality, a response to changes in the world. PMCs can provide important and necessary services, however unpalatable that fact may be in some quarters.

Attempts to Condemn and Control

Unsurprisingly, the United Nations has consistently been the most vocal opponent of PMCs (preferring to characterize them as 'mercenaries'). The UN is, after all, an organization of states and serves the interests of states. In the UN view, mercenary activity is a violation of the principles of sovereign equality, political independence, and the territorial integrity of member states as well as a threat to human rights. Several states (chiefly in Africa) had long urged the UN to take a greater interest in the issue and in 1987 the Commission on Human Rights appointed Enrique Bernales Ballesteros Special Rapporteur on Mercenaries. In his annual reports, Ballesteros has drawn attention to the growing number of hired fighters appearing in Zaire, Angola, Rwanda, Tajikistan, Armenia, Azerbaijan, Afghanistan, and former Yugoslavia. He also pointed out, in several reports, that mercenary activities are increasingly taking the form of security companies that provide military training and security services in return for money and mining and energy concessions. There has been, he said, a 'significant presence of mercenaries' in armed conflicts, especially in Africa. The reports showed special concern about the involvement of large, well-organized, and well-equipped private military forces such as Executive Outcomes.[16]

Despite all this concern, the international community has had very little success in attempting to halt or control the rise of PMCs. The Organization of African Unity (OAU) offered what was probably the first international agreement to ban mercenaries with its 1972 Convention for the Elimination of Mercenaries. The Convention never became international law, but its main provisions reappeared in the 1977 OAU Convention for the Elimination of Mercenarism in Africa.[17] That also had little effect, but much of the language was carried over to the Additional Protocol I of 1977 to the Geneva Conventions. However, the convention applies only in situations of international armed conflict. Most mercenary activity is in intrastate conflicts.[18]

The UN's 2001 condemnation of mercenaries echoed a 40-year history of similar statements. The General Assembly, the Security Council, the Economic and Social Council, and the Commission on Human Rights have condemned the use of mercenaries since the 1960s. Special Rapporteur Ballesteros has characterized them as politically disconnected from the societies into which they are introduced by governments. This, Ballesteros claimed, made them instruments for oppression, used to violate human rights and to impede the exercise of the right of people to self-determination. He asserted that mercenary initiatives by private companies registered as security firms in a third country were a threat to national sovereignty.[19]

UN reports also took note of the economic influence that was sometimes gained by the parent corporation, owners of the mercenary firm. 'Once a greater degree of security has been attained, the firm apparently begins to exploit the concessions it has received by setting up a number of associates and affiliates which engage in such varying activities as air transport, road building, and import and export, thereby acquiring a significant, if not hegemonic, presence in the economic life of the country in which it is operating.'[20]

The UN is not alone in these beliefs. A chorus of voices from academia and 'international civil society' has been equally loud in their belief that the mercenary phenomenon is potentially dangerous and destabilizing. The Center for Democracy and Development, a London-based public interest group, and a number of other organizations are equally vociferous.

For all of the collective outrage, remarkably little has been done to create international measures that could seriously hobble the activities of PMCs, much less drive them out of existence. The UN's own International Convention Against the Recruitment, Use, Financing, and Training of Mercenaries was finally adopted by the General Assembly in 1989, but did not manage to attract even the bare minimum of signatures needed for ratification until 2001.[22] This, of course, raises the obvious question of why no effective action has been taken.

The first part of the answer, oddly enough, is the fact that the UN as a body has not been notably interested in the subject of mercenary activity. Most of the outrage has been generated by a relatively small number of less influential countries, mostly in Africa, some of whom use mercenaries themselves. The rapporteur reports have often been academic exercises, theoretical considerations of the nature, role and impact of mercenary activities. This was interesting but not very useful as shown by the scant attention the Commission gave these reports. In 1995 the Commission even considered discontinuing the mandate since it seemed lack any substantive purpose. The 1998 renewal of the mandate was not even supported by the full Commission.

This indifference may rise from the low impact of the issue on many members and a general lack of support on the part of the great powers. Only a handful of UN member countries have any substantial 'mercenary' problem. None of the Convention signatories except Germany and Italy are major powers and none are significant suppliers of mercenaries or home to large international security firms. But at least three of the signatories, Angola, the Congo and Zaire, overtly use mercenaries in their internal struggles despite their own laws forbidding mercenary activity.

Another part of the answer may be found in the nature of the international legal efforts. They have focused almost exclusively on the elimination of mercenaries on the grounds that their activities threaten self-determination and decolonization. The UN Convention and the activities of its rapporteur on mercenaries are holdovers from the earlier era of old-fashioned mercenaries. International legalist Yvez Sandoz emphasized this when he stated, 'the basic approach is not relevant today… the problem of private security should not be essentially based on the mercenary issue as it was dealt with in the seventies'.[23] The situation is very different from the 1970s and so are international security firms. As noted earlier, some, like Dyn Corp and MPRI, are actually *de facto* arms of their national governments. Others perform useful services not provided elsewhere. It is also difficult to imagine how any outright ban on mercenaries would be administered and enforced. Even if it were, the likely effect would simply be to drive the practice underground.

Factually, the outsourcing of military expertise is a useful alternative for governments such as the US government, that wish to avoid placing their national armed forces in dangerous places such as Colombia. An example is the 1998 US decision to contract with DynCorp for verification monitors in Kosovo while other countries provided military officers.[24] Employing PMCs can help to overcome the political reluctance to become involved in situations where risks are high and there is little domestic constituency for the involvement of a state's professional armed forces. It can also help avoid oversight and control.

Using PMCs has enabled Washington to bring military influence to bear in Bosnia, Colombia and the Persian Gulf while continuing to reduce its armed forces. Georgetown University professor Herbert Howe, a specialist in military outsourcing stated, 'The military has dropped over 40 per cent in manpower and budget since the late 1980s. The US government is increasingly shifting over to outsourcing.'[25]

In addition, Professor Howe said, there is inevitably a public outcry whenever US troops are injured or killed in a foreign conflict. Much less attention is paid when privately contracted military trainers or specialists suffer the same fate. The government has minimal reporting requirements regarding casualties suffered by private contractors.[26] When a helicopter carrying US contractors performing anti-drug functions was shot down in Peru in the early 1990s, the loss caused barely a ripple in the international press.

Washington is not alone in appreciating the utility of PMCs. In March 1998, Sandline International, depicted by the press as 'a British mercenary force', helped restore the elected president of Sierra Leone to power after a military coup. Officers of the Sierra Leone army had seized control of the country in May 1997 and began a brutal murder campaign aimed at eliminating its possible political opponents. Despite continuing widespread and very public brutality, governments were unable to mount effective action. In October, when all diplomatic attempts to oust the mutinous generals had failed, the UN Security Council responded with an ineffective arms embargo. Finally, Sandline became involved. Although publicly depicted as a private security firm guarding 'mining and construction interests', Sandline told the press that it was asked by the British High Commissioner in Sierra Leone to help train and equip a local force capable of removing the generals. The American State Department was also apparently kept fully informed, and the US government lent at least its tacit support.[27]

Regulation and Realities

Given the realities of the situation, the capabilities, business nature, and success of the private military industry coupled with the lack of a effective regulation still raises important questions.

First, there is a basic question of accountability. Governments, including their armed forces, are at least nominally accountable to their people and their legislatures. Private corporations, on the other hand, have little or no responsibility to the public and are even shielded to some degree from government scrutiny.

This is indeed a problem, but as long as PMCs serve the purposes of the major powers and support the policies of these countries, no major power is likely to take a serious interest in creating legal restraints. Both the UK and the US already have laws on the books that forbid their citizens to fight as members of foreign militaries but these laws are seldom enforced.

Next, private military companies are not the freebooters that their critics often imagine. In reality they are restrained by several influences, beginning with their own government and the employing government. They are also restrained by their business nature, which requires them to seek good public relations and control the actions of their employees in order to obtain new contracts.

As long as the PMCs remain unthreatening they are also protected by what Jeffery Herbst calls their 'adaptation to the international environment of free trade'. Given their low asset base and lack of permanent employees, Herbst believes there 'is no compelling reason' for such firms to be headquartered in any particular place.[28] In the words of international legalist Juan Carlos Zarate, PMCs have 'developed a *modus operandi* compatible with the needs and strictures of the post-Cold War, state-based international system'.

The next question is less immediate. Over time, can the combination of corporate and military power create entities more powerful than states? According to Herbert Howe, 'I think the major worry that everyone has about this sort of thing is, will these forces become a force unto themselves, kind of rogue elephants?'[29] James L. Woods, a Washington defense consultant, agrees: 'If the international community cannot get its act together and help these countries keep themselves together and protect commerce and protect the citizenry, you're going to see more and more' examples of private contractors doing the job. Woods, a partner in the consulting firm of Cohen & Woods International, added that, over time, PMCs could become stronger than some of the sovereign states they are hired to protect.[30]

This seems unlikely for two basic reasons. For one thing, the actual military power of these companies is minuscule in comparison to even third-rate national armed forces. The military successes of the PMCs have occurred in places, chiefly Africa, where organized military opposition has been feeble or absent entirely.

Second, nation-states remain the locus of legal authority and are likely to remain so for the foreseeable future. There is no clear instance of a PSC accepting a contract without the consent of the state in which the contract was executed. Furthermore, given the amazing (indeed frightening) success of international corporations in wielding influence by economic means, there is no obvious reason for them to seek it through the wasteful and inefficient methods of military force. Finally, if corporate mercenaries were to gain anything like the degree of power and influence implied by Professor Howe's question, the great powers would certainly make it their business to implement legal constraints. Alternatively, the major powers might simply return to a policy of providing more military assistance via the professional military forces, thus negating much of the PMC's reason for existence and severely damaging their revenue stream.

The thrust of many attempts to control or eliminate PMCs is based on the mistaken belief that they are an aberration that should be put to rights. But the growth of PMCs may be part of a much larger trend. Mark Duffield suggests that while PMCs are booming both domestically and internationally, they are only bit players in the general trend towards privatization of social and economic activity. Seen this way, the rise of the PMCs is a consequence of widespread movement toward privatization and the neo-liberal restructuring of state activity.[31]

Certainly, it would be surprising if the changing role of governments, including the privatization of domestic welfare and security functions, was not also reflected in foreign policy.[32]

NOTES

1. For example, Karen DeYoung 'House Rejects Bush Request on Colombia', *Washington Post* (25 July 2001) p.A17 also Julian Borger and Martin Hodgson 'US Proxy War on Drug barons Unravels', *The Guardian* (2 June 2001) p.1. Critics were especially concerned over a provision in the proposed legislation that would allow private companies to use federal funds to purchase weapons and ammunition for 'defensive purposes' in the Andean region. Furthermore, the public and policy makers had been sensitized to the issue by a tragic incident in April when a light plane carrying a missionary family was misidentified as a drug aircraft and shot down by Peruvian fighters. A CIA radar plane operated by civilian contractors had guided in the fighters.
2. Abdel-Fatau Musah 'Liberia Conference on Private Military Intervention & Arms Proliferation in Conflicts in Africa' Report. (London, UK: Center for Democratic Development, June 2001).
3. <www.dyncorp.com/areas/index.htm>, accessed June 2001.
4. Article 47, Protocol Additional to the Geneva Conventions of 12 August 1949 and Relating to the Protection of Victims of International Armed Conflicts (Protocol I) of 8 June 1977. www.icrc.org/icrcnews/2ce2.htm
5. Both Vinnell and MPRI fall into this category.
6. For example, the late President Mobutu of Zaire apparently made at least two attempts to obtain help from PMCs and was turned down due to 'policy considerations of western governments'. Major Thomas J. Milton, USA 'The New Mercenaries – Corporate Armies For Hire', *Journal of the Foreign Area Officer Association* (Springfield, VA 1997), <www.faoa.org/journal/newmerc3.html>.
7. Herbert Howe, 'Global Order and Security Privatization', *Strategic Forum* (Washington, DC: Institute for National Strategic Studies, National Defense University, May 1998); also Kirsten Sellars 'Old dogs of war learn new tricks', *New Statesman* (25 April 1997).
8. 'The Russians Are Coming', *US News and World Report* (15 March 1999) via Internet

<www.usnews/issue/990315/15merc.htm>, accessed 28 Sept. 2001.

9. DSL has received a good deal of presumably unwelcome public attention in recent years, for example Howe (note 7); also, Pratap Chatterjee 'Guarding the Multinationals: DSL and the International Private "Security Business"', *Multinational Monitor* (March 1998) and Dean Andromidas, 'Defense Systems Ltd.: Crown Jewel', *Executive Intelligence Review* (22 Aug. 1997).
10. David Isenberg 'Soldiers of Fortune Ltd', Center for Defense Information Monograph, (Washington, DC: Center for Defense Information, Nov. 1997). This is an excellent treatment of the subject and recommended to anyone with an interest in PMCs.
11. For example, Herbert Howe, Interview, Center for Defense Information, Washington, DC, 2 Oct. 1997 <www.cdi.org/adm/1113/Howe.html> accessed 12 Sept. 2001.
12. Stephen P. Kinloch, 'Utopian or Pragmatic? A UN Permanent Volunteer Force', *International Peacekeeping* 3/4 (Winter 1996) p.171.
13. Howe (note 7).
14. Sean Greenaway and Andrew J. Harris, 'Humanitarian Security: Challenges and Responses', paper presented at the Forging Peace Conference, 13–15 March 1998, Harvard University, p.34, note 45. See also Larry Minear and Thomas G. Weiss, *Mercy Under Fire: War and the Global Humanitarian Community* (Boulder, CO: Westview Press 1995) pp.38–45.
15. Christopher Spearin 'A Private Security Panacea? A Response to "Mean Times" on Securing the Humanitarian Space' Canadian Center for Foreign Policy Development, Univ. of British Columbia, Second Annual Graduate Student Seminar 30 April–5 May 2000.
16. For example, United Nations, Press Release GA/SHC/3562 (16 Nov. 1999); 'Report of the Special Rapporteur on the question of the use of mercenaries as a means of violating human rights and impeding the exercise of the right of peoples to self-determination'; UN document E/CN.4/1998/31; 'Report of the Special Rapporteur on Mercenaries, etc.' UN document E/CN.4/1995/29.
17. OAU doc. CM/433/Rev.L., Annex 1 (1972); and Organization of African Unity Convention for the Elimination of Mercenarism in Africa, OAU Doc. CM/817 (XXIX) Annex II Rev. 3 (1977).
18. United Nations 'Report on the Question of the Use of Mercenaries as a Means of Impeding the Exercise of the Right of Peoples to Self-Determination, UN ESCOR, 44th Sess., UN Doc.
19. United Nations Press Release GA/SHC/3376 (5 Nov. 1996); United Nations General Assembly Resolution 47/84, 47 U. Supp. (No. 49) at 165, UN Doc. A/47/49 (1992); United Nations High Commissioner for Human Rights, 'Fact Sheet No.13, International Humanitarian Law and Human Rights' (Geneva Switzerland, July 1991).
20. United Nations, Press Release GA/SHC/3562 (16 Nov. 1999).
21. Abdel-Fatau Musah, 'Liberia Conference on Private Military Intervention & Arms Proliferation in Conflicts in Africa', Report. (London, UK: Center for Democratic Development, June 2001).
22. Background and current status of the International Convention Against the Recruitment, Use, Financing, and Training of Mercenaries courtesy of the US Mission to the United Nations, via FAX, 3 Oct. 2001. Comments on the signatories are the author's own and not to be otherwise attributed.
23. Yves Sandoz, 'The Privatisation of Security: Framing A Conflict Prevention and Peacebuilding Agenda', paper presented at Wilton Park Conference, 19–21 Nov. 1999.
24. Johnathan Steele, 'Private Military to Monitor Pullout', *The Guardian* (London) (2 Nov. 1998) p.1.
25. Tod Robberson, 'Contractors playing increasing role in U.S. drug war', *Dallas Morning News* (Sunday, 27 Feb. 2000), <www. peace.ca/ privatizingwar.htm>, accessed 11 Oct. 2001.
26. Ibid.
27. David Graves and Hugo Gurdon, 'US Says Sandline Experts Helped to Overthrow Rebels', *The Telegraph* (London) (14 May 1998) at <www.telegraph.co.uk>, accessed 13 Jan. 1999.
28. Dustin Chick, 'Mercenary Groups Discussed', *Business Day* (11 Dec. 1998) at <www.bday.co.za/98/1211/news/n9.htm>, accessed 3 Aug. 2001.
29. 'Private US Companies Train Armies Around the World', *US News and World Report* (8 Feb.

1997) p.13.

30. James L. Woods, private correspondence with the author, 17 May 1998.
31. Mark Duffield, 'Famine, Conflict and the Internationalization of Public Welfare', in Martin Doornbos, Lionel Cliffe, Abdel Ghaffar M. Ahmed, and John Marakis (eds.) *Beyond Conflict in the Horn: Prospects for Peace, Recovery and Development in Ethiopia, Somalia and the Sudan* (London: James Currey 1992) p.58.
32. Mark Duffield, 'NGO relief in war zones: Towards an analysis of the new aid paradigm', *Third World Quarterly* 18 (1997). In a similar vein, James Fennell, an advisor for Defense Systems Limited (DSL), observes: 'The increasing role of commercial security companies may be viewed in a similar vein to the increased policy and technical input of NGOs over the past two decades to the provision of official relief and development assistance…' James Fennell, 'Private Security Companies: the New Humanitarian Agent', presentation to the Conference on Interagency Co-ordination in Complex Humanitarian Emergencies, 19 Oct. 1999, Cranfield Univ./Royal Military College of Science, Shrivenham, UK.

Non-State Actors in Colombia: Threats to the State and to the Hemisphere

MAX G. MANWARING

The terrorist attacks on New York City and Washington DC on 11 September 2001 reminded Americans of realities long understood in Europe, the Middle East, Africa, Asia, and Latin America. That is, terrorism is a very practical, calculated, and cynical strategy of warfare for the weak to use against the strong. It is a generalized political-psychological asymmetric substitute for conventional war.[1] The intent is to coerce substantive political change.[2]

Now, for the first time since the end of the Cold War, political and military leaders are rethinking the United States' global role and supporting strategies. They are now discussing these issues in terms of the political and military transitions required to deal more effectively with the global security problems that were submerged in the morass of the East–West Conflict and unleashed by the Eastern European revolutions of 1989. In these terms, Colombia is emerging as the most compelling issue on the hemispheric agenda. That country's deeply rooted and ambiguous warfare has reached crisis proportions in that Colombia's 'Hobbesian Trinity' of illegal drug trafficker, insurgent, and paramilitary organizations are creating a situation in which life is indeed 'nasty, brutish, and short'.[3]

The first step in developing a macro-level vision, policy, and strategy to deal with the Colombian Crisis – in a global context – is to be clear on what the Colombian crisis is, and what the fundamental threats implicit (and explicit) in it are. This is the point from which political and military leaders can start thinking about the gravity of the terrorist strategy employed by Colombia's stateless adversaries. It is also the point from which leaders can begin developing responses designed to secure Colombian, hemispheric, and global stability. This paper, then, seeks to explain the Colombian crisis in terms of non-state threats to the state and to the region.

The Context of the Colombian Crisis

In the 1930s and 1940s, chronic political, economic, and social problems created by a self-serving civilian oligarchy began to create yet another crisis in a long list of internal conflicts in Colombian history. In 1930, Liberal reformists came to power and deprived Conservatives of the control of the central government and extensive local patronage. The Liberals also initiated an ambitious social agenda that generated increasing civil violence between Conservative and Liberal partisans.[4]

The catalyst that ignited the 18-year period called 'the violence' in April 1948 was the 'assassination' of Liberal populist, Jorge Eliecer Gaitan. That murder sparked a riot known as the *Bogotazo* that left much of the capital destroyed and an estimated 2,000 dead. Although the government was able to contain the situation in Bogota, it could not control the violence that spread through the countryside. Rural violence became the norm as an estimated 20,000 armed Liberal and Conservative combatants settled old political scores. Over the period from 1948 to 1966, *la violencia* claimed the lives of over 200,000 Colombians.[5]

It was in this unstable environment of virtually uncontrolled violence, rural poverty, political disarray, and government weakness that the illegal drug industry began to grow and prosper. That prosperity, in turn, provided resources that allowed insurgent organizations to grow and expand. And, later, as the Colombian government proved less and less effective in controlling the national territory and the people in it, the self-defense paramilitary groups emerged.[6] The thread that permitted these violent non-state actors to develop, grow, and succeed was – and is – adequate freedom of movement and action over time. The dynamics of the Hobbesian Trinity, within the context of the almost constant instability and violence over the past several decades, have substantially expanded freedom of movement and action, and correspondingly eroded that of the state.[7]

Virtually anyone with any kind of resolve can take advantage of the instability engendered by the ongoing Colombian crisis. The tendency is that the best motivated and best armed organization on the scene will eventually control that instability for its own narrow purposes.

Colombia's Three Wars

The problem in Colombia is that that country, and its potential, is deteriorating because of three ongoing, simultaneous and, interrelated wars involving the illegal drug industry, various insurgent organizations (primarily the Revolutionary Armed Forces of Colombia – FARC) , and 'vigilante' paramilitary groups (the United Self-Defense Groups of Colombia – AUC). This unholy trinity of non-state actors is perpetrating a level of corruption, criminality, human horror, and internal (and external) instability that, if left unchecked at the strategic level, can ultimately threaten Colombia's survival as an organized democratic state, and undermine the political stability and sovereignty of its neighbors. In that connection, there is now explicit recognition that Colombia's current situation has reached crisis proportions.[8] The critical point of this argument is that the substance, or essence, of the Colombian crisis centers on the general organization, activities, and threats of the major violent stateless actors at work in that country today.

The Narcos

The illegal drug industry in Colombia can be described as a consortium that functions in much the same way as virtually any multinational Fortune 500 company. Products are made, sold, and shipped; bankers and financial planners handle the monetary issues, and lawyers deal with the legal problems.[9] The consortium is organized to achieve super-efficiency and maximum profit. It has its 'capos' (chief executive officers and boards of directors), its councils, system of justice, public affairs officers, negotiators, project managers – and its enforcers. And, it operates in virtually every country in the Western Hemisphere and Europe.[10]

Additionally, the illegal drug industry has at its disposal a very efficient organizational structure, the latest in high-tech communications equipment and systems, and state-of-the-art weaponry. With these advantages, decisions are made quickly that can ignore or supersede laws, regulations, decisions, and actions of the governments of the nation-states in which the organization operates. Narcos have also assassinated, bribed, corrupted, intimidated, and terrorized government leaders, members of the Congress, judges, law enforcement and military officers, journalists, and even soccer players. As such, the illegal drug industry is a major agent for destabilizing and weakening the state governmental apparatus.

At the same time, narco cosmetic patronage to the poor, creation of their own electoral machinery, participation openly in traditional political parties, and financing of friendly election campaigns has facilitated even greater influence over the executive, legislative, and judicial branches of Colombian government. That activity exacerbates the necessity of meeting the narcos' needs and demonstrates the necessity of meeting their expectations and demands. Finally, all this mitigates against responsible government and against any allegiance to the notion of the public good and political equality. In that process, the consortium has achieved a symbiotic relationship with the state, and in a sense, is becoming a virtual super-state within the state.[11]

The Insurgents

The FARC insurgents are essentially a Marxist-Leninist *foco* – an insurrectionary armed enclave – in search of a mass base.[12] Because of the general lack of appeal to the Colombian population, the insurgents have developed a military organization designed to achieve the 'armed colonization' of successive areas within the Colombian national territory.[13] The intent is to liberate and mobilize the 'disaffected and the dispossessed' population into an alternative society.[14] That is, FARC responded to the lack of popular support, as did the communists in Vietnam, by attempting to dominate the 'human terrain'. In this effort, FARC has proved every bit as ruthless as the Viet Cong. Torture and assassination – to say nothing of kidnapping, extortion, intimidation, and other terrorist tactics – are so common as to go almost without comment expect in the most extreme cases.[15] Strategically, operationally, and tactically, the FARC approach is the Vietnamese approach.[16]

All this probably would have remained more or less out of sight and out of mind of mainstream Colombia in the under-populated and under-considered rural areas of the country if it had not been for the financial support provided by the illegal drug phenomenon. In 1982, a decision was taken by the Seventh Conference of the FARC to develop links with the Colombian drug industry that would provide the money, and manpower, necessary for the creation of a 'true democracy.'[17] As a result, FARC expanded from approximately 2,000 guerrilla fighters in 1982 to over 70 fronts (company-sized units) with approximately 18,000–20,000 fighters in 2001. This illicit funding has provided the FARC with the capability of confronting regular Colombian military units up to battalion-size, and of overrunning police and military installations and smaller units. Moreover, insurgent presence has spread from 173 municipalities in 1985 to 622 in 1995, out of a total of approximately 1,050 *municipios*.[18]

Thus, Colombian insurgents have taken control of large portions of the 'countryside' and placed themselves in positions from which to move into or dominate the major population centers. The stated intent is to create an army of 30,000 with which to stage a 'final offensive' against the regular armed forces and 'do away with the state as it now exists in Colombia'.[19] In these terms, through the control of large parts of the Colombian national territory, the insurgents are replacing the state. In that connection, the insurgents are denying the state its traditional 'monopoly on violence', and are challenging central government authority over the other parts of the country still under government control.

The Paramilitaries

The AUC 'self-defense' organizations are semi-autonomous regional alliances relatively independent of each other. Nevertheless, a central organization exists primarily to develop a national coordinated strategy against the insurgents. Additionally, the AUC national front organization provides guidance, training, and other help to member organizations as necessary. Strategy and tactics of the AUC, interestingly, mirror those of the insurgents. They seek to expand their control of grass-roots levels of government – municipalities or townships (*municipios*) and rural areas (*corregemientos*), and to exercise political influence through the control, intimidation, or replacement of local officials. And, like the insurgents, the paramilitaries profit from drug trafficking.[20]

These 'vigilante' groups began as self-defense organizations for the protection of family, property, and the law and order of a given geographical area. Because of the AUC's orientation against the insurgents, and willingness to provide fundamental justice and personal security to those defined as 'non-collaborators' with the insurgents, they have consistently improved their standing in the Colombian society. As examples, the number of small AUC groups have increased from 273 to more than 400, with an estimated current total of up to 8,000 active combatants. Moreover, the paramilitaries have organized, trained, and equipped 'shock brigades' that, since 1996, have become capable of successfully challenging insurgent military formations. Finally, in 2001, AUC groups are estimated to have an armed presence in about 40 per cent of the municipalities in the country.[21]

Despite paramilitary success against insurgents where the state has been absent or ineffective, and growing popular support, the Colombian government has disavowed the AUC. As such, the paramilitaries have become a third set of competing non-state actors along with the various insurgent organizations and the illegal drug consortium – challenging the authority of the state, and claiming the right to 'control' all or a part of the destabilized national territory.

Conclusion

Each of the three armed non-state players in the Colombian crisis generates formidable problems, challenges, and threats to the state and the region in its own right. What, then, of an alliance of the willing – even if that alliance represents a complicated mosaic of mutual and conflicting interests?

The Narco-Insurgent-Paramilitary Nexus

Within the past three or four decades, the nature of insurgencies has changed dramatically throughout the world with what Metz calls 'commercial insurgency and the search for wealth'.[22] One of the most far-reaching transformations began in the 1970s with the growing involvement of insurgent forces with narco-traffickers in the Middle East and Asia. Lebanon and the Golden Triangle come quickly to mind.[23] Thus, the narco-insurgent connection is not new, and it is not confined to Latin America. The question, then, is not whether there might be an alliance between the illegal drug industry, the insurgents, and the paramilitaries in Colombia. That has been understood and admitted since the 1980s.[24] The question is whether the threats associated with that union warrant real concern and a serious strategic response.

Motives and Linkages

The motives for the narco-insurgent-paramilitary alliance are straightforward. They are accumulation of wealth, control of territory and people, freedom of movement and action, and legitimacy. Together, these elements represent usable power: power to allocate values and resources in a society.

The equation that links illegal narcotics trafficking to insurgency and to the paramilitaries in Colombia – and elsewhere – turns on a combination of need, organizational infrastructure development, ability, and the availability of sophisticated communications and weaponry.[25] For example, the drug industry possesses cash and lines of transportation and communication. Insurgent and paramilitary organizations have followers, organization, and discipline. Traffickers need these to help protect their assets and project their power within and among nation-states. Insurgents and paramilitaries are in constant need of logistical and communications support – and money.[26]

Together, the alliance has the economic and military power equal to or better than that of most nation-states. This alliance also has another advantage. All three groups possess relatively flat organizational structures and sophisticated communications systems that, when combined, create a mechanism that is considerably more effective and efficient than any slow-moving bureaucratic and hierarchical governmental system. That combined organizational advantage is a major source of power in itself.[27]

Internal Objectives

The narco-insurgent-paramilitary alliance is not simply individual or institutional intimidation for financial or criminal gain. And, it is not just the use of insurgents and AUC groups as 'hired guns' to protect illegal drug cultivation, production, and trafficking. Those are only business transactions. Rather, the long- term objective of the alliance is to control or substantively change the Colombian political system.[28]

Narcos may not seek the overthrow of the government as long as the government is weak and can be controlled to allow maximum freedom of movement and action.[29] The insurgents, on the other hand, seek the eventual destruction of the state as it exists. Whether or not the insurgents are reformers or criminals is irrelevant. Their avowed objective is to take direct control of the government and the state.[30] Likewise, the paramilitaries want fundamental change. It appears that they are interested in creating a strong state that is capable of unquestioned enforcement of law and order.

Whether or not the vigilante groups are 'democratic' or authoritarian is also irrelevant. For their own self-preservation, they have little choice but to take direct or indirect control of the state.[31] The common narco-insurgent-paramilitary governmental change or overthrow effort, therefore, is directed at the political community and its institutions. In this sense, the nexus is not simply criminal in nature. It is more; it is a major political-psychological-moral-military entity. At the same time, the countryside ceases to be a simple theater for combat, and becomes a setting for the building of real local power.

The Latin American security dialogue does not generally refer to the narco-insurgent-paramilitary nexus in terms of their individual identities – at least in the sense of a business organization striving to control the price of drugs, weapons, or general protection. Rather, it tends to refer to the whole entity as greater than the sum of its parts. The security dialogue is concerned about a political-economic-military force that has become a major national and transnational non-state actor. That actor threatens national stability, development, and the future of the democratic system not only in Colombia but in the entire Western Hemisphere.[32] To be sure, this is a loose and dynamic merger subject to many vicissitudes, but the 'marriage of convenience' has lasted and appears to be getting stronger.

External Objectives

The narco-insurgent-paramilitary alliance appears to have developed a political agenda for exerting leverage in the international as well as the Colombian national arena. The perceived goal of a given national agenda is to promote an 'egalitarian social revolution' that will open up opportunities for 'everybody' – and give the organization the legitimate basis for controlling some sort of nationalistic 'narcocracy'. The objectives of the international political agenda are to establish acceptance, credibility, and legitimacy among the sovereign states with which the general organization must negotiate.[33]

In that connection, the spill-over effects of the illegal drug and arms trafficking industry have inspired criminal violence, corruption, and instability throughout Latin America in general and Caribbean transit countries in particular. For some time, the illegal drug industry has operated back and forth across Colombia's borders and adjacent seas. Colombian insurgents and paramilitary groups have also made frequent incursions into the neighboring countries of Brazil, Ecuador, Panama, Peru, and Venezuela. The resulting destabilization undermines the security, well-being, and sovereignty of these countries.[34] The 1992 report by the West Indian Commission captures the essence of the scope and gravity of this 'equal opportunity' phenomenon:

> Nothing poses greater threats to civil society in [Caribbean] countries than the drug problem, and nothing exemplifies the powerlessness of regional governments more. That is the magnitude of the damage that drug abuse and trafficking hold for our community. It is a many-layered danger. At base is the human destruction implicit in drug addiction; but implicit also is the corruption of individuals and systems by the sheer enormity of the inducements of the illegal drug trade in relatively poor societies. On top of all this lie the implications for governance itself at the hands of both external agencies engaged in inter-national interdicting, and the drug barons themselves – the 'dons' of the modern Caribbean – who threaten governance from within.[35]

Colombia is of particular importance in this situation because the narco-insurgent-paramilitary alliance represents a dual threat to the authority of that government, and to those of its hemispheric neighbors. It challenges the central governance of countries affected, and it undermines the vital institutional pillars of regime legitimacy and stability.[36]

The Internal and External Responses

Colombia, the United States, and other countries that might ultimately be affected by the destabilizing consequences of the narco-insurgent-paramilitary alliance in Colombia have tended to deal with the problem in a piece-meal fashion or even ignored it. For nearly 40 years the various Colombian governments dealt with the problem on a completely *ad hoc* basis – without a plan, without adequate or timely intelligence, without a consensus among the political, economic and military elites about how to deal with the armed opposition, and, importantly, within an environment of mutual enmity between the civil government and the armed forces.[37] With the promulgation of *Plan Colombia* in 2000, there is at least the basis of a coherent political project, but not much else.[38]

The United States has tended to ignore the insurgent and paramilitary problems in Colombia, except for making rhetorical statements regarding the peace process, terrorist activities, and human rights violations. The United States has focused its money, training, and attention almost entirely on the counter-drug campaign. It has seen the Colombian crisis in limited terms – the number of hectares of coca eradicated, and the number of kilos of coca that have been detected and destroyed. And, even though the United States and Colombia have achieved a series of tactical 'successes' in the coca fields, the laboratories, and on the streets, the violent non-state actors remain strong and become ever more wealthy. In the meantime, Colombia continues to deteriorate and becomes ever more fragile.[39]

Finally, the other countries that are affected by the nefarious activities of the narco-insurgent-paramilitary nexus tend to be doing little more than watching, debating, and wrangling about what – if anything – to do about the seemingly new and unknown phenomenon.[40] As a consequence, positive political sovereignty, territory, infrastructure, stability, and security are quietly and slowly destroyed – and tens of thousands of innocents continue to be displaced and die.

Conclusion

These are the realities of power operating in the Colombian Crisis. Seven years ago, Abmael Guzman reminded us that 'Except for power, everything else is illusion'.[41]

Where the Hobbesian Trinity Leads

Non-state criminal-terrorist organizations such as those that constitute the Colombian narco-insurgent-paramilitary nexus are significant political actors with the ability to compromise the integrity and sovereignty of individual nation-states. This is a fact that neither the public policy nor the academic international relations communities have completely grasped. Many political and military leaders see the violent non-state actor as a low-level law enforcement issue that does not require sustained policy attention. Many academicians are accustomed to thinking of non-state actors as bit players on a local stage. That may be the case in the early stages of their development, but is certainly not the case in Colombia today.[42]

Threats from the 'Hobbesian Trinity' at work in Colombia today come in many forms and in a matrix of different kinds of challenges, varying in scope and scale. If they have a single feature in common, however, it is that they are systemic and well-calculated attempts to achieve political ends.[43] In that connection, we briefly explore two of the many consequences the narco-insurgent-paramilitary union has generated. First, we examine the erosion of Colombian democracy; then we consider the erosion of the state.

The Erosion of Colombian Democracy

The policy-oriented definition of democracy that has been generally accepted and used in United States foreign policy over the past several years is probably best described as 'procedural' democracy. This definition tends to focus on the election of civilian political leadership and, perhaps, on a relatively high level of participation on the part of the electorate. Thus, as long as a country is able to hold elections it is still considered a democracy – regardless of the level of accountability, transparency, corruption, and ability to extract and distribute resources for national development and protection of human rights and liberties.[44]

In Colombia we observe important paradoxes. Elections are held on a regular basis, but leaders, candidates, and elected politicians are also regularly assassinated. As an example, numerous governmental officials have been assassinated *following* their election – 138 mayors and 569 members of parliament, deputies, and city council members were murdered between 1989 and 1999, along with 174 public officials in other positions. This is not to mention the judiciary. In 1987, alone, 53 members of the judiciary were assassinated.[45]

Additionally, intimidation, direct threats, and the use of violence on a person and his family play an important role *prior* to elections. And, as a corollary, it is important to note that although the media is free from state censorship, journalists and academicians who make their opinions known through the press are systematically assassinated.[46]

It is hard to credit Colombian elections as 'democratic' or 'free.' Neither competition nor participation in elections can be complete in an environment where armed and unscrupulous non-state actors compete violently to control government, before and after elections. Moreover, it is hard to credit Colombia as a democratic state as long as elected leaders are subject to control or vetos imposed by vicious non-state actors. As a consequence, Ambassador David Jordan argues that Colombia is an 'anocratic' democracy. That is, Colombia is a state that has the procedural features of democracy, but retains the features of an autocracy where the ruling elite faces no accountability.[47] Professor Eduardo Pizarro describes Colombia as a 'besieged democracy' and writes about the 'partial collapse of the state'.[48] In either case, the actions of the narco-insurgent-paramilitary alliance have pernicious effects on democracy, and tend to erode the ability of the state to carry out its legitimizing functions.

The Partial Collapse of the State

The Colombian state has undergone severe erosion on two general levels. First, the state's presence and authority has physically diminished over large geographical portions of the country. Second, the idea of the partial collapse of the state is closely related to the non-physical erosion of democracy. Jordan argues that corruption is key in this regard, and is a prime-mover toward 'narcosocialism'.[49]

In the first instance, the notion of 'partial collapse' refers to the fact that there is an absence or only partial presence of state institutions in over 60 per cent of the rural municipalities of the country. Also, even in those areas that are not under the direct control of narco, insurgent, or paramilitary organizations, institutions responsible for protecting citizens – notably the police and judiciary – have eroded to the point where they are unable to carry out their basic functions. Indicators of this problem can be seen in two statistics. First, the murder rate in Colombia is the highest per capita in the world at 41,564 in 1999.[50] Second, the proportion of homicides that end with a conviction is less than 4 per cent.[51] These alarming indicators of impunity strongly confirm that the state is not exercising adequate control of its territory or people.

In the second instance, non-physical erosion of the state centers on the widespread and deeply entrenched issue of corruption.

As an example, in 1993 and 1994 the US government alluded to the fact that former President Ernesto Samper had received money from narcotics traffickers. Later, in 1996, based on that information, the US withdrew Mr. Samper's visa and decertified Colombia for not cooperating in combating illegal drug trafficking. Subsequently, the Colombian Congress absolved Samper of all drug charges by a vote of 111 to 43.[52]

Not surprisingly, another indicator of government corruption at the highest levels is found in the Colombian Congress. The Senate decriminalized the issue of 'illicit enrichment' by making it a misdemeanor that could be prosecuted only after the commission of a felony.[53] Moreover, a former US Ambassador to Colombia asserted – in public and without fear of contradiction – that about 70 per cent of the Colombian Congress 'is bent'.[54]

Clearly, the reality of corruption in government favoring the illegal drug industry in Colombia is inimical to the public good.

Final Statement

Non-state actors using asymmetric terrorist strategies are pervasive in the world today. The general threat generated by the Colombian narco-insurgent-paramilitary nexus is only one case in point. In light of the dynamics of violent stateless actors, there is ample reason for worldwide concern and action.

NOTES

1. Michael Howard, *The Lessons of History* (New Haven, CT: Yale UP 1991) pp.174–5.
2. Field Manual 90-8, *Counterguerrilla Operations* (Washington DC: Headquarters, Department of the Army 1986).
3. This term was coined by Joseph R. Nunez in *Fighting the Hobbesian Trinity in Colombia: A New Strategy for Peace* (Carlisle Barracks, PA: Strategic Studies Institute 2001).
4. A classic book on this topic is Vernon Lee Fluherty, *Dance of the Millions: Military Rule and the Social Revolution in Colombia, 1930–1956* (Pittsburgh, PA: Univ. of Pittsburgh Press

1957). Also see: Dennis M. Hanratty and Sandra W. Meditz (eds.), *Colombia: A Country Study* (Washington DC: Federal Research Division, Library of Congress 1990).
5. Ibid. Also see: Luis Albert Restrepo, 'The Crisis of the Current Political Regime and Its Possible Outcomes', in Charles Bergquist, Ricardo Penaranda, and Gonzalo Sanchez (eds.) *Violence in Colombia: The Contemporary Crisis in Historical Perspective* (Wilmington, DE: SR Books 1992) pp.273–92.
6. Ibid. Also see: Angel Rabassa and Peter Chalk, *Colombian Labyrinth* (Santa Monica, CA: RAND 2001) pp.39–60; Eduardo Pizarro, 'Revolutionary Guerrilla Groups in Colombia', in Bergquist, pp.169–93; and Hal Klepak, 'Colombia: why doesn't the war end?' *Jane's Intelligence Review* (June 2000) pp.41–5.
7. These and subsequent assertions are consensus statements based on a series of author interviews with more than 90 senior US and Latin American civilian and military officials. These interviews were conducted from Oct. 1989 through July 1994; Sept. 1996; Dec. 1998; Nov. 2000; and Feb. 2001. To allow anonymity for those who have an objection to their names being made public, these are cited hereafter as Author Interviews.
8. Michael Shifter, *Toward Greater Peace and Security in Colombia* (New York, NY: Council on Foreign Relations and the Inter-American Dialogue 2000) pp.viii, 1–2, 18.
9. Author Interviews.
10. Ibid.
11. Ibid. and author interview with Ambassador Curtis Kamman at Carlisle Barracks, PA, on 7 Dec. 2000.
12. Ibid., and Thomas A. Marks, *Colombian Army Adaptation to FARC Insurgency* (Carlisle Barracks, PA: Strategic Studies Institute 2002).
13. Pizarro (note 6), and Rabassa and Chalk (note 6).
14. Ibid. and Klepak (note 6).
15. Ibid. and Kamman interview (note 7).
16. Author Interviews, Marks (note 7), and Thomas A. Marks, *Maoist Insurgency since Vietnam* (London and Portland, OR: Frank Cass Publishers 1996).
17. Rabassa and Chalk (note 6). Also see: Larry Rohter, 'A Colombian Guerrilla's 50-year fight', *New York Times* (19 July 1999); Larry Rohter, 'Colombia rebels reign in ceded area', *New York Times* (16 May 1999); Howard LaFranchi, 'Guerrilla commander says, 'This is a means''', *Christian Science Monitor* (19 July 1999); Serge F. Kovaleski, 'Rebel Movement on the Rise: Colombian Guerrillas Use Military Force, Not Ideology to Hold Power', *The Washington Post* (5 Feb. 1999); Gary M. Leech, 'An interview with FARC commander Simon Trinidad', *NACLA Report on the Americas* (Sept./Oct. 2000); Clifford Krauss, 'Colombia's rebels keep the Marxist Faith', *New York Times* (25 July 2000); Alfred Molano, 'The evolution of the FARC: A guerrilla group's long history', *NACLA Report on the Americas* (Sept./Oct. 2000); and *Jane's Information Group*, 'FARC: finance comes full circle for bartering revolutionaries' (19 Jan. 2001). Hereafter cited as Newspaper Reports/Interviews.
18. Ibid. and *The Economist*, 'Survey of Colombia' (21–27 April 2001).
19. Ibid.
20. Rabassa and Chalk (note 6). Also see: David Spencer, *Colombia's Paramilitaries: Criminals or Political Force?'* (Carlisle Barracks, PA: Strategic Studies Institute 2001); Juan Forero, 'Colombian Paramilitaries Adjust Attack Strategies', *New York Times* (22 Jan. 2001); Juan Forero, 'Rightist Chief in Colombia Shifts Focus to Politics', *New York Times* (7 June 2001); and Tod Robberson, 'Militia leader's revelations igniting fear in Colombia', *Dallas Morning News* (17 Dec. 2001).
21. Ibid. and 'Survey of Colombia' (note 18).
22. Steven Metz, *The Future of Insurgency* (Carlisle Barracks, PA: Strategic Studies Institute 1993) pp.13–15.
23. Mark S. Steinitz, 'Insurgents, Terrorists, and the Drug Trade', *Washington Quarterly* (Fall 1985) p.147.
24. Newspaper Reports/Interviews.
25. Peter A. Lupsha, 'The Role of Drugs and Drug Trafficking in the Invisible Wars', in Richard Ward and Herold Smith (eds.) *International Terrorism: Operational Issues* (Univ. of Chicago

Press 1987) p.181. Also see William J. Olson, 'International Organized Crime; The Silent Threat to Sovereignty', *The Fletcher Forum of World Affairs* (Summer/Fall 1997) pp.70–4.

26. Ibid. and Author Interviews.
27. Ibid.
28. Ibid. and Peter A. Lupsha, 'Towards an Etiology of Drug Trafficking and Insurgent Relations: The Phenomenon of Narco-Terrorism', *International Journal of Comparative and Applied Criminal Justice* (Fall 1989) p.63.
29. Author Interviews.
30. Ibid. and Newspaper Reports/Interviews.
31. Rabassa and Chalk (note 6), and Spencer (note 20).
32. Author Interviews.
33. Ibid.
34. Ibid. Also see: Stephen E. Flynn, *The Transnational Drug Challenge and the New World Order* (Washington, DC: Center for Strategic and International Studies 1993); and William O. Walker III, 'The Foreign Narcotics Policy of the United States since 1980: An End to the War on Drugs', *International Journal of Narco-Diplomacy* (Winter 1993–94) p.64.
35. Cited in Ivelaw Lloyd Griffith, *Drugs and Security in the Caribbean: Sovereignty Under Siege* (University Park: Pennsylvania State UP 1997) p.1.
36. Ibid. and Walker (note 34).
37. Author Interviews.
38. Ibid.
39. Max Manwaring, 'U.S. too narrowly focused on drug war in Colombia', *The Miami Herald* (15 Aug. 2001).
40. Author Interviews.
41. Quoted from 'El Documento Oficial de Sendero', in Rogger Mercado U., *Los Partidos Politicos en el Peru* (Lima: Ediciones Latinoamericanas 1995) p.110.
42. Author Interviews. Also see Martha Crenshaw (ed.) *Terrorism in Context* (University Park: Pennsylvania State UP 1995).
43. This observation was made in 1986 by former-Secretary of State George P. Shultz in an address before the Low-intensity Warfare Conference at the National Defense University on 15 Jan. 1986 in Washington DC.
44. David C. Jordan, *Drug Politics: Dirty Money and Democracies* (Norman: Univ. of Oklahoma Press 1999) p.19.
45. Author Interviews. Also see Ana Maria Bejarano and Eduardo Pizarro, 'The Crisis of Democracy in Colombia: From "Restricted" Democracy to "Besieged" Democracy', unpublished manuscript, 2001.
46. Author Interviews.
47. Jordan (note 44) p.21.
48. Bejarano and Pizarro (note 45) and Pizarro (note 6).
49. Jordan (note 44) pp.158–70, 193–4.
50. *Annual Report 1999* (Washington, DC: Inter-American Development Bank 2000) p.141.
51. Data taken from Mauricio Rubio, 'La justicia en una sociedad violenta', in Maria Victoria Llorente and Malcolm Deas, *Reconocer la Guerra para construir la paz* (Bogota: Ediciones Uniandes CERED Editorial Norma 1999) p.215.
52. Jordan (note 44) p.161.
53. Ibid.
54. Kamman interview (note 7).

Kashmir, Pakistan and the War by Terror

JASJIT SINGH

Militant violence has been tearing apart the polity and society in the state of Jammu and Kashmir for the past 13 years. During that time, almost 28,000 people have been killed, mostly Muslims, and nearly half a million Hindus and Sikhs have been refugees in their own country for over a decade – driven out from the valley of Kashmir by extremist militancy in the name of religion. This overlapped with the conflict of transnational terrorism, perpetrated by religious extremism in the adjoining border state of Punjab from 1984–93, when 30,000 people died.

India and Pakistan have fought three full-scale wars since 1947 over this multiethnic, multi-religious, erstwhile princely, state, that legally, politically and practically emerged as an independent country during the two months after the British withdrawal from India. The central reason why the dispute has remained so intractable over the decades is that the perception of the nature of the dispute on either side is so fundamentally different. The passage of time has only made it more complex.

The current violent phase began on 31 July 1988, as per the leader of the Pakistan-based separatist organization JKLF (Jammu and Kashmir Liberation Front). Since then, it has gone through a number of escalatory stages, of which the events of 1 October (terrorist attack on the Kashmir legislature) and 13 December 2001 (terrorist suicide attack on the Indian parliament in New Delhi) have been climaxes in the latest stage. Continuing violence and terrorism across the frontiers has further complicated attempts to any solution.

The Genesis

The problems began at the time of transfer of power by Britain. This was sanctioned by the Indian Independence Act, passed by the British parliament in 1947. It led to India's independence and the creation of Pakistan, which claims that Kashmir is an 'unfinished agenda of the partition' of India.

The agenda of partition was essentially to carve out a Muslim majority state as the new country. And as the state of Jammu and Kashmir had a 77 per cent Muslim population, the claim that it be part of Pakistan gathered support in Pakistan and even abroad. However, the British ruled only some 53 per cent of India directly, mostly organized as 'provinces' in areas that were strategically important. The remaining part of the country composed of princely states ruled by their own kings and queens (maharajas and maharanis). They were tied to British rule by separate treaty arrangements, where the rulers accepted British paramountcy, especially in matters of defence, foreign affairs and communications.

The Indian Independence Act 1947 included the transfer of power to India as the successor state; the creation of Pakistan; and the lapse of the principle of paramountcy over some 564 princely states legally and constitutionally, making them independent countries. They were advised to join one country or the other while taking geographical contiguity into account. These states were not to be allocated on the basis of religion, cast or creed, and the decision of the ruling monarch in the exercise of his sovereign rights would be the sole criteria.

Therefore, while it may be argued – as indeed many Pakistanis do – that the idea of Pakistan (a state carved out of Muslim majority areas of India) supports the contention that Jammu and Kashmir should have been part of Pakistan, the principle of democratic equality and the rules for the transfer of power (and partition) did not require this. The West Pakistani leadership were unwilling to accept the verdict of the first-ever election held on the basis of adult franchise in the country in 1970.

Hence, rule by majority finally led to the domestic instability, military repression and genocide by the army in its Eastern wing. It also led to the break-up of Pakistan and the emergence of Bangladesh, seriously damaging the ideology by which the Pakistani claim to Jammu and Kashmir is built. This appears to have intensified the desire to possess Kashmir by any means, partly in a spirit of revenge.

In political terms, the Indian National Congress (the dominant Indian political party) adopted a position that decisions on accession should also conform to the will of the people. The Muslim League, however, which had sought partition – and Pakistan – argued that the decision of the ruler must be treated as final. Once the decision to grant independence and transfer of power was made public in the summer of 1947, high-pressure politics went into action when the Muslim League tried to woo the Hindu rulers of Western India to join the new country and the Congress pressed for the idea of consultation of the people.

It is in this context that the prime minister of the interim government of India, Jawaharlal Nehru, insisted that political leaders jailed in Jammu and Kashmir State must first be freed and democracy installed at the earliest opportunity, before any decision on accession by the Hindu ruler of the states could be taken. The government even made it clear to the ruler of Jammu and Kashmir in June 1947, through the British Viceroy of India, Lord Louis Mountbatten, that the Indian government would have no objection to Jammu and Kashmir joining Pakistan, but that it should accede to one country or the other.

It is under these circumstances, when Jammu and Kashmir (J&K) had legally and constitutionally become an independent country, that Pakistan imposed an economic blockade in violation of its own bilateral Stand Still Agreement and planned a direct military invasion. However, this was scuttled by the British threat to withdraw their officers (who occupied all the top- and middle-level positions in the Pakistani military), and the plans were changed to conducting a covert war.

This involved a mix of tribals from Pakistan and troops on leave. When this looting, raping and pillaging force was almost at the gates of Srinagar, the state capital, the ruler formally acceded to India – which then sent in the military in the nick of time. Pakistan followed this up with the formal induction of its military forces to back what by then was a failed invasion. And the Kashmir dispute was etched into the history of the subcontinent.

India's complaint to the UN led finally to the UN Commission on India and Pakistan (UNCIP) adopting a resolution on 13 August 1948, which was accepted by both India and Pakistan. The substance of the resolution was based on four inter-linked linear steps. Pakistan agreed to withdraw its military forces from the state; all efforts would be made to withdraw the tribals from the state; all steps would be taken to restore normalcy (for which India was to maintain a certain level of military forces in the state); and finally, when normalcy was restored, a plebiscite would be held to decide the final accession of the state to India or Pakistan (with no provision for independence). At the time of the UN-brokered ceasefire Pakistan occupied nearly one-third of the state. It did not withdraw as required by the UN resolution, and so the conflict is continuing.

Changed Dynamics of the Conflict

The dynamics of the conflict altered fundamentally in the 1980s. Two interrelated strands stand out. Perhaps for the first time, the alienation of the people of the valley of Kashmir started to grow, and soon thereafter terrorist violence emerged in the state, which has so far resulted in over 28,000 deaths and has made any solution even more intractable.

Growth of Alienation

While many would argue that Pakistan engineered the alienation of the Kashmiri people in pursuit of its long-standing goal, the truth is that the real reasons for alienation (essentially of the people of the valley) were basically indigenous and emanated from a complex interaction of realities.

First, the changing socioeconomic development of the state generated a sense of relative sense of deprivation among the people of the state. The Buddhist majority Ladakh and the Hindu majority Jammu region felt they were being discriminated against by the focus of development in the Muslim-majority Kashmir valley, although overall development of the state during the three decades since the 1950s indicated a tremendous advance. Population below the poverty line had fallen to 25.2 per cent by the early 1990s as compared with the all-India average of 36 per cent. This performance was almost on a par with states like Kerala and Haryana, which were in the upper range of rising prosperity in the country. Per capita income, although low, was Rs. 3,816/- toward the end of 1980s, which compared well with the average for the whole country. Infant mortality rates had dropped in the state to levels well below the national average and stood at 45 per 1,000 births by late 1990s compared to the all-India average of 72 per 1,000 births at that time.

The statistics go on. But the problem was also the lack of adequate employment beyond that generated by tourism and agriculture. The insulation of the state was partly due to the special status under Article 370 of the Indian Constitution. With the exception of private enterprises owned by dominant political-social élites of the state, almost all industrial enterprises in the state are government-owned since private enterprise not indigenous to the state cannot set up private industry within the state.

Gross industrial output remained a mere one-sixth of the national average. The average daily number of factory employment (per 100,000 people) in the late 1980s was a paltry 300 as compared with the all-India average of 1,050. The mountainous terrain of the state no doubt reduces the potential for industrialization, although there is scope for specialized industries. But in contrast, in the neighboring state of Himachal Pradesh, which is more mountainous, the average was 1,175 at that time!

As regards tourism, over 85 per cent of visitors come from the remaining parts of the country. This received a tremendous boost in the 1970s from regulations which authorized government employees to travel on holiday at government expense to any place in the country once every four years. Thus it became possible for even the clerical staff in the remotest parts of India to travel to the fabled valley of Kashmir for a brief holiday. The valley people traditionally never moved out to look for employment outside the valley. Tourist traffic, mostly by middle-class Indians, generated an impression of a far more prosperous India outside the valley and inevitably contributed to a sense of relative deprivation.

But the real impact on the minds of people came from the spread of the information revolution, the first phase of which has been in television and satellite communications. By the end of 1980s, nearly 90 per cent of the population of the state was covered by television (while the national average was still below 80 per cent). Daily newspaper circulation by the end of 1980s stood at over 40 per cent compared to the national average of 28 per cent (with neighboring Himachal Pradesh a mere 3 per cent).

The impact of the information revolution, as on the rest of the world, has been to increase awareness among people of a quality of life that simply is not available in reality. This has given rise to a revolution of rising expectations, with the gap between expectations and satisfaction levels rising rapidly. This in turn has given rise to a deepening sense of relative deprivation.

A complex set of factors has led to an increasing revival of religion and its resurgence in political life across the developing countries. Coupled with low employment opportunities, especially for increasingly aware and partially educated youth, this has led to increasing frustrations and alienation.

Resort to violence comes easily to frustrated youth and it should not come as a surprise that the bulk of the militants and terrorists worldwide and in Jammu and Kashmir state are from 15 to 25 years in age. Maladministration, corruption and political opportunism, especially during the 1980s, added to growing frustration and alienation. This in turn provided a fertile ground for religious extremism and separatist ideologies to grow. It is in this context that Pakistan began to employ terror as an instrument of politics by other means.

Rise of Terrorism

Global and regional trends of terrorism based on religious extremism in pursuit of political goals have converged, making Afghanistan-Pakistan the epicenter of international terrorism along with the rise of jehadi culture inside Pakistan. Global trends in international terrorism complemented and derived mutual support from the strategy pursued by Pakistan in Kashmir. The more significant of these trends are outlined below:

- For a variety of reasons, targeting of civilians has been increasingly legitimized during the past two centuries, especially after air power was used for the firebombing of cities and the dropping of nuclear weapons. Doctrinally, society had become totally inclusive according to the total war paradigm.
- Globalization has expanded and deepened the scope and extent of opportunities for terrorism that now span the globe. One has only to look at the international connections of Al-Qaeda to grasp the scale and extent of global networking.

- Terrorism is being increasingly used as an instrument of politics and foreign policy. This is a pernicious reversal of the civilized approach to dispute settlement in general, and the current trend of democratization and cooperative security in the world in particular. Its effectiveness has been increasing because of the ever-greater vulnerabilities of modern society to acts of terrorism, where liberal democracies are especially at risk to such application of violent force.
- The state has been losing its monopoly of the instruments of violence, and many states have been promoting diffusion of sophisticated weapons. During the Cold War the superpowers pursued this as part of their strategy for dominance. Afghanistan was the classic example, where covert warfare was promoted by encouraging the spread of weapons, narcotics and violence into society on the strength of religious sentiments. These in turn were used by Pakistan to pursue its own agenda. The debris of the Cold War has further eroded the control of the state over weapons.
- The center of gravity of international terrorism has been shifting toward Southern Asia since the 1970s. Afghanistan-Pakistan progressively became the epicenter of international terrorism, driven by religious extremism and funded by the narcotics trade and transnational crime. Afghanistan-Pakistan is one of the world's three largest narcotics producing and exporting regions in the world.
- Terrorism is shifting from its traditional political orientation to religious ideology-driven violence. Compared to their near absence three decades ago, religious groups now constitute over two-thirds of the militant/terrorist entities in the world. Religion is coming to play an increasing role in politics even in states that have pursued liberal democratic or socialist ideologies. International security is consequently affected seriously, because '… the combination of religion and politics is potentially explosive. The combination of religion and nationalism is stronger, but a blend of the three has an extremely destructive potential.'[1]

The history of the covert war in Afghanistan has been detailed extensively even by Pakistani former senior military officers. Pakistan was the 'front-line state' for the US war against the USSR in Afghanistan during the 1980s where it conducted a covert war and acquired the expertise and material resources to continue a sub-conventional war through terror, well after the Soviet Union withdrew from Afghanistan.

Two major elements in the process of legitimizing sub-conventional war and the sanction of religion can be clearly identified in the run-up to the actual operationalizing of covert terror wars. Immediately after its creation, Pakistan decided to invade the state of Jammu and Kashmir in order to incorporate it within its territory. The driving rationale for its plan was strategic and geoeconomic.

A newly created Pakistan had an economy almost wholly dependent on agriculture, which received irrigation from canals drawing water from three major rivers. These three rivers flowed from the state of Jammu and Kashmir into Pakistan. The argument went that if the state acceded to India, then India would be able to throttle Pakistan's lifeline at any time. Possession of Kashmir became important if Pakistan's economic survival was to be ensured. (The problem incidentally was resolved through the World Bank-brokered Indus Waters Treaty of 1959, which defines the share of river waters between the two countries.)

A security imperative also played its role in the attempt to justify the goal. If Jammu and Kashmir acceded to India, Indian military deployed on its western borders would always be dangerously close to almost all the major cities of Punjab in West Pakistan. Islam was brought in to provide the central motivation that could stand the test of time, especially after the Indus Waters Treaty and the UN-sponsored ceasefire in 1949.

Since the British commanders made it clear that all their officers would be withdrawn in case the army is used for the attack on Kashmir, an alternative plan to use tribals, army officers on leave and demobilized soldiers was put into action in the invasion of the state. Once the state acceded to India on 26 October 1947, and the Indian military went in to defend the state against Pakistani invasion, regular forces of the Pakistan army were inducted into the battle a few weeks later.

The pattern of covert war followed by overt military war was again employed in 1965 when a 'Force Gibraltar' was infiltrated into the state and when it appeared to falter, a regular armor-led invasion, codenamed 'Grand Slam', was put into action on 1 September 1965. Pakistan's army chief, General Aslam Beg, had admitted that these attempts had failed essentially because there had been no clearly defined strategy when he was heading the army. In substance he articulated this in terms of the new doctrine of 'offensive defense'. Nuclear weapons have been seen as a key element in that strategy.

It is not coincidental that terrorist violence in Punjab and J&K was initiated when Pakistan acquired what General Beg described as a 'credible deterrent'. The expectation has been that cross-border terrorism provides Pakistan with a 'low-cost' option, while the nuclear deterrent neutralizes India's conventional superiority. This has been considered as the 'Sword of Damocles' hanging over Pakistan. Thus, terrorism was seen as an option for conducting'low-intensity' war under the nuclear umbrella.

The confidence induced by this strategy had finally led to the launching of the war in Kargil across the high Himalayas during 1998–99. The original plan had almost been put into action in 1987 but was held back at the last moment possibly because the nuclear deterrent was not fully operational. But the covert-overt strategy was once again operationalized.

The second issue was the legitimization of the use of irregular warfare, covert war and terrorism in pursuit of ideological-political goals. Steve Cohen, who has studied Pakistan army extensively and deeply over the decades, wrote that Pakistani army officers undergoing courses of instruction at US military institutions paid special attention to irregular warfare. The difference was that, while the US/NATO officers focused on how to fight against guerrilla warfare, Pakistani officers searched for ways in which to wage such wars. As noted above, the Pakistani army adopted a strategy of employing irregular warfare as the primary method of conducting wars.

The creation of Pakistan on the basis of religion also led to its army having to 'adapt to Islamic principles and practices'.[2] This in itself had started to alter the secular apolitical moorings inherited from the British Indian Army. But it was the Islamization pursued under President Z. A. Bhutto in the mid-1970s, and taken to greater extremes by General Zia ul-Haq after he usurped power in 1977, that started to provide religious legitimacy for military action and finally for terrorism. Zia ul-Haq jailed Bhutto (who was finally hanged in 1979) and ruled for many years under martial law, which he declared as the army chief.

There is little doubt that he was a devout Muslim. But he propelled religion into politics and intensified its role in society and its governance largely to legitimize his rule. American scholars in fact assessed as early as the beginning of 1980s that as Islamization deepened in Zia's Pakistan, Kashmir, which had really been off the Pakistani political radar horizon and was not an active issue in relations with India after 1966, would come back to the center stage. Indians unfortunately did not pay adequate attention to these trends and other factors, such as the increasing alienation of the people in Jammu and Kashmir state.

Pakistan projected the war in Kashmir as an indigenous war between the Indian state and the people of the state. Conventional wisdom would have us believe that there is a struggle for freedom in Jammu and Kashmir. One look at the empirical evidence disproves such assumptions. No freedom movement would be expected to destroy the basic infrastructure of the state. But between 1989 and 1999, the destruction of 765 schools/education institutions, 1,271 government buildings and, above all, the destruction of 344 bridges (almost entirely in Kashmir valley) by the militants and the Mujahideen in the state are proof of the real nature of the war. Militants also destroyed 9,488 private houses. And by the end of the 1990s, more than two-thirds of the jehadi fighters in Kashmir were foreigners.

War by Terror

Perhaps the most important facet of legitimization of religion in covert war and terrorism began with the publication of a fundamentally erroneous interpretation of the teachings of the Holy Quran. Brigadier S. K. Malik of the Pakistani army wrote *The Quranic Concept of War,*[3] in which he concluded that the Holy Quran enjoins all believers to use terror as a weapon of war. He concluded that 'The Quranic military strategy thus enjoins us to *prepare ourselves for war to the utmost in order to strike terror into the hearts of the enemies, known or hidden...*' (emphasis in the original).[4]

The book teaches that terror must be struck during the preparatory stage, in the run-up to war, during war, and for war termination. Terror struck into the hearts of the enemies, therefore, 'is not only a means, but is an end in itself. Once a condition of terror into the opponent's heart is obtained, hardly anything is left to be achieved. It is the point where the means and the ends meet and merge'. War, the book argues, must be total. General Zia-ul Haq encouraged such efforts and wrote the foreword to the book, recommending it. General Aslam Beg as the army chief and other army leaders in subsequent years inevitably cited the book to exhort military officers when addressing them.

The operationalization of this concept and the strategic doctrine was carried out initially in Afghanistan, then in Punjab in India from 1984 and then Jammu and Kashmir from 1988 onward. The 'success' of the Mujahideen in defeating one superpower provided a great boost to the rationale for the pursuit of this strategy, especially since it was seen as a low-cost option where not only was India not in a position to retaliate with a strong military punitive action, but was also on the defensive diplomatically and politically because of the issues of human rights and its own failure to project the real issues at stake.

Initially, indigenous groups were being supported by Pakistan's intelligence agencies in the name of self-determination and even independence. However, Pakistan had virtually lost the war through terrorism by 1991 when it was forced to begin supplementing the indigenous militants with the Mujahideen from Pakistan and even from Afghanistan. Pakistan certainly got the better of India in the information war until the end of 1990s when the terrorist war in Kashmir began to merge with the international terrorism emanating from Afghanistan-Pakistan.

By the time the strategy of war through terrorism was initiated in Kashmir, extensive experience had been gained by Pakistan in prosecuting a Mujahideen covert war in Afghanistan. This was waged through Mujahideen groups, managed by a combination of Pakistan's army and

Inter-Services Intelligence (ISI). Enormous quantities of sophisticated modern portable and non-portable weapons were accumulated in the process. The weapons and equipment came as a result of proliferation by state (intelligence) agencies to non-state actors and groups like the Mujahideen and jehadi groups. They included sophisticated, military-specification small arms and light weapons, which more often than not excelled in quality compared with those of the security forces.[5]

The case of Stinger surface-to-air-missiles in the hands of the Mujahideen is symptomatic. Most accounts agree that Pakistan had siphoned off over 60 per cent of the weapons and equipment meant for the Mujahideen. The Ojheri ammunition dumps that blew up in 1988 in Rawalpindi were associated with the destruction of substantial stocks, so that the CIA could not carry out the planned audit. One ISI head has been quoted as saying in 1995 that the organization was holding three million AK-47s 'greased and packed' for future use.

The ISI obtained phenomenal flows of funding through drug trafficking and money laundering. The case of the Bank of Credit and Commerce International (BCCI) is only one instance.[6] Mehran Bank in Pakistan was active in the matter. There are credible reports of large sums of money being placed at the disposal of the army chief and the president of Pakistan for support to terrorist groups fighting inside India.

The transnational militancy prosecuted by Pakistan in Punjab since 1984 had concentrated on the two districts of Punjab on the border with Pakistan. This area also constitutes the region through which pass the surface lines of communications (road and rail) between Jammu and Kashmir and the rest of India (the other route via Lahaul-Spiti is more tenuous and closed during winter). These two districts also represent the area from where India had traditionally launched its counterattack to relieve the pressure of Pakistani armored thrusts into the Jammu region.

The War Within

Ethno-sectarian violence and terrorism driven by religion extremism within Pakistan have also been expanding during the past two decades. Much of this is due to indigenous factors of declining human development indices, increasing disparities in a feudal society, and the growth of religious extremism used to fuel the war abroad. Since the beginning of 1980s, General Zia ul-Haq's regime has promoted Sindhi separatism through its intelligence agencies under the political platform of the Mohajir Quami Movement (MQM). (The MQM was created as a political party composed of the 'mohajir' (refugee) community of Muslims who migrated from India and settled in Sindh.) This was meant to counter Benazir Bhutto's campaign for democracy, centered on her Pakistan People's Party (PPP), and to undermine her base in the southern province of Sindh.

Her aim was to dislodge the military rule of General Zia. At the same time, Islamization of society under General Zia increasingly led to the polarization of Muslim sects, leading finally to sectarian violence among the minority Shia and majority Sunni population of Pakistan. Ethnic conflicts among various communities and among Pathan refugees and settlers from the frontier areas also added to the rise of violence in society. Increasing economic chaos aggravated the problems.

The phenomenal spread of small arms and light weapons within Pakistani society and the impact of the narcotics trade may have enabled the intelligence agency to conduct its covert war outside Pakistan, but its spread to Mujahideen groups was also the beginning of the diffusion of sustaining armed conflict within the country. The result was an escalating process of violence in society.

Pakistan's economy began to deteriorate from the mid-1980s, with growth deteriorating markedly in the 1990s. As against an average growth rate of 6 per cent in the 1980s, real GDP growth slowed to an average of 5 per cent and further to 4 per cent during the first and second half of the 1990s, respectively. Fixed investment as per cent of GDP declined significantly in the 1990s. As against an average rate of close to 17 per cent in the 1980s, fixed investment declined to 15.3 per cent in the second half of the 1990s. During this period, public sector investment declined sharply compared to the private sector. As against an average of 9 per cent of GDP, it has declined to 6 per cent in the second half of the 1990s while private sector investment stagnated at around 8 per cent.

Large fiscal deficit continued to pose a serious threat to macroeconomic stability. Declining economic growth, persistence of severe macroeconomic imbalances, lack of social safety nets, and poor governance in the 1990s have had adverse effects on the country's poor and most vulnerable. All these factors have been the major cause of poverty in many low-income countries and Pakistan is no exception. The incidence of caloric-based poverty has increased from 17.3 per cent in 1987–88 to 22.4 per cent in 1992–93 and, further, to 32.6 per cent in 1998–99. In other words, the number of poor people who cannot meet their daily minimum nutritional requirements and fall below the poverty line increased from 17.6 million in 1987–88 to 43.9 million in 1998–99.

Entrenched poverty and rising income inequality can themselves be impediments to growth. Similar trends are observed in rural and urban poverty. According to the basic needs approach, poverty increased from 28.6 per cent in 1986–87 to 35.9 per cent in 1992–93 and, further, to 35.7 per cent in 1993–94, but at a greater pace in the rural areas than in the urban areas. Income distribution has also worsened in the 1990s, especially in the rural areas.

Fiscal deficit has emerged as one of the major source of macroeconomic imbalances in Pakistan. Persistent slippage on both revenue and expenditure sides has contributed to mounting financial imbalances. The serious macroeconomic imbalances that persisted in the 1980s in terms of large fiscal deficit (7.1 per cent of GDP) continued in the first half of the 1990s, despite several revenue measures introduced in the successive budgets on the one hand, and cutting development expenditure on the other. Fiscal deficit remained, on average, at 7.1 per cent of GDP in the first half of the 1990s. It declined slightly to 6.4 per cent of GDP in the second half of the 1990s, mainly by further reducing development expenditure. In other words, the quality of slight fiscal adjustment has been poor, as it was not achieved by enhancing tax efforts (tax-to-GDP ratio), but mainly at the cost of future growth potentials.

At the same time, religious radicalization of society had been increasing. Pakistan has been a breeding ground for Islamic militants for the past two decades.[7] In the 1980s, General Zia ul-Haq promoted the madrassas as a way of garnering support from the religious parties (against demands for restoration for democracy), and of recruiting fighters for the anti-Soviet war in Afghanistan. Hundreds of thousands of madrassas (religious seminaries) provided a training ground for the jihad outside Pakistan, but also inevitably fueled domestic ethnosectarian violence. As many as one-third of the 50,000 madrassas train jihadi fighters for religious wars in places as far away as Chechnya, Afghanistan, Kashmir and the Philippines. Nearly three million young people study in these seminaries where militant Islam is at the core of the curriculum in most cases. The problem for Pakistan has been that it is difficult to promote and prosecute a jehadi war abroad without promoting ethnosectarian violence within.

By early 2001 Pakistan's policy of pursuit of terrorism as an instrument of foreign policy and ideology had started to become counter-productive.[8] The Taliban had become a serious liability, both in international terms as well as from the 'Talibanisation' of Pakistan itself, which became a matter of deep concern to many Pakistanis. Pakistan's isolation was already acute. Its strategy of covert-overt war in Kargil in the summer of 1999 had backfired badly. It had become a target of international sanctions imposed on the Taliban (whom it had created in order to perpetuate its control over Afghanistan in pursuit of its goal of 'strategic depth'). The war through terrorism was no longer able to deliver Kashmir, and India had begun to look for options for offensive action even if limited to the political-diplomatic arena. It is in this context that the terrorist attacks on the US on 11 September offered an opportunity to reshape the decades-old strategy.

Pakistan's willingness to cooperate with the United States in fighting international terrorism may have surprised some, but had to be seen against the backdrop of Gen. Pervez Musharraf's attempts to change gears at least since June 2001. This dramatic turnaround in strategy had the support of the élites, and found no objections from the masses, since the feeling that the path of religious extremism had brought only problems for Pakistan was deeply shared.

Meanwhile, the process of reversal of the terror-war threatened to marginalize vested interests within the army, the Inter-Services Intelligence (ISI) and the élites. The terrorist attacks on the Kashmir legislature on 1 October 2001, and the more serious, suicidal attack on the Indian parliament on 13 December, galvanized Indian policy into taking the political-diplomatic offensive and heightened international concerns. After pressure built up over a month with the mobilization of the military forces for possible war by India and high-pressure diplomacy by the United States, General Musharraf in a landmark speech on 12 January 2002 spelt out the parameters of the reversal of the sub-conventional war strategy.

In essence, Musharraf committed Pakistan to abandon religious extremism and assured the world that Pakistani territory would not be used for terrorism anywhere in the world, including in Kashmir. He has promised severe action for violation of the new norms and terrorism inside or outside by Pakistanis. At the same time, he has condemned terrorism and religious extremism in the strongest terms we have heard from a Pakistani head of state and government so far.

The focus is essentially on the domestic situation; but the winding down of jihadi terrorism within Pakistan will also help in its decline across the borders, because of the consequent loss of legitimacy suffered by terrorism, as a tool of state policy in the name of Islam, from Zia's time. Musharraf has ordered a crackdown on sectarian violence, and has imposed restrictions and registration of mosques, and on religious teaching that spreads hatred. He has also announced a new madrassas policy that is expected to come into force through the year. Mosques and *madrassahs* will be regulated through a new ordinance to be announced.

The thrust of the new policy has been to control the war within, and to alter the dynamics of the war without. This will take time, but Musharraf has promised that Pakistan will not give up political diplomatic support for its stated position on Kashmir.

NOTES

1. Falih Abd al Jabbar, 'The Gulf War and ideology: the double-edged sword of Islam', in Haim Bresheeth and Nira Yuval-Davis (eds.) *The Gulf War and the New World Order* (London: Zed Books 1991) p.217.
2. Stephen P. Cohen, *The Pakistan Army* (New Delhi: Himalayan Books 1984) p.34.
3. S.K. Malik, *The Quranic Concept of War* (Lahore: Wajidalis 1979).
4. Ibid. pp.58–9.
5. For a detailed study on covert war in Afghanistan operations see (Brig.) Mohhamad Yousaf and Major Mark Adkin, *The Bear Trap: Afghanistan's Untold Story* (Jang Publishers: Lahore 1992); for a study of the role of small arms see Tara Kartha, *Tools of Terror* (New Delhi: Knowledge World 1999); for details of narcotics trafficking see official US and UN reports on the subject.
6. Jonathan Beaty and S.C. Gwynne, *The Outlaw Bank* (New York, NY: Random House 1993) p.279.
7. Massoud Ansari (in Karachi), 'The Jihad Factories', <www.flonnet.com/fl1816/18160650.htm>.
8. Jessica Stern, 'Pakistan's Jehad Culture', *Foreign Affairs* (Nov./Dec. 2000).

Part Three

Counter-OPFOR Strategies

Battlespace Dynamics, Information Warfare to Netwar, and Bond-Relationship Targeting

ROBERT J. BUNKER

In the coming wars between nation-states and non-state entities, both traditional and advanced forms of weaponry and concepts will be employed.[1] Increasingly, however, advanced forms of war-fighting will play a dominant role in counter-OPFOR (opposition forces) strategies because of the new capabilities which they offer. This chapter will discuss three new types of strategies: battlespace dynamics, information warfare to netwar, and bond-relationship targeting.

Of these strategies, only information warfare is widely recognized as playing a role in future conflict and war and, even then, it has been extremely difficult for nation-state militaries to fully grasp the disruptive implications netwar will have upon their hierarchical organizational structures and the Western conduct of war. Strategies based upon battlespace dynamics and bond-relationship targeting are discussed far less than information warfare or even netwar and, as a result, they are virtually unknown to the majority of defense planners and policy makers.[2]

Battlespace Dynamics

The first strategy is derived from battlespace dynamics. This understudied area of analysis emerged in 1996 as a conceptual tool to support US Army future war-fighting perceptions. It suggests that war and conflict take place within defined space-time boundaries.[3] These boundaries have significantly expanded in Western warfare over the last two and one-half millennia as the art and science of war have progressed. Generally classical warfare was based on two dimensional space-time derived from x (line) and t (time) operations and medieval warfare was based on three dimensional space-time derived from x & y (square) and t (time) operations. Greek phalanxes and Roman legions were 'line' fighters because of the limited area foot soldiers could cover in open ground. Medieval knights and their retainers could be characterized as 'square' or 'field' (battlefield) fighters because the mobility provided by the horse allowed them to fully exploit y-space, unlike their classical predecessors.[4]

Modern warfare based on four-dimensional space-time derived from *x*, *y* and z (box) and *t* (time) define current nation-state operations. The z-space dimension was ushered in by the development of the firearm and cannon during the European Renaissance and later expanded by the emergence of more sophisticated forms of artillery, rocketry, aircraft, and missile systems over the ensuing centuries. Modern military forces, beginning with firearm-using mercenaries, can be thought of as 'box' fighters. This characterization was still viable even during the 1991 Gulf War when the killing zone for Iraqi forces created by Coalition forces was represented by a 'battlespace box' which existed for hundreds of kilometers.

Ultimately, dimensional expansion is derived from more powerful motive sources applied to war and conflict (such as human, animal, and mechanical energy paradigms). Research suggests that we are now in a shift from a mechanical to a post-mechanical energy paradigm. This means that fifth dimensional space-time derived from *x*, *y* and z (box), *t* (time), and *c* (cyber) operations are now emerging. Forces, such as terrorists, which engage in this form of conflict can be viewed as 'cyber' or literally 'out-of-the box' fighters. As an outcome, we can expect to see limitations placed upon both state and non-state forces operating in modern (four-dimensional) battlespace to be overcome for advanced war-fighting purposes.

A number of examples of overcoming these limitations exist.[5] While many are primitive in nature, these new capabilities show the potential fifth-dimensional battlespace has to offer:

Spatial Expansion

This capability allows two physical objects which are meters away from each other to be reoriented so that they are thousands of kilometers away from each other. The classic example of this capability is based upon terrorist use of stealth masking. By violating Western rules of warfare and removing soldier uniform and insignia, this criminal-soldier can make himself or herself invisible to US military and law enforcement personnel. Even when standing a few meters away, terrorists are for all intents and purposes thousands of kilometers away because they have blended in with the non-combatant civilian populace. Western attempts at gaining this capability are currently based upon advanced stealth technology which has been applied to fighter aircraft making them invisible to radar systems or reducing their radar cross section (RCS) significantly so as to make them blend in with background clutter such as small birds.

Spatial Contraction

This capability is based on taking physical objects and collapsing the distance between them. In this case, two objects, thousands of kilometers away from each other, would be brought together. This capability arose during the Vietnam War, when battlefield images were broadcast directly into American living rooms.

It has since become much more sophisticated, with real-time 24-hour Cable News Network (CNN) broadcasts. This imagery has been exploited by unconventional forces time and again by subjecting the civilian populace of Western nation-states to the horrors of the battlefield for bond-relationship targeting operations (covered in a following section). The Internet, with its live streaming website feeds and real time webcams for virtual reach-back operational support (such as telemedicine or bomb tech support), are other examples of the spatial contraction capability.

Temporal Acceleration

The employment of lasers for their counter-optical and destructive effects, rather than their targeting capability, will elevate them to weapons (that is, laser-arms). This will allow normal time-of-flight limitations to be overcome along with other ballistic limitations such as flight curvature. Before a soldier is done pulling the trigger on a laser-arm, it will have struck its target. No-time-of-flight exists in this case because light travels at absolute speed. While counter-optical weaponry designed for human targeting is currently banned by international law, it is expected that this ban, like the medieval bans on the crossbow and wheel lock pistol, will fail and these weapons will eventually proliferate into the hands of non-state soldiers.

Temporal Deceleration

This capability is expected to develop, but no technologies that are ready to be fielded were identified. It will be based on the ability to slow time rather than compress it. Such torsion weaponry is currently more science fiction than science fact, and may take decades, if not longer, to develop. Still, temporal deceleration represents a logical fifth-dimensional capability which is expected to eventually emerge and should be explored.

Dimensionally Shifted Attack

Some forms of advanced weaponry, specifically acoustic weapons, have the ability to circumvent modern conventional defenses. For example, US mechanized forces such as M1A2 Abrams tanks are impervious to most forms of anti-tank weapons possessed by criminal-soldiers, older Soviet armor, RPGs, and small-to-medium-caliber infantry weapons. On the other hand, infrasonic projecting weapons have the ability to bypass the armor of an M1A2 Abrams tank because their attack is 'out of phase' with it. This allows for the acoustic waves they generate to directly reach past the armor and influence the crew inside the tank. Outcomes can range from disorientation and nausea to more severe bioeffects. Fielding limitations appear to be based on energy sources; current mechanical based ones in use are too constrained in their power generation ability.

Mass Disruptive Attack

New battlespace dynamics based upon mass disruption, rather than mass destruction, have also emerged. Omnidirectional energy projectors such as software weapons (viruses) and radio frequency weapons allow mass disruptive targeting to take place via replicative and expansive processes, respectively.[6]

This form of attack would allow large segments of Western infrastructures to be disrupted without causing the high levels of destruction associated with traditional forms of weapons of mass destruction. This new operational capability is far different than seizure and destruction methods relied upon in modern war-fighting. It provides an OPFOR the ability to send a society into chaos by means of targeting the bond-relationships between things rather than the things themselves.

Energy Barriers

The ability to create non-physical force fields is another emerging capability. It is currently based on weaponry which generates energy barriers of various types. Early forms of this weaponry are the eye-safe Laser Dazzler, which creates an 'optical wall' or 'optical shell' in front of or around military personnel, respectively, and the Short Stop system which creates an 'electronic umbrella' which prematurely detonates incoming mortar and artillery rounds.

Another type of weaponry would create 'acoustic curtains' over bridges and sewers for access denial purposes. Holograms could be used in the same manner but, rather than denying access, they would stealth-mask those objects (and thus overlap with the spatial expansion capability). While the maturity of acoustic and holographic weapons may be in debate, the area denial system (ADS) is not.[7] This classified program was made public in March 2001. It is meant to operate as an area denial device via the creation of an energy barrier. The ADS functions as a millimeter wave projector, has good standoff range, and creates pain in the exposed skin of its targets.

These new capabilities would seem to confirm that a temporal and spatial breakdown of modern battlespace is now taking place. This breakdown explains why the older military forces of the nation-state (armies, navies and air forces) will be unable to defend it from criminal-soldier attacks based upon terrorism and cyberwar techniques. Currently, the agents of these attacks are stealth-masked and, as a result, completely invisible within the parameters of the traditional battlespace paradigm. The older defending military forces are rendered ineffective because the attacking forces are 'out of phase' and thus able to bypass them with impunity.

An example of this phenomenon would be the ability of radical Islamic terrorist forces to successfully attack the World Trade Center and the Pentagon during their September 11 hijacked airliner suicide operations. This analysis conceptually accounts for the fact that, within the modern military paradigm, those target sets were completely safe from attack and in a post-modern military paradigm they were left defenseless. Such operations can be regarded as the ultimate form of asymmetry.

While 'asymmetric war-fighting' is the current term used in Washington, DC, the concept should go beyond current technique or weapon of mass destruction (WMD) based definitions. Rather, it should be expanded to bring in dimensionality. The term 'dimensional asymmetric war-fighting' is a far more accurate characterization of the threats and potentials post-modern war-fighting represents.

In many ways, non-state 'cyber forces' should be viewed much like early manifestations of the raiders of old who took down the Western Roman Empire. Concern thus exists that the modern battlespace breakdown will ultimately undermine the foundations of our modern world based upon the nation-state form. If this is the case, then understanding battlespace dynamics will be integral to counter-OPFOR initiatives. It will represent a focal point of study which will allow the nation-state, or its successor form (such as the European Union experiment), to develop effective defenses against increasingly sophisticated 'dimensional asymmetric war-fighting'-based attacks and ultimately engage in such attacks against hostile entities themselves.

Information Warfare to Netwar

The strategy of information warfare at its most basic level is based upon the defense and attack of information and information systems. While such techniques have always been an aspect of warfare, the importance of this form of conflict has been magnified many times over with the computer and Internet revolutions of the last few decades. It has now become an accepted fact that information warfare is vital to current military operations and that such attacks may represent a potential strategic vulnerability to a nation's critical infrastructure. In law enforcement operations focused on countering non-state forces, these perceptions are gradually starting to take hold but are still years behind military thinking.

Past and current disagreements over information warfare center on the term itself and its impact on war-fighting.[8] Some groups consider computers, software, and the Internet (and intranets) as the principal domain of information operations. Others are more inclusive and may bring in deception, propaganda, psychological operations, electronic warfare, and/or even organizational conflict (hierarchies vs. networks) to this definition.

Views on its operational level war-fighting impact can be divided into two schools of thought. The Force Multiplier School views information warfare as something which will allow conventional military forces, focused on seizure and destruction, to do their jobs even better. It appeals to Western nation-state militaries because of their current battlefield dominance based on the high levels of firepower they possess. The New Capabilities School views this form of warfare as a means to engage in disruptive attacks against opposing forces and/or target sets. It appeals to the militaries of weaker non-Western states and to non-state entities which are actively challenging Western nation-state institutions.

For counter-OPFOR purposes, the Force Multiplier School ultimately represents an evolutionary dead end. Non-state entities, as earlier pointed out, cannot now or in the future engage in direct four-dimensional 'battlespace box' combat with Western military forces. They have no hope of surviving such dimensionally symmetric force-on-force combat. This brings us back to New Capabilities School views based on disruptive attacks as the path to follow.

An acceptance of the view of information warfare's more pronounced impact needs to be anchored to some form of definition of what it comprises. The question becomes whether it is based on just computers and their electro-optical networks or whether other techniques such as electronic warfare should be included. The correct answer is neither. Such definitions are too traditionalist and even backward looking in their thinking. Our concern is not how modern warfare was waged but how post-modern warfare is and will be waged. Accepting that we are facing coming wars between nation-states and non-state entities, 'organizational conflict' is required to be our focus.

In these 'wars over social and political organization', concepts relating to netwar, a term coined by John Arquilla and David Ronfeldt in 1993, are of immense significance.[9] These concepts have already helped with the formation and expansion of the Los Angeles County terrorism early warning (TEW) Group model and fit well into non-state threat analysis found in works on non-trinitarian war, fourth-generation warfare, and fourth epoch war.

Netwar in 1993 was originally described as:

> … information-related conflict at a grand level between nations or societies. It means trying to disrupt, damage, or modify what a target population 'knows' or thinks it knows about itself and the world

> around it. A netwar may focus on public or elite opinion, or both. It may involve public diplomacy measures, propaganda, and psychological campaigns, political and cultural subversion, deception of or interference with local media, infiltration of computer networks and databases, and efforts to promote a dissident or opposition movements across computer networks.[10]

In 1996 the definition was:

> … an emerging mode of conflict (and crime) at societal levels, involving measures short of war, in which protagonists use – indeed, depend on using – networked forms of organization, doctrine, strategy, and communication. These protagonists generally consist of dispersed, often small groups who agree to communicate, coordinate, and act in an Internetted manner, often without a precise central leadership or headquarters. Decision making may be deliberately decentralized and dispersed.[11]

The latter definition is more useful in helping to determine counter-OPFOR courses of action. It suggests that networked forms of organization, doctrine, strategy, and communication all need to be studied prior to the start of conflict. These and other factors are starting to be considered for intelligence preparation of the battlespace (IPB)/ operational space (IPO) against non-state entities.

Organizations, be they hierarchical or networked, at all levels can also be viewed as information systems. This takes us back full circle to the 'defense and attack of information and information systems' definition used for information warfare. These systems can be said to engage in observe-orient-decide-act (OODA) loops based on Col. John Boyd's well known analysis. Networks have far better OODA loops than hierarchies (their use and processing of information is far superior) and for that reason, along with many others, they represent a form of organization far better suited to post-modern conflict. In 'not crime-not war' operational environments, networks quickly seize the initiative.

In information war and netwar scenarios, OODA loops will likely represent one of the key avenues of attack and defense. OPFOR OODA loops will be required to be mapped out based on the network structures involved (for example, chain, star, all-channel) and then disrupted. Friendly hierarchical and networked organizations will also have to have their OODA loops modeled and defenses put into place. While techniques such as distributed denial of services attacks, combined cyberarms approaches based on overcoming security systems, and even dual-dimensional battlespace synergies based on physical and cyber-attacks will represent important forms of this type of warfighting, their use will only be truly meaningful and effective after non-state threat entity mapping and analysis based on netwar concepts has taken place.

Bond-Relationship Targeting

The third strategy is based on the operational concept known as bond-relationship targeting (BRT). This concept was originally developed by the author in 1997 for US military use against non-state (criminal) soldier based entities, but law enforcement applications soon emerged. It had become pretty clear that attrition, maneuver, and even precision guided attack doctrines were insufficient against the future threat of networked non-state OPFORs.

The concept was derived from reverse engineering the target set effects of non-Western warfare (such as terrorism), and merging those perceptions with the recent Department of Defense (DOD) definition for non-lethal weapons which had appeared.[12] More recent concepts of 'effects-based weaponry and/or targeting' appear to be in harmony with some BRT perceptions.

Bond-relationship targeting is defined as:

> Rather than gross physical destruction or injury, the desired end state is a tailored disruption within a thing, between it and other things or between it and its environment by degrading, severing or altering the bonds and relationships which define its existence.

Non-state forces lack traditional 'destructive combat power' so they instead have been forced to rely upon 'disruptive combat power'. The best modern example of this fact is the Vietnam War. American forces used their destructive prowess to achieve battlefield victory after battlefield victory over the Vietcong. The Tet Offensive resulted in a crushing defeat for the OPFOR. From a military destruction and seizure viewpoint, the US won the war. However, from a political bond-relationship targeting viewpoint, the Vietcong won hands down. They were able to turn the American people, government, and military against itself. By the war's end, the bonds and relationships which held together these components of our nation were badly degraded. Terms like 'stab in the back', which characterized military perceptions of the government, and 'baby killers', which characterized the populace's perceptions of the military, are but two examples of this degradation process.

Terrorism works the same way. The attacks themselves are minimal in their destructive power, like pebbles thrown into a pond; it is the shock waves they set off which are the real danger. These ripples attack a nation's bonds and relationships, causing varying forms of disruption to take place. The taking down of the World Trade Towers was about as good as a terrorist network can ask for, short of a weapon of mass destruction attack. It is much like throwing a rock into a pond. The point of impact is larger but it is the disruptive nature of the choppy waves which are still the real danger.

These perceptions complement current DOD thinking on non-lethal weapons. This thinking views NLW as using '... means other than gross physical destruction to prevent the target from functioning.' The advanced nature of the upper tier of these weapons and their unique nature allow mass disruptive attacks to be launched.

This overlap of 'disruptive combat power' is far too coincidental. It is emerging from both low-tech non-state (criminal) forces using terrorism, and high tech forces using advanced weaponry derived from five-dimensional battlespace dynamics. This suggests that disruptive targeting is becoming a critical war-fighting capability. Like networked structures, it will become a key component in the nation-states wars against non-state entities. In the future, we can expect our networks to increasingly engage their networks with disruptive targeting.

To conduct bond-relationship targeting, a non-state threat entity is required to be mapped out for a given battlespace (opspace). Similar mapping perceptions are also derived via netwar analysis. This entity can range from a low-level threat such as an anarchist group like the Black Bloc, to a high-level threat such as a drug cartel or guerrilla network. The entity is composed of 'things' such as people, groups, and resources like money and weaponry. Such mapping is no different than what is done in current military and law enforcement operations.

This mapping is where the similarity ends. In a conventional operation, these things are targeted for destruction and seizure. A drug load can be viewed as one example. If federal law enforcement comes across a drug load, it is confiscated and those transporting it are arrested. The operation is deemed a success. This 'bale count' thinking is really no different than the old 'body count' thinking employed in Vietnam. However, no real harm has been done to the drug trafficking entity. The loss of some mules (transporters) and loads have long been factored into the cost of doing business. Another example is that of combating a street gang. Traditional methods of cracking down would be for the local police to sweep an area and lock up the neighborhood gang members for various infractions for a few days. This has little effect because jail time is considered a badge of honor by these individuals.

A final example would be a military confrontation with a guerrilla network. In this scenario, one of the secret terrorist C^2 (command and control) doctrine websites has been discovered. A standard option would be to go to the Internet provider and shut down the site. If that was not possible, it could be hit with denial-of-service attacks depending on the legality of such an action. A more sophisticated military might try a third method, which would be to monitor the site and collect intelligence. The first two targeting methods have little benefit since the site can always reappear somewhere else. The third method is far better but represents passive intelligence gathering rather than an offensive attack.

Each of these examples can now be looked at via the prism of bond-relationship targeting. In the case of the first, the drug load represents a relationship between the sender at one end and the receiver at the other. The mules may work directly for the sender as an employee or be free agents. Rather than seizing the load and arresting the mules, the load itself could be secretly tampered with in some way. If it was shorted (part taken away and replaced with an inert substance) and allowed to continue onto its destination, it would have the effect of destroying the trust between the sender and receiver and possibly turn them against one another. If the mules survived the wrath of the receiver, they would now be likely turned against their employer or contractor who in turn would blame them for shorting the load. The level of disruption created by means of this method far exceeds the act itself.

With regard to the second example of the gang members being locked up, this response has already been replaced in some municipalities by the 'gang injunction'. This is a judicial method which makes it illegal for gang members to publicly assemble together. The bonds of communication between the things (the gang members) have been severed by this technique. As a result, it paralyzes the gang's criminal activities.

The third example based upon the secret guerrilla group website would be best served through the bond-relationship targeting prism by engaging in data pollution. The information relationship for the whole network is the target set. The website could have its information subtlety compromised over time with term and/or character changes. This would not be noticeable early on but would eventually create a cascading effect. The intent is to corrupt as much of the information of the guerrilla network as possible. This could be tied into time-delayed viruses that subtly corrupt data further in computers which have logged onto the website. The idea would be to engage in an attack with strategic rather than tactical or operational benefit.

As an outcome of these bond-relationship targeting examples, it is clear that mapping out the things which comprise a non-state threat entity is but half the equation. The next step is determining the invisible bond-relationships which hold those things together and anchor them to their environment. This is where bond-relationship targeting goes beyond traditional notions of psychological operations and even terrorism. It provides the rationale behind a tangible targeting template. The bonds between the things, once isolated, can then be weighted for their importance. Targeting priorities can then be determined and capabilities matched to them.

One drawback to bond-relationship targeting is currently based on determining its effectiveness after its application. Criminal-soldiers face the same problem when employing terrorism against Western states (but realize its effectiveness so engage in it anyway). Since 'battlefield damage' is principally non-physical, traditional forms of damage assessment can not be used for validation purposes. Measuring destruction is relatively easy compared to measuring disruption. Still, degradation of OPFOR operational tempo is not something a military commander or law enforcement officer in charge needs to have quantified. The operational results speak quickly for themselves.

The second drawback to bond-relationship targeting can at times be an ethical one. Some techniques or technologies required to obtain specific bond-relationship degradation, severance or alteration may be deemed illegal. These need to be worked through legal counsel to ensure that they confirm to the rules of engagement that are in effect, or may require a reassessment of those legal conventions with which they are in variance.

Summary

Battlespace dynamics, information warfare to netwar, and bond-relationship targeting all represent viable strategies which can be utilized by nation-states against non-state entities. They are not stand-alone solutions to combating networked OPFORs, but rather can be combined with each other and with additional strategies based on non-lethal and hyper-lethal weaponry, with better use of intelligence and planning prior to the engagement of hostilities, and with friendly C^4I networks for operational support and direct operational impact in 'not crime not war' operational environments.

NOTES

1. The 11 Sept. 2001 attack on the World Trade Towers and the Pentagon by the radical Islamic networked organization Al-Qaeda will, in the years to come, probably be viewed as the first of these new wars of the 21st century. Their early emergence, however, can be seen in Colombia with the rise of the Medellín cartel as a direct challenger to that sovereign state.
2. Battlespace dynamics and bond-relationship targeting are more recent attributes of Fourth Epoch War theory. That theory was originally developed by this author and T. Lindsay Moore in 1987.

3. Early works include Robert J. Bunker, 'Advanced Battlespace and Cybermaneuver Concepts: Implications for Force XXI.' *Parameters* 26/3 (Aut. 1996) pp.108–120., and *Five-Dimensional (Cyber) Warfighting: Can the Army After Next be Defeated Through Complex Concepts and Technologies?* (Carlisle Barracks, PA: US Army War College, Strategic Studies Institute. 10 March 1998) pp.142. It should be noted that *t* (time) was not added as a dimensional component until 1998.
4. An exception would be Alexander the Great and Hannibal. The exploitation of y-space by their cavalry forces would help to explain their stunning victories over OPFOR phalanx and legion forces, respectively. They were able to exploit 'dimensional bubbles' into *y*-space against contemporaries solely configured for *x*-space warfighting. With the addition of viable cavalry forces these great military leaders also enjoyed a temporal advantage over their adversaries which translated into quicker reaction cycles or operational tempo.
5. Other capabilities isolated but not discussed are *organic structure replication* (via cloning), *organic structure alteration* (via transgenic engineering), *physical structure alteration* (via cocaine smuggling technology), and *physical structure debonding* (via liquid metal embrittlement).
6. Robert J. Bunker, 'Weapons of Mass Disruption and Terrorism', *Terrorism and Political Violence* 12/1 (Spring 2000) pp.37–46.
7. Refer to the John B. Alexander and Charles 'Sid' Heal contribution on 'Non-Lethal and Hyper-Lethal Weaponry' for more on the significance of the Area Denial System.
8. For an overview of these debates, see Robert J. Bunker, *Information Operations and the Conduct of Land Warfare*. The Land Warfare Papers, No. 31. (Arlington, VA: Association of the United States Army, The Institute of Land Warfare. Oct. 1998).
9. John Arquilla and David Ronfeldt, 'Cyberwar is Coming!' *Comparative Strategy* 12/2 (Spring 1993) pp.141–65. For additional research see John Arquilla and David Ronfeldt, *The Advent of Netwar*. MR-789-OSD (Santa Monica, CA: RAND 1996), *In Athena's Camp: Preparing for Conflict in the Information Age*. MR-880-OSD/RC (Santa Monica, CA: RAND 1997), and *Networks and Netwars: The Future of Terror, Crime, and Militancy*. MR-1382-OSD (Santa Monica, CA: RAND 2001).
10. Arquilla and Ronfeldt, 'Cyberwar is Coming!' (note 9).
11. Arquilla and Ronfeldt, *The Advent of Netwar* (note 9) p.5.
12. Department of Defense, *Policy for Non-Lethal Weapons*. No. 3000.3 (9 July 1996).

'Cleansing Polluted Seas': Non-State Threats and the Urban Environment

RUSSELL W. GLENN

Thutmose III's exhausted Egyptian soldiers found that the fighting was far from over after their day of slaughter on the Jezreel Plain. Canaanite leaders opposing their pharaoh had escaped the battlefield and fled into the nearby city of Megiddo, a key location along the trade route between Egypt and the fertile valleys of the Tigris and Euphrates. It would take another seven months of operations before the battle reached its ultimate end when that objective fell in 1279 BC.

Nearly a millennium later, Alexander the Great's soldiers and sailors also labored seven months before capturing the port of Tyre. Bypassing the city would have unacceptably exposed Alexander's line of communications. Further, Tyre was the finest of the Phoenician ports and the parent city of Carthage. Its conquest swelled Alexander's reputation and that of his army, granting him a decided advantage as he thereafter continued his exploits in Asia and Africa.[1]

The Iberian Peninsula presented multiple challenges for the Roman Publius Cornelius Scipio when he arrived in 210 BC. The interior held separate Carthaginian armies, each alone capable of defeating Scipio's legions. The young but wise general instead chose to capture that point most important to the enemy's lifeline: the port of New Carthage. His surprise attack brought him possession of the critical supply base, the initiative in the struggle for the peninsula, and an initial victory in the successful military career of 'Scipio Africanus'.

Rome had long stood as the political, economic, social, and religious center of an empire that had reigned supreme for centuries before the Vandals captured it in AD 455, looting the city of much of its wealth before departing two weeks later. The fall of the capital and symbolic heart of that empire signaled the final collapse of Roman power in the west.[2]

The causes underlying such attacks on ancient urban areas have proved durable, applying in similar measure to more recent eras. Paris was the target of German intentions in both twentieth-century world wars because of its status as France's head of government, a major transportation hub, centerpiece of the nation's economy, and reputation as one of the world's great metropolises. Twentieth-century attackers were attracted to Manila, Leningrad, Stalingrad, Berlin, London, Seoul, Hue, Saigon, Panama City, and Mogadishu for these and many of the reasons that precipitated assaults on Megiddo, Tyre, New Carthage, and Rome.

There will be no diminishing of this interest in the years to come. Major concentrations of population will continue to wield local, regional, national, and often international influence. Approximately half of the world's residents now live in urban areas. The movement from rural to more densely populated regions is nearly universal, but rates in developing nations exceed those of their more economically fortunate counterparts. Cities and towns are sources of wealth. Migration from the countryside carries promises of higher wages, freedom from dependence on the weather, and relief from a social isolation especially unattractive to the young. The resultant growth often outpaces urban economies' capabilities to provide housing, utility infrastructure, and human services support for the recently arrived.

The factors that draw armies into urban areas do much to explain why villages, towns, and cities are similarly the foci of non-state actor attentions. Concentrations of dissatisfied newcomers make it easy to understand why many are successful in their pursuits. Disgruntlement born of unmet expectations grows in a soil enriched by observations of the wealthy living in close proximity, by oppression of those whose arrival economically threatens longer-term residents, and by the collocation of groups harboring long-standing antipathies. Little wonder that dominant personalities and promises of betterment win hearts and minds, especially among youths suddenly free of traditional rural social mores. It is no surprise that those desiring to raise a challenge to the established order are drawn to these concentrations of economic power, bureaucratic failure, and social inequity.

Fish in the Sea: Non-State Actors' Urban Environments

Most attempts to categorize non-state actor threats do so by focusing on the nature of the groups themselves: member motivations, ends sought, demographic characteristics, or methods employed. It is perhaps more revealing to consider an alternative perspective, one that looks at the nature of the urban population in which these organizations operate.

Non-state organizations often require support from their environments to a greater extent than do regular military forces. Mao addressed the need in his depiction of the relationship between members of a population and guerrillas: 'The former may be likened to water and the latter to the fish who inhabit it.'[3]

Non-state actor characteristics can, without too greatly misshaping the pegs, be put into five 'holes' or categories. The nature of few groups is such that they fall within but a single category; virtually all demonstrate the properties of two if not more. The categories draw their defining elements from the nature of the support provided by the urban population. No less than with Mao's revolutionaries, non-state actor successes are functions of the seas in which they operate.

Controlling the Sea

Organized criminal elements driven by economic gain are the longest standing non-state organizations in many densely populated areas. Survival is in considerable part due to the establishment of an environment conducive to their desired ends. These groups have in some cases established such 'legitimacy' that their authority has been recognized by local and even national governments. The New York City Mafia essentially controlled that city's docks in the World War II era. The American government asked for and obtained Mafia support in securing the New York port area against threats posed by Axis forces during the war years.[4]

Yet it is acceptance of their legitimacy by those residing in their operating areas that is fundamental to such non-state actors' welfare. This is obtained in myriad ways, to include winning support by 'policing' neighborhoods to rid them of undesirables such as drug dealers and prostitutes or coercively via the enforcement of 'laws' that require payment of protection money (taxes). Control may include co-opting government officials such as police, judges, politicians, and other public authorities to further create an environment amenable to the criminal organization's freedom of action. Such creation and maintenance of stability compares favorably with that achieved by many national governments. The result is a community in many ways reliant on and often supportive of the controlling entity.

This success is neither gained nor maintained without at least occasional resistance. Organizations so challenged have to adapt to survive. They relocate to and influence other seas when community resistance makes movement prudent. They attempt to maintain a low profile so as not to become a target for law enforcement authorities or the locally politically ambitious. They further legitimize their economic activities by integrating those illegal with others accepted by or even beneficial for the community. In short, they thrive by controlling the sea that is fundamental to organizational survival and success when such influence is feasible and by adapting when the waters sour.

Urban gangs are related to yet can in general be distinguished from more traditional organized criminal organizations. Whereas the traditional criminal actor employs a rapier, gangs more often employ blunt instruments of coercion. Their inter-group relations are more frequently characterized by violent confrontation than are those of traditional entities. Gang success is nonetheless akin to that of the earlier-mentioned urban criminal groups in that they seek social and economical integration with their communities.

Safe Pools in Dangerous Waters

Organizations in this second category seek to capitalize on the predisposition and influence a portion of the population residing in their operational area. That they focus on only a part of the sea is due to its makeup: while some members of the larger population share goals and beliefs in common with the non-state actor, a considerable number do not. Both the Irish Republican Army (IRA) and the Palestinian Liberation Organization (PLO) operate in areas in which subsets of the population are sympathetic to their goals while the greater part is apathetic, uncooperative, or antipathetic.

The seas in which these organizations swim have fairly extensive pools of friendly waters. This size provides sufficient robustness to ensure that the non-state actor virtually always has a support base, even when it alienates or for other reasons loses a portion of its indigenous foundation.

Alienation can have several consequences. It can underlie the formation of permanent splinter groups or have the transient effect of causing temporary dissatisfaction within the supporting community because of individual poorly conceived actions. Both the IRA and PLO have suffered losses to spin-off organizations whose members disagree with the parent organization's political agendas or related military policies. The IRA has suffered a contraction of its support base due to a growing intolerance of violence in the Catholic community stemming in part from acts of violence that even long-time supporters find unjustifiable. Despite these losses (and diminishing support in the Irish Republic), the size and consequent heterogeneity of the Northern Ireland Catholic community is such that the IRA retains sufficient backing to sustain its agendas.

Local Ponds and Remote Seas

Non-state actors in this third category have no large indigenous support base in their target urban areas, nor do they tend to maintain other than very limited numbers of organization members there. They are therefore forced to rely on local urban nodes for assistance rather than general largesse. The IRA and PLO share some characteristics with other groups in this category in addition to their benefiting from a large and supportive indigenous infrastructure in the region where they conduct most of their activities: both on occasion also choose to strike where local aid is limited. Irish Republican Army attacks on London targets and PLO terrorist activities in Israeli Jewish communities are not uncommon.

Unlike the IRA and PLO, however, the Liberation Tigers of Tamil Elaam (LTTE or Tamil Tigers) have no high-profile urban targets in northern Sri Lanka where Tamils dominate the population. The region has no equivalent of a Belfast or Jerusalem in which targets are numerous and indigenous support plentiful. The Tigers instead export violence to the Sri Lankan capital of Colombo. The Tamil Tiger support base in the city is limited, and those favoring LTTE actions may be members of a Tamil diaspora rather than native residents. Assistance comes from a smaller segment of the population than is the case in Northern Ireland or Palestinian-controlled areas of Israel, easing monitoring and detection by adversary security forces. Tiger bombing and assassination cells therefore tend not to be based in Colombo for extended periods. The local sea in which they swim is like separate ponds surrounded by uncooperative if not outright threatening ground.

The cases of the IRA, PLO, and LTTE are revealing for another reason: all rely on considerable economic support from sources outside their homelands. This reliance means that the non-state actors have to work carefully at cultivating a popular external image, one that precipitates a sustaining of these sources of income. Their reliance on sources of support outside of their area of operations demands maintenance of more than a purely coercive capability. Establishing legitimacy beyond the bounds of their immediate community requires a fairly sophisticated diplomatic, political, and public relations infrastructure. The non-state actor must be able in manipulating international as well as local public opinion, a capability that implies existence of a central authority sufficiently dominant to ensure that violent activities act to support other initiatives as part of a coordinated and consistent campaign.

These three groups all obtain direct contributions from diaspora overseas, but funding from foreign commercial and charitable enterprises complements the donations. Fundraising by the Irish Northern Aid Committee (Noraid), allegedly a charity collecting for IRA prisoners, was notably less successful only after continued Department of Justice attention and extensive media coverage of a 1982 US federal trial in which Noraid's director and other defendants admitted to shipping arms to the IRA.[5]

To overcome a reliance on the vagaries of voluntary donations alone, the LTTE developed a system in which its representatives lend seed money to Tamil diaspora businesses. Subsequent profits are shared with the lenders who use them to fund rebel force activities. A recent article in *The*

Economist estimates such annual income as $24 million from the United States and the equivalent of $7.8 million and $1 million from Switzerland and the United Kingdom respectively. The estimate of Canada's contributions is C $24 million.[6]

This geographical separation of non-state actor organizations from their support bases means that these financial sources are largely out of reach of government authorities who would seek to terminate them. Political and diplomatic firewalls generally allow Tamil Tiger, IRA, and PLO leaders to operate with little concern that their enemies will be able to interfere with overseas fundraising. Such independence facilitates the development of sophisticated and long-standing financial sources. It also has direct operational impact. Extensive external financing lessens group member reliance on local support in a target area, thereby reducing the chance of compromise that such association could precipitate.

Swimming Amongst the Enemy and the Unwitting

The fourth category encompasses groups that perform unexpected one-time or only occasional actions such as the bombing of the federal building in Oklahoma City or the 11 September 2001 attacks on the World Trade Center and the Pentagon. These organizations are not based in the targeted communities. They lack virtually any measure of overt, witting local assistance. Their attacks are therefore all but devoid of dependence on direct support from sympathetic elements in the target region.

The sea may be hostile to the group's intentions, but it is nevertheless dense and heterogeneous, a condition making it fairly easy for attackers to conceal themselves. Unlike in rural environments, those speaking a foreign language and unfamiliar with local customs are commonplace in many urban areas. Daily contacts are characteristically superficial. Unusual behaviors may go undetected due to the high density of activities; the 'hum' of urban daily life veils what would immediately attract attention in less frenetic domains.

Non-state actor financial support is likely extraterritorial, as are its sources of training and equipment. Actions directed at interdicting this external support can be complicated by the lack of an identifiable diaspora or other demographic base. Intelligence collectors will therefore be severely tried during efforts to determine sources of backing and how they might be terminated. The non-state actor representative's lack of reliance on a support foundation in the target area also reduces the likelihood of compromise. Uncovering a planned attack may be virtually impossible barring infiltration of the organization itself or a mistake on the part of the perpetrators.

Yet even members of these groups swim in a sea. It is the population of the urban area in which they prepare for and execute their tasks. At a minimum, this indigenous population provides concealment via its considerable numbers. It likely provides sustenance through routine commercial exchange. The residents of most cities are little concerned and receive at best limited guidance regarding how to detect threats from unfriendly non-state actors. They are therefore unlikely to take action when seeing unattended articles, marginally unusual behaviors, or other signs that would signal potential danger to the better educated. The sea may be inherently unsupportive in character, but it is benign, even supportive, in effect.

Puddles on the Pavement

Members of the final group, like those just described, have but an ephemeral presence in a target area, but in this fifth case the non-state actor often capitalizes on the predisposition of the local populace. Anarchists and others that employ public demonstrations as a means of pursuing illegal ends are representative. The transient nature of their operations abets success: the non-state actor tends to conduct activities only for the duration of the high-profile event that is the raison d'être for its presence in the city. It thereafter departs with no intention of returning.

The majority of local residents may be ambivalent regarding the overt goals of such groups (for example, resistance to international trade agreements or support for marginal environmental causes), but harbor an innate belief that the right to demonstrate is worthy of preservation. The sea is therefore predisposed toward tolerance as long as its members believe the non-state actor is but exercising legitimate rights.

That the covert objectives of these organizations are outside the bounds of legal behavior necessitates further actions on the part of the non-state actors to conceal their actual intentions. They may seek to employ unwitting accomplices to screen illegal activities, actively recruiting the participation of other (law-abiding) organizations in demonstrations or simply capitalizing on the presence of naive onlookers. The greater the success in massing the unwary in the vicinity of planned gatherings, the larger the immediate sea that allows those with ill intentions to escape arrest. Many of the legitimate protestors are from outside the immediate geographical area; they are therefore as unknown to local law enforcement officials as are the problem elements.

It is thus difficult to identify troublemakers prior to outbreaks of violence or other undesirable behaviors. Determination is further complicated in that the actions of those who eventually perpetrate illegal acts generally remain within the bounds of the law until the sea that conceals their activities is in place. They then defeat immediate efforts at identification and arrest via such simple expedients as donning masks and striking selected targets quickly, thereafter removing the concealment and reentering the greater mass of humanity.

Law enforcement personnel find themselves in a conundrum: bold and immediate action is essential to make arrests, but the dense gathering of legitimate demonstrators and onlookers precludes the rapid movement of large numbers of security personnel without risking injury to the innocent. Any inadvertent injuries are likely to be captured by the omnipresent media whose apparatus and personnel may inadvertently help to further shield criminal activities and block security force movements. The anarchist and similar organizations are also careful to limit the extent of the threat they pose. While their actions are undoubtedly embarrassing for local and even national government officials, they rarely threaten loss of life or other than minor damage to property. They as such remain below the level of major security organizations' serious concern, tending to escape focused national and international intelligence attentions that could deny them success.

Water Treatment: Addressing the Urban Non-State Actor Threat

All non-state actors operate in a sea of some kind as they pursue their urban objectives. Organizations that rely on maintaining a presence in their target area have to ensure that they can withstand the occasional draught precipitated by law enforcement crackdowns or alienation of some segments of a previously supportive population. Those that have no intention of maintaining large on-station representation may take advantage of local diaspora, their members temporarily immersing themselves in the friendly population and moving within it as would a single fish in a school, visible yet virtually impossible to individually identify and isolate. Others create transient ponds that evaporate after a target event has passed.

Treatment of the waters on which these threats depend offers a means of limiting their influence. Removal of oxygen from a river causes its fish to die. Public officials can stunt or kill undesirable elements in their troublesome seas, pools, ponds, or puddles, but the remedy has to be tailored. A general poisoning will destroy legitimate and illegitimate enterprises alike. What comprises effective treatment will vary depending on the nature of the threat and the sea on which it depends. It will inevitably include the following three elements in some form.

Focusing Treatment: Identifying Critical Points

The initial step in a treatment process involves the identification of those key elements, or critical points, that offer a way of most effectively influencing the target in the manner desired. Members of non-state actor threat groups are themselves both targets and a means to controlling or eradicating undesirable entities. Eliminating, compromising, or turning sufficient numbers of a group may eventually cause an organization to fail.

Key components of the supporting sea are likely more lucrative targets in that they offer greater chances of success. If an organized criminal entity is the threat, turning a highly placed member is a desirable but rare coup. An anti-corruption campaign seeking to remove police, politicians, inspectors, and others that have aligned themselves with the threat offers better promise and the added benefit of winning support from the local populace, especially if that public is recruited and thus shares responsibility for the victory. Expelling the pollutants provides an environment in which desirable life forms can once again thrive. Convincing citizens to rely on honest public officials for basic needs further undermines the criminal organization's foundation.

If it is a disenfranchised or disenchanted portion of a larger sea that is providing the support base, as is the case with the IRA and PLO, critical points include these dissatisfied members of the community. Such cases may be immune to rapid treatment; long-standing antipathies have spawned in-bred hatreds that permeate the disgruntled waters. Other parts of the sea may also resist the treatment methods, perceiving that state resources are being unwisely spent on those who have long supported an adversary.

Yet well considered, multi-faceted initiatives hold promise. The British have demonstrated considerable patience in improving the economic and political status of Northern Ireland's Catholic population despite resistance from Unionist elements. Slowly, ever so slowly, living standards, education levels, and other measures of basic well being are improving through mutually supporting economic, social, political, and military efforts. There is evidence that the IRA is being deprived of its oxygen; the once friendly pool shows signs of desiring to purge itself of that group's violence. The Palestinian situation is not completely dissimilar, but attempts at treatment have thus far proven unsuccessful, perhaps because it too greatly ignores the sea from which the treatment is to remove the pollutants.

Critical points may be distant from the immediate waters in which the threat operates. Loss of the external support on which it depends would dramatically handicap a group such as the IRA, PLO, or LTTE. As has been noted, in these cases critical points may be beyond the political jurisdiction of the nations most threatened by the non-state actors. Addressing them can be problematic. Efforts by the Sri Lankan government to convince other countries that they should more rigorously police those supportive of Tamil Tiger operations have had limited results. Success comes more easily for nations with greater diplomatic, economical, or coercive influence. In either case, an information campaign directed at the citizens and leaders of selected nations will deny the non-state adversary unchallenged access to those waters.

The critical point may in some instances be the sea at large. The city of San Diego was notably successful in containing the influence of disruptive demonstrators during the 2001 Biotechnology Industry Organization's annual trade show because its officials recognized that the key target group was the sea in which the threat had chosen to demonstrate. A preemptive educational campaign directed toward the city's residents undermined the non-state actor position prior to the conference.[9] An informed and law-abiding citizenry and city police force together refused to tolerate incursions on the property and other rights of fellow residents, choosing instead to support law enforcement efforts to restrict the activities of demonstrators with other than legitimate agendas.

Forcing the Threat into Shallow Waters

A fish in the shallows finds it more difficult to remain unseen by potential predators. Actions taken to limit tolerance of illegal acts can have the dual effects of selectively poisoning a threat's sea and draining it of supporting waters. Non-state actor success relies on adequate resources, vulnerable targets, and freedom of action during preparation periods. The IRA, PLO, and LTTE operate surreptitiously until striking a blow for much the same reasons organized criminal elements seek to maintain a low profile. Terrorists' innocuous behavior before their 11 September attacks denied intelligence authorities knowledge of their intentions. Those intending to use demonstrations as forums for violence tend to overtly remain within the confines of the law until the event itself. All of these groups attempt to make early detection problematic by seeming to be but an innocent part of the sea.

Yet illegal actions, either those recurring or others necessary to prepare for single major illegal acts, fall outside the norm of accepted and routine behavior. Those activities too often go undetected or unreported due to complicity, complacency, concealment, or ignorance. It is within the power of security authorities to address all of these shortfalls. The threat's ability to operate unimpeded can first be restricted by actions taken to identify critical points. Examples include the already mentioned elimination of a previously supportive population's sources of discontent, the conduct of education programs directed at inciting intolerance for illegal acts, and public awareness campaigns directed at increasing public understanding of criminal methods.

These initiatives act to make the seas unwelcome for threat elements. Those elements must then seek support from the increasingly small segments of the population that remain willing to assist them. Sources of provisions shrink accordingly; they can be further reduced by the monitoring of products thought to be of value to the non-state actor (such as explosives ingredients or components of sophisticated trigger devices). Actions taken to limit threat freedom of movement, such as curfews or restricting routes open to vehicle traffic, act with these other measures to force those with ill intentions into increasingly shallow waters where they are more readily detected and removed.

Forming the Net

Removal of non-state actor urban threats will depend in considerable part on cooperation between disparate governmental and at times governmental and non-governmental agencies. Denying diaspora or other external support will involve multiple international jurisdictions. Lessons learned at considerable economic cost and embarrassment in Seattle and Genoa should be passed on to those overseeing the sites of impending events that are likely to attract demonstrator involvement.

Few local urban governments have the financial or other capabilities essential to expelling a non-state actor threat alone. Cooperation weaves a net of shared expertise, intelligence, and supportive action far more likely to clear the waters of unwanted elements. Federal governments should act to coordinate national programs with the objective of countering threat initiatives; they should also be the conduits for the dissemination of lessons learned by local, national, and international authorities. Non-governmental elements, most notably the public itself, should be invited to play a role. The greater the number of those supporting actions to limit the activities of non-state urban threats, the tighter the weave on the net woven to sweep them from supporting seas.

Conclusion

Understanding the nature of the various urban seas in which the non-state actor swims, and identifying those elements most critical to its support, are vital first steps toward gaining advantage and eventually expelling pollutants from the waters. Employing education and otherwise acting to remove nutrients on which the threat depends simultaneously starves the fish and reduces the depth of the waters on which they depend for protection from detection and attack. Such actions may themselves precipitate the targets' demise. If not, ultimate removal will rely on a net woven of cooperation between local, regional, national, and international agencies and the people who comprise the seas essential to threat survival. Focusing on the non-state actor alone risks ineffectiveness, outright failure, and long-term alienation of the citizenry. Actively cultivating the cooperation of the people during treatment efforts acts to both advance the adversary's defeat and calm the waters for the years to come.

NOTES

1. J.F.C. Fuller. *The Generalship of Alexander the Great* [1956] (New York, NY: Da Capo 1989) p.203.
2. Though puppet emperors would rule for nearly another quarter century, Rome the empire had all but disappeared. See, for example, Michael Grant, *The Army of the Caesars* (New York, NY: M. Evans 1974) p.285.
3. Mao Tse-Tung, *On Guerrilla Warfare*. Trans. Samuel B. Griffith (Garden City, New York, NY: Anchor 1978) p.83.
4. Carlo D'Este. *Bitter Victory: The Battle for Sicily, 1943* (Glasgow, Scotland: Collins 1989) pp.624–5.
5. Robert D. McFadden. '5 are acquitted in Brooklyn of Plot to Run Guns to IRA', *New York Times*, Section 1, 6 Nov. 1982, p.31; and Jimmy Burns, 'Noraid defiance fails to move US Justice Department', *The Financial Times* (London), 6, 30 May 1994.
6. 'Migrant Communities: There is Another Country …', *The Economist* 356 (19 Aug. 2000) p.26. See also Antony Davis, 'Asia, Tamil Tiger International', *Jane's Intelligence Review* 8/10 (1 Oct. 1996) p.4.
7. Non-state actors employing demonstrations to further their aims may openly advertise their pending presence at future events. Advertising their intentions to protest compromises the locations and times at which demonstrations will take place. However, as recruiting other groups (essential for concealment) and ensuring media coverage are crucial to the non-state actors' agendas, this loss of secrecy is viewed as necessary despite the negative security implications. It is therefore possible for security authorities to fix the timing of threat actions with near certainty. This in turn should facilitate study of demonstrator methods and consequent adaptation by governmental authorities.
8. The author thanks Tom Sward for his advice to expand the concept of educating members of the population to encompass a larger information operations campaign.
9. Seth Hettena. 'Hundreds Protest Biotech Conference.' *The Cincinnati Enquirer*. (25 June 2001) accessed 26 Oct. 2001 at <enquirer.com/editions/2001/06/25/fin_hundreds_protest.html>.

Non-Lethal and Hyper-Lethal Weaponry

JOHN B. ALEXANDER and
CHARLES 'SID' HEAL

The future of conflict: is small, smart, fast, precise, unconventional, and death is optional. The main danger facing today's military leaders is preparing to fight the war they want to fight versus the war they are going to fight. While the technology advantage will belong to US and its allies, decisions about when and where engagements will occur are likely to be relinquished to the adversaries. Not that they want it that way, but a host of external pressures will circumvent many decision-making processes. That is the nature of asymmetric warfare.

On 11 September 2001, a defining day in American history, the worst fears of our military planners were realized. Hijacked airplanes were turned into suicide bombs, three of which inflicted incredible damage resulting in more than 3,000 fatalities. Despite several studies and repeated warnings about the vulnerabilities of the US homeland, a very successful attack was launched without any weapons systems being involved and caught the intelligence apparatus off guard. In a period of a few minutes, the world changed forever. It also portended the necessity for a unique juxtaposition of complimentary weapons systems, non-lethal and hyper-lethal.

There was a distinct downside to the impressive technology demonstration of 'Desert Storm' and the 11 September attacks part of the legacy. Most potential adversaries took home the message that it is not smart to fight the US in a direct confrontation on an open battlefield. You will lose. That is why future adversaries will strike at soft targets and keep our attempts at mobilization and coalition building in as much turmoil as possible. While multinational action may be desirable, there will exist difficult situations in which unilateral capabilities are necessary.

Less than a decade after 'Desert Storm', the effectiveness of American airpower was severely tested in Bosnia. Despite an overwhelming technical advantage, and coupled with relative freedom of the skies, very few critical targets were actually destroyed with the large number of precision standoff weapons that were dropped. A combination of poor weather conditions and innovative decoys confounded the best efforts of our combat aviators.

Further complicating the prosecution of the air campaign were the requirements of international target selection processes and complex command and control systems. Then there was the overt political overlay placed on military leaders. The lessons learned from Bosnia were that adversaries could effectively influence international decision-making processes and defeat the advantage of precision-guided systems with relatively cheap countermeasures. Airpower alone was insufficient and combat decisions made by committees with political agendas were fraught with problems. More importantly, the aura of invincibility had been shattered.

Then, beginning early that fateful Tuesday morning the world as we knew it changed forever. Not only could adversaries evade our best attempts to hit them, they brought war to mainland America, events not experienced in the entire twentieth century. War had always been over there. Even the earlier 1993 bombing of the World Trade Center had not galvanized our citizens as did this. Most apropos are the words attributed to Admiral Yamamoto after receiving word of the successful attack on Pearl Harbor: 'I'm afraid all we have done is to awaken a sleeping giant.'

Emerging Threats

> *The future is not the son of Desert Storm, but the stepchild of Somalia and Chechnya.*
>
> General Charles C. Krulak, 31st Commandant, USMC

While discussed in more detail elsewhere in this collection, the nature of emerging threats is of preeminent concern and worth mentioning here. There is agreement that some traditional threats will remain. To defeat those potential adversaries our troops must be equipped with massive overwhelming firepower capabilities. The old Cold War axiom, to fight outnumbered and win, will take on new meaning. As the seventh largest military in the world, the US must rely on technical superiority if they are to be capable of engaging any threat.

Geographically dispersed threats require a rapid deployment capability. Inherent with rapid deployment are situations in which the forces on the ground are placed in tenuous situations until sufficient combat power can be established to make those elements self-sustaining. Adequate strategic transport capability has always been the long pole in the tent for planning purposes. The bad news is that the situation will not change in the foreseeable future. Worse news is that we will deploy forces into difficult situations and they will remain vulnerable during early entry operations.

However, it is far more likely that we will engage new enemies in less than optimal circumstances. Fighting in cities, however undesirable, is most likely. Experiences in Hue, Panama City, Mogadishu, Chechnya, and many other places indicate just how difficult such combat can be. While the Army currently emphasizes the need for weapons with precision strike capability at tens of kilometers, these battles are fought at tens of meters.

Further, changing social structures will dictate that actions be taken against subsets of population groups while not permitting extensive collateral casualties to noncombatants. In such circumstances non-state actors, with the ability to affect our national interests, will be collocated with others not sharing these views or ambitions. Identification by race, religion, ethnicity, or place of birth will be insufficient to name them as enemies.[1] These changes in social structure will play a key role in determining the amount and type of force that may be employed under a given set of circumstances. In turn, that will drive the weapons requirements process.

Other issues in the changing missions of the military will include involvement in peace support operations abroad and confronting domestic terrorism. While the Bush administration of 2001 indicated that they do not desire extensive engagement in peace support operations, the reality is that involvement by the US is driven by circumstances beyond their control. The power of the CNN effect is such that visible suffering will eventually cause a public outcry for intervention. Unfortunately factors such as race, religion, and historical relationships will determine the amount of pain and misfortune that is deemed tolerable. Based on experiences in Cambodia and Rwanda, we have proven that Americans will allow genocidal levels of atrocities provided we are not openly confronted by the news media.

Homeland defense and counterterrorism also present unique conundrums because peace and individual freedoms may be competing interests. There is a delicate balance between rights protected under our democratic process and the perceived need for domestic security. In the past decades Americans have accepted increasing invasions of privacy and personal inconveniences in order to feel safe. The most obvious example is airport security. With the bombings of the World Trade Center (1993) and the Murrah Federal Building in Oklahoma City US citizens were shocked into the reality that it can happen here. With standoffs at Ruby Ridge, Waco, Pine Ridge and recently Santa Clarita, the public both understands that confrontations can happen locally and questions the appropriateness in use of deadly force.

Then, on 11 September 2001, a day of infamy and transcendence in America, the balance shifted dramatically and forever.

From the police side of the equation things have changed significantly. The amount of force available for law enforcement agencies was severely tested in the now-infamous shootout at a bank in North Hollywood. During the holdup and televised aftermath the robbers were equipped with complete body armor and fully automatic weapons. Although eventually killed they outgunned the police and held them at bay for a considerable period of time. Even then questions were raised about whether or not the police did enough to protect the lives of the assailants resulting in at least one lawsuit on behalf of one of the suspects.

There is a convergence of operational capabilities between law enforcement agencies and some military operations. In question will be the weapons systems provided to each and the circumstances under which they may be employed. Improved technology will be part of the solution to future conflicts. Also necessary are excellent training, skilled leaders, established policies and an informed public. All of this rests on improved intelligence about illegal activities and the intent of our adversaries.

Effects-Based Weapons

There are competing, almost incongruent forces, that will emerge in future weapons systems. The common factor will be that they emphasize the effects produced by the weapon rather than killing power. These factors will run from death and total physical destruction to compliance through intimidation and show of force. The spectrum is very broad but might include such diverse effects as temporary physical incapacitation, dazzling light, pain, muscle tetanization, electronic upset or burnout, tire degradation, decomposition of materials or a host of others either singularly or in any combination.

While many are currently being developed as independent items, there will be a strong need to consolidate technologies and produce integrated weapons systems. They will include advanced target identification and acquisition, controlled effects, and combat assessment capabilities.

The effort to control collateral casualties will be predicated on three factors, identifying the right target, precision guidance, and optional lethality payloads. These systems will permit commanders to tailor their combat power based on local circumstances. In fact, the biggest increase burden may be on the commander's decision-making requirements so that he can insure both mission effectiveness, assume reasonable troop safety risks, while minimizing collateral casualties.

While currently known as non-lethal weapons, this nomenclature will eventually be subsumed in the broader context of effect-based systems. Non-lethal outcomes will be part of the continuum. While these systems currently need special identification to ensure continued research and development in a harsh budgetary environment eventually they will compete with all other weapons capabilities. Otherwise they will remain a boutique item, selected piecemeal and falling well short of their full potential.

The first major non-lethal weapons systems have recently been announced. Probably of most interest has been the vehicle mounted area denial system (VMADS) – just renamed the area denial system (ADS) as consideration is being given to configurations that do not include a vehicle. Nicknamed the people zapper, the ADS – is a millimeter wave projector that operates with pain as the mediating effect. At about 95 gigahertz (GHz) this very short-wave system strikes exposed skin and attacks the pain receptors. As one who has experienced this effect, it is noted that only a brief exposure is required to convince a person that they want to be out of the path of this weapon.

The frequency of the ADS is important. At 95 GHz it can pass easily through the atmosphere. However, the wavelength is so short that it does not penetrate the body more than 1/16th of an inch. This fact should allay fears that there is a dial in effect switch that can be turned up and cooking will occur. Extensive animal and human testing was conducted before the decision to go forward with this system. Eye effects are of particular concern. To determine what damage might occur to a cornea, test animals were exposed to dosages far above anything considered for the weapon without any appreciable permanent injury. These tests are continuing.

The ADS holds great promise for many reasons. One of the biggest problems in peace support operations has been the commingling of a few snipers in a crowd of civilians. In Mogadishu, those people played the role of willing hostages and proved they were prepared to die for their cause. The ADS would quickly strip away snipers from hostages. The pain is sufficiently intense that snipers would not be able take aimed shots at our forces. This gives ADS a potential role in military operations in urban terrain (MOUT) by defeating the most persistent and pernicious of all urban threats.

One concern being addressed is determination of what crowds will do once exposed to the ADS beam. Clearly it will not be able to dwell on a civilian population even if they are demonstrating intent to riot. Once exposed the people must be given an opportunity to vacate the area. Operational considerations will include being able to disperse a crowd without having people trampled to death.

A major advantage of ADS over any existing non-lethal weapons system is its range. Soldiers have been using the rock test for some time. They want weapons that can influence people at distances beyond the rock-throwing distance of a teenager – considered to be about 180 feet, not counting bounces. The exact distances that ADS will be effective have yet to be fully determined. However, it will pass the rock test several times over.

Initially developed at the US Air Force Phillips Laboratory for base security applications, other ADS operational uses are possible and offer significant advantages. Following the 12 October 2000 attack on the USS *Cole* in Yemen, the US Navy began looking for better methods to protect ships in port. ADS is one possible measure. There are also proposals for placing an ADS on several airborne platforms. This would allow fast delivery of the ADS in situations that develop rapidly, as has been experienced by our troops engaged in peace support operations. Such a system would have changed the outcome in Mogadishu, and prevented injuries in Bosnia.

Clearly ADS is a multi-role system that can be effective in crowd control, perimeter security and in MOUT. The biggest hurdle will be gaining acceptability by both the military and political leaders. The ill-informed media just about instantly decried the VMADS when information was first released in March 2001. When one considers the alternatives, such as the large number of civilians mowed down by helicopter miniguns and machine-guns in Somalia, the pain inflicted by the ADS becomes a very attractive and responsible alternative.

Another major non-lethal weapons system under consideration is the advanced tactical laser (ATL). Being developed by Boeing, this is a chemical oxygen iodine laser (COIL) transported on an airborne platform that can strike targets with extreme accuracy at many kilometers.

It is believed that advances in adaptive optics allow laser capabilities previously unattainable. It is reported that the COIL will be able to place a four-inch spot on targets at 20 kilometers. The proposed approach to this type of system is the advanced tactical laser (ATL). Although still in the conceptual development stage, ATL would utilize a COIL and operate at a wavelength of 1.315 microns. The laser, its chemical fuel, and laser beam director would be sized to fit on an aircraft platform such as an Osprey tilt-rotor craft or a C-130 transport. A soldier who views the scene through a separate aperture co-aligned with the laser beam director would select the target. In more advanced versions of ATL, target selection could also be accomplished automatically using target-recognition and tracking software.

Such a system could be lethal if directed against human beings. Their use as non-lethal weapons is intended for applications such as bursting automobile tires, rupturing fuel tanks, selectively cutting through electrical or communications lines, or setting fires. The advantage of such a system would be its ability for selective and precise targeting. A frequently cited example is a military convoy operated by armed soldiers holding civilian hostages. The laser system would rapidly sweep along the convoy, selectively targeting vehicle tires, tracks, and weapons, while avoiding injury to the hostages. If achievable, this capability would be very useful.

There are several issues associated with atmospheric propagation that are likely to limit the effectiveness of ATL as currently envisioned. The first is atmospheric absorption. At the COIL wavelength, atmospheric absorption will heat the column of air through which the beam passes. This heated air will de-focus the beam through a mechanism known as 'thermal blooming' and reduce the intensity on target. Thermal blooming may be compensated to some extent with adaptive optics, but that approach introduces significant complications to the system design.

The second issue concerns the ability of ATL to be pointed precisely. A limiting effect is atmospheric turbulence along the beam path. This turbulence causes high frequency beam 'jitter' which also reduces the intensity on the target. Vibration disturbances on the aircraft platform itself will also contribute to beam jitter, further reducing intensity on target. There are also serious logistics issues that would need to be addressed in order for ATL to operate in the field. The COIL fuel is comprised of caustic chemicals that require careful storage and handling.[2] Nevertheless, reviews by the developer and military suggest that this can become a viable system, one that would greatly enhance combat effectiveness. The Boeing proposal indicates the ATL could engage 172 targets in 40 seconds, which is the total capacity of the chemical laser. The number of targets engaged would be dictated by the dwell time necessary to defeat each object.

There is another class of high-energy laser systems proposed for antipersonnel application. These are designed to produce a kinetic shock through a laser-induced plasma. One such system is the pulsed energy projectile (PEP) being developed by Mission Research Corporation. PEP would utilize a pulsed deuterium-fluoride (DF) laser designed to produce an ionized plasma at the target surface. In turn, the plasma would produce an ultrasonic pressure wave that would pass into the body, stimulating the cutaneous nerves in the skin to produce pain and induce temporary paralysis. The proposed PEP system would accomplish this at ranges up to 500 meters.

So far, laboratory tests at short range have produced 270 joules and acoustic (pressure) levels of 170 dB.[3] Still in early development, the PEP is quite controversial. It would pack a very significant wallop with instantaneous time of flight. The ability to cause temporary paralysis of selected targets would be an attractive attribute. Nonetheless there are issues to be addressed in the developmental and operational concept processes.

Nearly every study of non-lethal weapons places high-power microwave weapons near the top of their list. The most important capability is to cause electronic disruption to disable or destroy electronic equipment. All sensitive electronics are potential targets including computers, cell phones and radios, television global positioning system (GPS) receivers, and some engine ignition systems. Some HPM systems would provide this capability without accompanying blast effects, physical damage, or death to nearby personnel characteristic of conventional explosives. HPM systems designed to produce these effects would utilize conventional millimeter-wave and RF generators combined with a suitable transmitter such as a microwave horn or antenna. Unconventional approaches to generating and delivering HPM include explosive devices that would produce a single, intense pulse usually referred to as electromagnetic pulse (EMP) devices.[4]

Explosive-drive HPM systems allow the cruise missile to fly within close proximity to the intended target. A single pulse is generated and because of the local target, the amount of energy output required is far less than a system with area coverage. If the operating frequency of the targeted electronics is known, then the weapon can be tailored and require even less energy to do substantial damage. With explosive-driven HPM there are some shrapnel effects. A big advantage, however, is that there is no problem with fratricide to friendly equipment. If the promises of the HPM community ever come to fruition, a major step will have been taken in combat effectiveness.

Magic Dust has always been a dream as a non-lethal weapon. Not yet fully defined, this would be a substance that would cause temporary incapacitation with 100 per cent safety. It would be even better if the incapacitation would initiate an instantaneous catatonic state so that muscles freeze and prevent the leasing of a dead-man's switch. That is, 'How do you stop a terrorist who has pulled the pin on a grenade?'

There is good news and bad news with incapacitants. The bad news is that Magic Dust does not exist and probably never will. The difference between incapacitation and death is very small as is attested to by the insurance rates of anesthesiologists. The good news is that advances have been made in the field of incapacitants. One useful approach is the administration of both the paralytic agent and the antidote simultaneously. This allows the targeted subject to be temporarily taken down but begin the recovery process almost immediately. Since dosage is a key factor, there will be limitations on widespread usage. In some hostage rescue situations, however, the risks may well outweigh the potential losses. After the 11 September hijackings, there are new rules of engagement and willingness to accept even friendly losses in extreme situations.

At this point we will not address all of the operational and philosophical issues associated with the use of incapacitants or calmative agents. It must be understood that these will probably never be perfect systems. They will offer highly desirable combat and rescue capabilities. They will also offer the potential for abuse. Two major concerns will be raised. One involves the use of calmatives for suppression of dissension by civil groups. The second will be the use of these agents to incapacitate adversaries, thus allow them to be executed. Both issues, however, have policy and legal implications. Regardless technologies are on the horizon that will allow these capabilities to be explored.

Problematic in peace support operations is finding persons who are wanted for criminal activity. Since humans have a mental bias that permits them to identify others of their racial origin more easily than those of other groups, identifying and arresting criminals of other races has proven difficult. It was suspected in Bosnia that wanted criminals were stopped and released because of the security forces' inability to quickly and reliably identify an individual.

Recent developments in automated facial identification, however, will change that. These devices already exist and are being employed by police agencies. From a military perspective we can anticipate that future security units will be armed with biometric sensors that quickly scan facial characteristics, retinal features and fingerprints and compare them with a database of known criminals. The soldiers would then be alerted as to the true identify of the targeted person and can arrest them on the spot. This will have great utility at checkpoints and in crowd surveillance in identifying and arresting suspects and removes the age-old sanctuary of anonymity.

Not all of the effects-based weapons will be non-lethal. In fact, some of them are potentially very lethal. Two areas are of particular concern to the military. One, already mentioned, was the vulnerability of early entry forces while they are establishing a foothold. The second is deeply buried facilities that are impervious to traditional bombing and missile attacks.

To protect early entry units and special operations forces Raytheon has developed a concept called Big Gun. The intention is to provide small forces on the ground with the capability to direct very heavy firepower that can be delivered precisely and quickly. Big Gun calls for an orbiting aircraft high above the area of interest. On board are up to 1,500 guided munitions. On demand they are simply dropped from the aircraft and guided to the target.

Big Gun envisions a person or a robot sensor locating a target on the ground. They then relay both the automated GPS coordinates and an authentication code to the aircraft. They provide the GPS location, direction, range, and target imagery for automatic target recognition. Within seconds the bomb is on its way using GPS for relative accuracy since both the designator and weapon are using the same GPS constellation. For moving targets, such as tanks or other armored vehicles, there is a terminal seeker on the weapon. Of course multiple rounds may be dropped if several targets are designated.

One major advantage to Big Gun is that common, currently available munitions can be employed. These include XM-982 INS/GPS guided weapons, TERM (tank extended range munition) with a GPS add-on, MRAAS 105mm, and an Advanced PGMM (precision guided mortar munition) with terminal seeker. Since they are dropped there is no need for a firing mechanism. From an aircraft orbiting at 40,000 feet a radius of 16 miles can be covered. Higher altitudes provide even greater range.

Deep buried targets have presented a serious problem for several decades. During 'Desert Storm' specially designed penetrating munitions came of age. They were used to destroy the near state-of-the-art aircraft bunkers that held the Iraqi Air Force planes. Since they could not fly, as that was certain death, the aircraft were systematically destroyed in place.

However, there were other targets, such as underground command and control centers, that required even bigger bombs. Developed in short order was the guided bomb unit-28 (GBU-28), a 5000-pound laser guided bomb with a 4,400-pound penetrating warhead. The first weapons were actually made from Army artillery tubes that were packed with high explosives. Called the 'bunker-buster', it was over 19 feet long. The accelerated development program was nothing short of miraculous. The program was started on 1 February 1991 and the test bombs were delivered on 20 February. On 27 February, two operational bombs were delivered and subsequently dropped by an F-111, destroying the target. Since then, many additional bunker-busters have been added to the inventory and additional research has gone into developing effective deep penetrating munitions as they will be key in striking similar targets.

There have also been controversial proposals for obtaining penetration capability. Several are potentially space-based weapons systems. Placed in space, these bombs could be de-orbited and directed with great precision to a target. Coming from space they would reach velocities in excess of 4,500 mph and have the advantage of striking targets more rapidly than conventional aircraft could reach them.

Currently there is great debate about whether or not weapons should be placed in space. Treaties aside, sooner or later this will happen. Having penetrating munitions stored there would provide a great advantage in time from decision to attacking the target. In today's rapidly changing circumstances, that differential may be critical. In fact, in the near future it is likely that there will be very high real estate value parked in space. But it will be industry, not governments who will own this property. If history tells us anything, it should be clear that some form of protection will be necessary. That will likely mean placing weapons in space.

In addition to penetrating munitions there will be advances in explosives. Among those will be fuel air explosives (FAE) that proved devastating in Chechnya though it was first developed by the US and used in Vietnam. FAE disperses a cloud of fuel that is then ignited. This causes a blast overpressure that will destroy virtually all soft targets including vehicles, aircraft, bunkers and even minefields. Exposed personnel are very vulnerable and pliable body armor will not protect and may even add to the seriousness of injuries. The rapidly expanding shock wave literally flattens everything in the proximity of the epicenter. When used in enclosed areas the damage is even greater than in the open. The effects include, blast, burning and crushing. In fact, they are so great that FAE has been compare to low-yield nuclear weapons in destructive power.

One change that will occur is an emphasis on total systems development. Too many of the effects-based weapons rely on independent target acquisition before they can be employed. Further, combat damage assessment can be very imprecise when attempting to determine the extent of damage done internally. Therefore, future systems will be characterized by fully integrated target acquisition, precision guidance, nodal exploitation, controlled effects, and automatic combat damage assessment.

Policy Issues

Weapons technology cannot be viewed in a vacuum. There are extensive policy issues that must be considered with the development and deployment of all weapons. Contrary to the protestations of Colin Gray, the nature of conflict has changed.[5] There are shifts to non-state adversaries, the objectives of all parties may not be conquest, and how the conflict is prosecuted do lead to the conclusion of transformation.

All of the weapons mentioned are subject to dictated rules of engagement. The problem with many effects-based weapons is that they blur the boundaries that have been previously established. In peace support operations it may well be junior officers or NCOs who make decisions that impact national policy. Therefore, the tendency has been to withhold authority for use of such weapons to unreasonably high levels of command. It is the soldiers on the ground who know if their lives are in jeopardy; they should have authority to use the force necessary to accomplish the mission while safeguarding themselves. What these weapons dictate is a need to think through the rules of engagement in great detail, conduct extensive training so that soldiers know what is expected of them, and let them do their job based on military, not political decisions.

Treaties play a significant role in the development of some of these weapons. Unfortunately, many predate current technology and thus require the unnecessary taking of life. Further, many potential adversaries are not signatories to the treaties and some countries that have signed treaties are in flagrant violation. As conclusively shown in the recent terrorist attacks, these adversaries care not for the rules of land warfare, nor the opinions of civilized people. It is time to revisit the notion of weapons treaties and determine a course of action that makes sense in today's world.

Summary

September 11, a day that will truly live in infamy, conclusively demonstrated that asymmetric warfare has fully arrived. No one anywhere in the world will ever be totally safe again. Disregarding all notions of appropriateness civilians are targets, infrastructures are at risk, and humanity is the poorer for it. The oft-predicted emerging terrorist threats moved from their shadowy lairs and into Manhattan and Washington.

To decisively respond it will be necessary to develop weapons systems that function at both ends of the force spectrum. There will be fearsome hyper-lethal weapons that deliver surgical blows with extreme power and metric accuracy. On the other end, non-lethal weapons will meet the need to control violence in urban areas, some of which will be on the US mainland. Some of these weapons have been described, others have not. More will be developed.

NOTES

1. For a more in depth analysis of the impact of social organization see John B. Alexander, Appendix A, *Future War: Non-Lethal Weapons in Twenty-First-Century Warfare* (New York, NY: St Martin's Press 1999).
2. Naval Studies Board Review of Non-Lethal Weapons and Technology (Oct. 2001).
3. Ibid.
4. Ibid.
5. Colin Gray, *Weapons for Strategic Effect: How Important is Technology?*, Occasional Paper No. 21, Center for Strategy and Technology, Air War College (Jan. 2001).

Intelligence Preparation for Operations

MATT BEGERT and DAN LINDSAY

Intelligence Preparation for Operations (IPO) is the implementation of a concept of readiness by preparation, observation and analysis. The purpose is to identify a threat in time to dissuade, detect, deter, or engage as soon as possible or, failing that, to mitigate and recover as fast as possible with the least resultant destruction or disruption. It is a concept of active defense achieved through constant surveillance and vigilance. It is a support function that offers several synergistic advantages in the active defense of any operating area. It can be implemented in a local political jurisdiction, an area of responsibility (AOR), a region, in stability and sustainment operations (SASO), peacekeeping or any variety of missions or public safety responsibilities, domestic or external.

The objective is to support tactical-level or first-responder action in time and space and to clarify critical thinking for course of action (COA) decision at a strategic or political level. These advantages are possible because of the potential to speed decision and action. It is investigative, preparatory and analytical and works best in a network, not a hierarchy. It is complementary to, not competitive with, existing ways of operating.

Intelligence preparation of the battlefield (IPB) is a well-known, well-documented and well-studied advantage in military operations. Sun Tzu in *The Art of War* recognized it more than 2,000 years ago by emphasizing knowledge of the terrain, the weather, the enemy, and the skillful use of spies. Recent study has appropriately focused on intelligence for military operations in urban terrain (MOUT) and has recognized the additional complexity of the environment and the shortfalls of current IPB doctrine. Previously, IPB subject matter had only dealt with constant or reasonably predictable elements like terrain and weather, and with conventional military doctrine, equipment and intent. Modern military doctrine has a well-defined role for IPB for nation-state conventional force-on-force action. Some parts of IPB are applicable to emerging threat environments, but IPB is incomplete when dealing with an asymmetric threat.

IPB addresses modern nation-state use of force. But this world has been post-modern since 9/11 and new challenges require post-modern thinking. The distinction between crime and war is blurred. The new security environment does not segment neatly inside and outside American borders. It does not obey political boundaries or nations' rules of war.

IPO is more complex both because of the threat and because of the target set. IPB has been designed for symmetry. It assumes two conventional forces, uniformed, outfitted and trained for head-to-head conflict. Post-modern conflict looks to be less force-on-force (symmetrical) and more a game of encounters, using stealth and surprise (asymmetrical), with no clear concept of victory. This battlespace could be anywhere and could be five-dimensional. IPO must deal with asymmetry and it must be asymmetric.

This concept disregards the distinct institutional boundaries between domestic public safety and national defense because that model does not work in this new security environment. The governmental institutions built for yesterday's security environments are not designed for the current and future threats. Public safety requires a more active defense, an effective method for using intelligence and a system that is preemptive and proactive as well as reactive and punitive. Military forces will need to develop an asymmetric offensive capability, which will require rethinking the national defense strategy. The future will see some degree of merger between these two protective functions.

Common Terms

A common set of terms and descriptions can simplify the task of introducing or describing emerging concepts. Intelligence preparation for operations (IPO) is described in a context of an ancient and classic view of war and conflict, an entrepreneurial view of operations and a straightforward concept of decision-making. These concepts may or may not stand the test of time and utility. The intent is to make a starting point for the required entrepreneurial thinking of the near future.

The ancient study of war is that of Sun Tzu. Asymmetry, preparation, unconventional operations and tactics, understanding and using terrain, the advantage of intelligence, the use of spies and the concept of winning without ever beginning a war are enduring and applicable concepts.[1]

Clausewitz wrote *On War*, which is a foundation document for modern Western militaries. It describes conventional and formal force-on-force nation-state warfare, which is the forte of the United States but is less useful in the emerging security environment of the post-modern world. Clausewitz identified, described and refined three levels of activity in war and conflict that are useful in explaining intelligence preparation for operations (IPO): tactical, operational and strategic.

Tactical refers to individual action or procedure, and is generally analogous to first response in public safety work. *Operational* level is the use in time and space of assets in order to use that tactical or first response capability. It is often referred to as an 'art' because it requires a working knowledge and a responsibility for the effective use of tactical assets and people. Operational 'artists' are usually selected and promoted for their responsibility, with experience.

Strategic levels of activity involve broad concepts, and are often constrained by policy and interaction outside the system. In military organizations, this is the arena of generals. In the civilian and public safety sectors, this is the arena of chiefs, sheriffs and political leaders. IPO offers something of utility at each of these levels, but it is best implemented at the operational level where it can be used to counter, by speed or surprise, the actions of an opponent. The purpose of IPO is to aid in the speed and accuracy of decision thereby limiting enemy opportunity for speed or surprise.

Tactical, operational and strategic action is interconnected. An example is the definition and implementation of rules of engagement (ROEs). ROEs are implemented at the tactical level, but it is strategic policy that defines ROE, often based on diplomatic and political criteria. Strategic activity also involves high level or critical decision-making or politically or diplomatically influenced decisions. Events that are tactical, operational or strategic can have influence or consequence outside of their respective level. That is, a tactical event may have a strategic consequence, or an operational decision may affect tactical employment. These levels of activity are not boundaries.

Network Operations

A network organization speeds decision and action in comparison to a hierarchical structure. Networks offer several advantages but are entrepreneurial because of institutional reluctance to modify hierarchical, and inherently slower, organizational behavior. A government or institution which has invested time and effort in developing effective hierarchical process does not easily transmute to a network that gives the appearance of dissipated and decentralized control. This is a weakness that an asymmetrical opponent who is not bound to a similar hierarchical structure can exploit. A possible solution is to graft a network to support the operational level of activity in a hierarchical organization.

A network supports Intelligence Preparations for Operations in two ways: It supports the gathering, collection and dissemination of information and intelligence and, it speeds up this process so that the network system can increase tempo in a decision cycle.

The Decision Cycle Model

The model for the decision cycle is the OODA loop, conceived, studied and developed by US Air Force Colonel John Boyd. His work and study has influenced operational thinking in the US Department of Defense, and specifically, the Marine Corps. Use of his concepts helped develop priority capability of jet fighters for aerial combat and influenced the development of the F-15 and F-16. OODA is an acronym for 'Observe, Orient, Decide and Act'.

Boyd described human activity and interaction as a continuing loop of those four activities. Conflict or interaction between two OODA loops results in a win and a loss, to describe it in its most straightforward terms. The faster loop has the better chance for a 'win'. Therefore, anything that quickens the observation, orientation, decision and action increases the chance for a win. Although deceptively simple to describe, the OODA Loop is actually a complex, intricate and continual process.

A soccer team that develops and executes play by leveraging individual skill (tactical) to form a play on the move downfield (operational) for the purpose of executing the coach's instruction to increase tempo (strategic) to outpace the other team is an example of OODA loops engaged in competition.

Colonel Boyd, in a series of lectures, described decision making in those four steps and emphasized that it was a continual process and always imperfect. All other things being equal, the shorter loop wins. Better, faster or more accurate intelligence is a key to shortening the loop.

These concepts: three levels of activity, asymmetry of force, the OODA loop and network organizations, are defined in order to frame the importance and utility of Intelligence preparation for operations. Innovative and entrepreneurial thinking is required for implementation. Clear perception and definition of a security environment and the understanding of an opposing asymmetrical enemy is essential to create and maintain a networked intelligence gathering and response capability.

IPO is an essential part of an active defense both inside and outside political borders. It may be the single most important imperative to operationalize the concepts of critical infrastructure protection, homeland defense and security and counterterrorism.

Intelligence must be fused with operational capability to be effectively used as a countermeasure to opposing enemy or opposing force (OPFOR) action. Knowledge of terrain, weather, activity and culture, along with an unbiased view of strengths and weaknesses are all elements to consider.

The Purpose of Intelligence Preparation for Operations

The use of intelligence is not a new concept for either military or law enforcement operations. This new security environment requires a hybrid intelligence focus that is part of both of these differing intelligence concepts.

The language of intelligence is specialized. Military intelligence analysts think and talk in terms of orders of battle referring to size, shape and capability of the enemy and their work is replete with maps, organizational symbols and knowledge of weather and terrain. It is intended for unit-on-unit action in a recognized operational area of war and most often used as part of offensive action. The perfect product of this activity is the accurate prediction of enemy intent.

Criminal intelligence has a different focus of effort. The criminal intelligence analyst talks in terms of evidence, clues, leads and motive. The perfect product of this effort is linking time, place and activity with evidence and certainty. In so doing, it is more often retrospective and is often restrained by civil liberties. The goal is to lessen and dissuade crime, thereby keeping social order and minimizing illegal activity motivated by the baser human characteristics such as hate and greed. It goes to supporting a social system defined by law and, in a democratic society, by a tenet to maintain as much personal freedom as possible. Intelligence preparation for operations addresses the gray area between crime and war and therefore uses some elements of each of these differing concepts and uses of intelligence.

IPO should exist to achieve the objective of detection and elimination of the opposing threat. In its purest sense, its most valuable but elusive capability is to identify enemy/OPFOR intent before the fact. That intent may be unveiled at the strategic, operational or tactical level. The goal is to discourage, preempt or interfere with enemy activity before it can gain relative superiority to achieve a goal of disruption or destruction. Failing that, however, IPO is valuable at any point along the continuum from threat detection to consequence management and restoration. The ultimate goal is to deter because of fear of certain failure. Deterrence achieved through IPO would be a collection and analysis capability that prevents any attempt of action by the enemy/OPFOR and identifies and defeats this criminal-soldier before he can act.

The assessment and analysis of environment is an essential element for IPO. Terrain and weather have always influenced human activity, but planning for intelligence preparation for operations in complex urban terrain involves other influencing factors that have been identified but may not be well understood. Both Sun Tzu's *The Art of War* and the Marine

Corps' *Small Wars Manual* cite density, population, activity, cultural anthropology and other influences as important when collecting and analyzing information on the environment.

Cities develop as an overlay to existing terrain and thereby shape and mold human activity patterns. Weather and climate affect this development and activity. Urban overlay adds complexity and internal volume to terrain, and successful activity, cultural influence and specific activity such as migration, commerce, politics and social attitudes all go to shaping the character of an urban center. Modern and industrial cities have a pace and rhythm that is signature; and it is different from an older or less multicultural urban center.

The ability to discern normal activity from abnormal activity or unusual occurrence is valuable intelligence gathering capability that could be maintained through a cooperative effort of networked local public safety agencies. Technology has enabled the creation and existence of cities with more complexity, density, vertical development and internal volume, even in places that could not support such density and human activity in the past. IPO should be able to characterize a city, region or operational area.

IPO requires a system with at least three components. It must have a capability for self-evaluation of the operating area, a method for observing and reporting for the purpose of gathering intelligence, and a method for analyzing and synthesizing that intelligence so that it is useful for decision making.

The assessment of terrain and activity must be compared to intent and capability of the OPFOR. The OPFOR's intent and willingness to act defines, to some degree, the strengths and vulnerabilities of an operating area, its protective forces and its emphasis for intelligence collection.

In perfect form, it yields indicators and warnings of impending threat possibility and probability. This offers the opportunity to speed decision and action to intercede before the act occurs or before the action has the chance to gain sufficient momentum.

It is imperfect, constantly requires attention and is asymmetrical because it pits knowledge and critical thinking against the intent to act. It aids operations by identification and quickens decision and action. Intelligence preparation for operations is an asymmetrical and preemptive pre-event response to threats.

IPO is a networked system for assessment, analysis, forecasting and decision making. IPO has reconnaissance, assessment, psychological, analysis and prediction components. It is not of itself a direct operational task, but it is inextricable from operations and may leverage operations for information collection. Its purpose is not to interfere with operations, but rather to augment and enhance operations using information to speed decision.

Creating a networked system with information, surveillance and assessment capability is the starting point for intelligence preparation. The core elements are a useful base of knowledge, a means to gather and store information, a method for analysis and the ability to develop and describe courses of action based on those capabilities. Effective preparation requires an in depth and critical examination and understanding of the environment or terrain. Urban terrain, especially modern urban terrain with high density, internal volume and diverse activity, is complex, which makes assembling and distributing knowledge and information challenging.

Implementation of intelligence preparation requires methods to collect information and acquire and maintain knowledge. Information ranges from broad details on the complex urban terrain, to specifics on facilities, venues or sections of that terrain. Knowledge is that educated and intuitive understanding that gives the perspective required for assessments and courses of action for operational decisions.

The rhythm and pace of human activity, the influence of weather on activity and the timing and flow of traffic along major lines of communication (roads and highways) are examples of information. An understanding of the operation of power and water systems, a working appreciation of how to deal with hazardous materials, an ability to use a public health system information network and expertise on threat weapon systems are examples of required knowledge.

The ability to obtain specialized knowledge is also especially important, specifically during times of heightened threat. The ability to find a structural engineer with specific knowledge of building design or a specialist in biological science could be critical. The ability to quickly contact experts by 'virtual reachback' is an important component of a complete system for IPO.

IPO is a basis for critical decision making. In its broadest sense, IPO is the foundation for creating an extensive understanding of a specific and often complex operational area. It is also a straightforward evaluation of probable and potential targets within that area. It requires a continual method of sensing and reporting on activity in the operational area. The goal is to identify a norm in order to sense and identify abnormal events. The goal of an asymmetrical opponent is to find weakness and exploit it, rather than confront strength. IPO is the countermeasure. It defeats that exploitation with knowledge and the ability to orient, decide and act.

IPO is a constant operation. The potential for changing threat conditions, as well as the potential to improve threat detection always exists. IPO should be constantly improved.

Boyd emphasized that the interaction of OODA loops was constant and complex. His statement, 'You're never there, you're always getting there',[3] was meant to emphasize that the continual interaction of opponents was a constant duel of observe, orient, decide and act. Therefore, seeking improvement in the IPO is also always constant.

The core element in intelligence preparation for operations is a system ability to analyze and synthesize information and knowledge to identify an accurate threat picture. The thrust of effort in intelligence preparation for operations should be to develop, maintain and improve a core competency of analysis. The initial products of analysis are indicators and warnings of threat based on the best discernable OPFOR intent, willingness and capability. Determining the definitions of normal activity, detecting abnormal threat activity, identifying appropriate deception action, directing the collection of essential elements of information and creating useable courses of action (COA's) are priority activities of intelligence preparation for operations.

These results support, in various ways, the goal of speeding the OODA loop. This system is additive, not competitive, with the existing hierarchical operational system. It is a network system that can bolt on to a hierarchy to speed decision and action by enhancing operational art.

As the threat becomes more defined with analysis, active defense and response can become more focused to that threat, training and rehearsal can be more economical in time, effort and funding, and operational art can gain acceptance as an institutional requirement.

Intelligence analysis for the purpose of predicting enemy/OPFOR intended action is done through the forecasting of action based on the ability to identify patterns linked to probable intent. The forecast need be neither perfectly accurate, nor does the preparation or response to a suspected event have to be perfect. It only has to be recognized, assessed and acted upon faster than the opposing action.

Creating a networked system with surveillance and assessment capability is the starting point for intelligence preparation. The core elements are knowledge, information, analysis and the ability to develop and describe courses of action based on those elements. A network creates more than a speed advantage. Over time, different functional groups integrate operations as a result of being associated in a non-hierarchical system.

Development and enhancement of tactical capability and operational art requires cooperation among different specialists. Special Forces operations, for example, require cooperation of manpower intensive ground operations in urban terrain with specialized technical operations of satellites to speed the OODA loop with communications, navigation and information flow. The same is true, and is required, to speed decision and action in a domestic safety network of policing, fire and public health.

Tools or methods to organize information and the development of a rehearsal capability are two examples of ways to continually improve IPO capability. Information tools for rapid retrieval of essential knowledge are a requirement to speed orientation. An example would be a target folder for a specifically identified site, facility, infrastructure or activity. The target folder contains information essential for pre-planning, crisis planning and crisis response.

Some means to organize a rehearsed response to a specific threat is required to make best use of intelligence preparation for operations. This is implemented as a rehearsal to probable and possible threats. If indications and warnings of threat change, the rehearsal to the threat must change to address that threat.

An example of a rehearsal is a playbook designed and tested for a specific threat. Both pre-planning for specific threats and rehearsal of playbooks in preparation for that threat are tools and actions that can speed the OODA loop, exercise a cooperative, networked response and identify shortfalls. Playbooks addressing the differing threats of weapons of mass destruction (WMD) would outline differing responses to those threats. The exercising of those contingencies through rehearsal is a valuable process for improvement in intelligence preparation. A decision to pre-stage consequence management assets to reduce response time to a forecast event might be a lesson learned from pre-planning a rehearsal, for example.

Rehearsal encourages proactive planning, innovative thinking and reveals shortfalls in preparation. It also strengthens confidence and adaptability and reinforces the new skill sets required to confront asymmetric and emerging threats.

The value of IPO is to build a capability to deny or partially deny the enemy/OPFOR an asymmetrical advantage of surprise or stealth. A success is the absence of an intended disruptive or destructive event and it is also the interruption of an event. It is also the identification of the parts of the operational area that are either vulnerable, the focus of enemy intent, or both. The focus of effort of IPO is on the identification of ways to dissuade, interrupt or stop the opposing force by identifying intent before the fact.

Results

There are compelling reasons to do intelligence preparations for operations. Deterrence, the ultimate goal, is a high benefit result from an asymmetrical approach to the problem of heightened threat. This approach requires surveillance and critical thinking instead of the maintenance of a force-on-force response, which requires time and intensity of manpower and resources. In contrast, IPO is asymmetrical in that it looks for weakness, rather than only creating and maintaining a buildup to counter the enemy/OPFOR strength.

The foremost goal is to identify, through indicators and warnings, and to have enough information to stop an intended action before it can gain momentum or cause disruption or destruction. This investment in knowledge and understanding is more of a force multiplier than the simple addition of more resources.

Operational art is the ability to use capability to counter a threat and it relies heavily on the ability to clearly assess a situation. It is often attributed to a combination of experience, critical thinking and accurate intelligence. Quickly retrieving or getting the right information at the right time is a feat that is often difficult in unthreatening times and always impossible in times of immediate need. IPO is preparation before emergency requirement. It is economical and pragmatic.

The reason to do intelligence preparation for operations is to achieve an advantage against an unknown threat before it becomes an event. In addition to maintaining an asymmetric advantage, IPO is a means to sustain a safe and civil society without unduly restricting civil liberty and personal freedom. Increased intelligence by means of surveillance for pattern recognition melds well with the traditional and accepted process for criminal intelligence.

Success in monitoring, with appropriate restraints, encourages networking operations with adjacent operational areas. The use of crime mapping, for example, to characterize areas at risk in communities is non-intrusive but reveals significant and useful information about crime and its correlation with terrain and urban activity. Threat mapping, like crime mapping can graphically coalesce information that, by itself, is seemingly unimportant, but when put together creates a picture, a pattern or a trend.

Summary and Conclusions

IPO should be used as a long term strategy to address balancing the requirement for appropriate protection with the expectation of personal freedom in an advanced civilization. Intelligence is a powerful tool and must be used appropriately as well as be properly constrained. The rules of engagement for hunting the criminal-soldier inside and outside our political boundaries will spark an extended debate. IPO may be a useful model in understanding and developing an appropriate measured response to this present and future security threat.

IPO's greatest value, over time, will be to shape critical thinking to identify the asymmetrical threats of an enemy/OPFOR. That knowledge can be used to disrupt OPFOR action at any point, from planning through preparation and execution. It will reveal the vulnerabilities of OPFOR thinking and action and it can help shape, predict, interfere, stop or mitigate that action.

Implementation, however initially adequate, is the keystone to initiating operational support through IPO. Simple initial organization, critical evaluation and improvement over time will lead to a more sophisticated and effective model and operation. Obstacles to this momentum are in-place hierarchical structures, political interest over operational imperatives and simple resistance to change. It is essential for effectiveness that IPO be used locally, wherever that may be, and that political division, jurisdiction or other artificially constructed 'seams' not create obstacles. Specific attention should be focused on the elimination of obstacles that can be exploited by the OPFOR.

The fusion of accurate intelligence and operational capability in a networked structure holds the best possibility for an effective asymmetrical active defense for the near future. Any discovery of an impending threat to an operating area will probably be because of skillful analysis of intelligence in a region that has invested time and effort in intelligence preparation for operations. Planning, equipping, training and intelligence preparation within an operating area must be a local or regional capability.

The opportunity to speed the OODA loop is the greatest at the point of intended action. Although follow-on response may be rapid and adequate, it will always be in trail of initial local intelligence, preparation, rehearsal and critical thinking. This is equally applicable to deployed military units, local public safety networks or, in the most likely future, the combination of both. It is possible and feasible that in the near future a deployed Special Forces unit could collect and pass intelligence to a regional intelligence network in a US county that could be immediately useful in both situations.

NOTES

1. Sun Tzu, *The Art of War*. Translated by Thomas Cleary (Boston, MA: Shimbhalla Press 1988).
2. John Arquilla and David Ronfeldt, *The Advent of Netwar* (Santa Monica, CA: RAND 1996).
3. John R. Boyd, Lecture, US Naval Institute Seminar, Washington DC (Sept. 1996).

Networked Force Structure and C^4I

JOHN P. SULLIVAN

The world of today and tomorrow is one dominated by a conflict between those who have and those who do not. The 'outsiders', that is those with a conflicting social or cultural focus, are likely to challenge our superiority according to *their*, not our, rules. Their operations blur and will continue to blur the distinctions between crime and war, criminal, combatant and non-combatant. Their actions will seek to exploit the capability gaps and organizational seams of the modern state's internal and external security structures. These emerging challengers will embrace unconventional operations not amenable to conventional responses.

Over the past decade, analysts, academics, and practitioners in the United States and elsewhere postulated that the nature and form of conflict was changing. By assessing evolving trends, this cadre of military and civil researchers observed the evolution of a new form of warfare, embodied by the blurring of crime and war, the increasingly lethal terrorism, and the emergence of new, predatory networked forms of organization.[1]

Within this conundrum, terrorism has evolved, shifting from the well recognized 'classic terrorism' into 'post-modern terrorism', characterized by a wider range of groups (sometimes acting as networks) embracing violence as a political tool. In essence, social, cultural and economic factors are joined with political and often criminal objectives contributing to a *guerre civilisationnelle*, which results in a particularly dangerous and elusive form of conflict.

On 11 September 2001, the notional conflict left the realm of forecast and analysis. In the surprisingly graphic, coordinated, near-simultaneous attacks on the World Trade Center (WTC) in New York City and the Pentagon in Washington DC, the scourge of global networked terrorism brutally assaulted the American homeland, savagely dismantling the barriers between crime and war. Violating conventional criminal law and the laws of armed conflict (international humanitarian law)[2] these attacks severed the distinction between military and civilian, soldier, police officer and firefighter as these – normally *hors de combat* targets – were attacked by Al-Qaeda a networked adversary.

The current terrorist conflict, where non-state actors occupy a key role (and at times *de facto* capture states) is part of our evolving operational space (opspace). As this conflict evolves – and perhaps broadens – the following challenges can be anticipated:

- Enhanced influence of networked forms,
- Potential capture (or co-option) of states,
- Increased criminal-terrorist overlap.

To this add an increased incidence of terrorism in the continental United States (the firewall has finally been intractably broken), erosion of the distinction between 'international' and 'domestic' terrorism, and finally further erosion of the distinction between crime and war.

Links between religious extremists, criminal organizations (such as narcotics traffickers) and rogue state partners complicate civil and military responses to conflict. These new adversaries, a complex opposing force (OPFOR), are diverse and linked in unfamiliar ways.[3] A range of actors such as Osama bin Laden's Al-Qaeda and a loose coalition of criminal actors, guerillas and insurgents have challenged and can be expected to continue to challenge national security capabilities that were designed to operate within a nation-state framework. Outside that framework, our traditional structures have great difficulties.[4]

Pulsing, Swarming and Netwar

The range of actors found in this emerging Fourth Generation Opspace (terrorists, transnational criminal organizations, militant anarchists, bandits and warlords) typically operate in small dispersed units. They exploit our vulnerabilities, exploit flexibility, and have the ability to deploy in a range of locations, perhaps in simultaneous operations. Pulsing and swarming across geographic, political and geographic boundaries they challenge traditional, hierarchical structures. As described by Ronfeldt and Arquilla, they use network forms of organization to:

- swarm and disperse,
- penetrate and disrupt,
- elude and evade.[5]

The rise of networks (and hence networked adversaries) results from the migration of power to non-state actors that are able to organize into multiorganizational networks (particularly 'all-channel' networks where every node is connected to every other node) more readily than hierarchical, state actors. As a result of this trend, network-based conflict and crime are a growing threat. As Ronfeldt, Arquilla and others have often noted, hierarchies have a difficult time fighting networks. Thus, to combat networks, that is to master counternetwar, the police, military and security services must first understand the nature of the networked threat, and then as described later forge the proper balance between networks and hierarchies to combat these emerging threats.[6]

Essentially, it is not just the challenge of facing networked adversaries, it is the challenge of determining which type of network we face, and then determining the actual composition and links within that network. Most analysts describe three types of networks:

- *Chain* (line) where nodes are linked laterally/horizontally and communication must flow through an adjacent node to get to the next;
- *Hub* (star or wheel) where nodes are all connected to a central node and each node must communicate through the central node to reach others;
- *All-channel* (fully connected/full-matrix) where each node is connected to each other and all can directly communicate.

Finally, a hybrid organization or combination of a network and hierarchy must be recognized as a potential organizational form.

Military theorist Robert J. Bunker has identified the operational advantages of networks within conflict to include factors of speed, offensive, defensive, and combat multipliers.[7]

- ***Speed*** (as evidenced by the ability to quickly negotiate the decision cycle or OODA loop (decision cycle) as described by Colonel John Boyd[8]) provides an advantage by serving as an information multiplier by increasing information flows. Speed also results from reduced information seams and decreased organizational gaps (best in an all-channel organization) and through increased information fusion (as a result of better filtering and fusing of information to reduce noise). Finally, speed results from the increased processing capacity provided by parallel processing and multitasking. This is especially valuable during surge periods, such as a crisis or during an attack.

- ***Offensive*** benefits include swarming capability, distributed 'sensor-to-shooter' links, bond-relationship targeting (BRT), and the use of deception in the form of attack masking. Swarming is important because it allows an adversary to quickly gather and concentrate its forces at a decisive point facilitated by the use of a sensor grid that allows nimble individual action toward a common goal. This can mass the source of an attack and can be enhanced through attacks and the links or bonds between and among structures or forces.

- ***Defensive*** advantages include increased stealth (such as stealth masking to protect critical nodes); reduced vulnerability to decapitation; reduced vulnerability to precision force; and enhanced information redundancy. Networks can pulse and swarm rather than rely upon mass, thus reducing exposure of critical nodes, furthermore; a robust cellular structure can enhance survivability of C^4ISR (command, control, communications, computers, intelligence, surveillance and reconnaissance) structures.

- ***Combat Multipliers*** include collective vision, adaptive behavior, ease of growth and mission tailoring. These factors can contribute to increased returns as the network grows. Scalability as embodied in ease of growth and mission tailoring can be exploited as a modular or 'plug and play' organization suited to the particular threat or operation encountered at a given point in time.

Complexity and Urban Expeditionary Operations

Post modern security forces can expect to face networked adversaries in a variety of settings, many in an urban environment. The threat envelope described in this paper is essentially what General Montgomery C. Meigs describes as 'a shift in the nature of the art of operations'.[9] General Meigs, Commander of US Army Europe and Seventh Army, noted a number of consequences of the information age that are influencing the changing operational landscape. These include rapid advances in information and communications systems, improved sensors, precision guidance systems and the availability of novel off-the-shelf technologies. These technologies are double-edged since they are also readily available to our adversaries. This technological situation, combined with political and cultural factors, media intensity, and the vulnerability of Internetted command and control lead to new strategic realities.

Among the contemporary realities cited by Meigs is the employment of forces, usually in an incremental manner, in joint, combined or multinational formations. These joint/combined forces are likely to face an entrenched adversary fighting on his own turf with an initial numerical and *intelligence* advantage in a complex opspace. In his own words:

> We will be operating on a very complex battlefield that combines the challenges of difficult and unfamiliar terrain, terrorists and paramilitaries, and refugees and unfriendly civilian organizations (some possibly having links to internationally networked organized crime).[10]

This observation implicitly acknowledges the continued expeditionary nature of future conflict. To that, it is necessary to add that much of this potential complex op- or battlespace will be urban, likely necessitating urban expeditionary operations from the littorals. Some of these urban expeditionary operations may even be at home, requiring coalition operations in support of domestic law enforcement and public safety agencies.

RAND analyst Russell W. Glenn, in a series of works, has explored the challenges imposed by the multidimensional urban battlespace of the future.[11] As Glenn observes, the urban environment is characterized by a density of people and terrain features. Urban terrain, with its subterranean, surface and building or rooftop features poses a challenge to military commanders, and their operational and intelligence staff, not to mention the forces on the ground.

Structures of a variety of types, including many vertical, converge with roadways, boulevards, and alleys above ground, to create multiple avenues of approach, firing positions and obstacles. Underground subways, tunnels, sewers and basements form another dimension. These features (picture a makeshift shantytown of cardboard boxes, packing crates and scrap metal poised on top of high-rise office towers or housing projects) diminish lines of sight and inhibit standard sensors and communication capabilities.

Density of people accompanies terrain (after all, terrain is adapted to meet the needs of the populace). Thousands, up to tens of hundreds of thousands, of inhabitants per square kilometer (or in Glenn's view 'cubic kilometer') occupy urban space obscuring the OPFOR, non-combatants, and friendly forces alike. Complexity is the result.

Urban operations are fraught with complexity. Increased operational tempo (due to the multiplicity of interpersonal and terrain interactions), compressed decision times, and a density of potential C^2 (command and control) systems complicate matters. Command and control are chaotic in intense urban situations. Communications and intelligence are often subject to degradation in these settings, since urban clutter limits the effectiveness of sensor and communications technologies. As a result, control often devolves to a small-unit or squad level, increasing demand for accurate, real-time situational awareness at all echelons, a situational awareness that is both elusive and hard to achieve.

Many intelligence tools, such as IMINT (imagery intelligence), SIGINT (signals intelligence), COMINT (communications intelligence) and MASINT (measuring and signature intelligence) are available but difficult to exploit in an urban setting since their data is masked or obscured by noise or density. As a consequence, urban operations are subject to the influence of 'deception', complicating the intelligence picture.[12]

Consequently, intelligence for urban operations is dependent on HUMINT (human intelligence) and novel means such as OSINT (open-source intelligence), CyberINT (cyber-intelligence), and rapid/automated decision support (intelligence preparation for operations, including Urban IPB and critical node analysis) to focus and direct intelligence collection efforts to meet essential command needs such as the rapid dissemination of intelligence, surveillance and reconnaissance (ISR) products that frame a common operating picture.

Forging an appropriate response to this evolving threat envelope is a complex and demanding task, demanding significant deliberation in order to develop a balanced approach. Yet this deliberation must occur quickly as the conflict is already in progress and promises to widen. Serious attention must be given to a revision of the entire US national security structure (as well as that of Great Britain, France, the European Union and international structures) to break down the bureaucratic obstacles to action. Entrenched bureaucratic obstacles are in a true sense real-time barriers to effective efforts to combat terrorism and, if left untended, promise to serve as a force multiplier to the opposing force.

Collaboration and partnership, such as interagency, interdisciplinary partnerships with law enforcement agencies to explore and experiment with novel intelligence applications and approaches for the emerging threat environment should be explored. We need to focus sharply on what lies ahead, seeking discourse about emerging and future conflict. We need to further develop our open source intelligence, HUMINT and cultural intelligence capabilities and integrate them. To meet the threat of 'now and future' warfare, our intelligence must focus more on cultural and social paradigms, not just the military order of battle.

Novel Approaches to Intelligence and Operations Needed

Our adversaries span the globe in a shifting constellation of competitors, sometime allies, non-combatants and criminal opportunists. We can expect to meet them in a range of settings including humanitarian stability and support operations (SASOs), terrorist incidents, consequence management operations for complex emergencies, and response to intrastate ethnic conflict and riots.

To address this complex mix of responses, it is imperative that we adapt and develop new intelligence applications and approaches to these emerging and evolving threats at the intersection of crime and war quickly, because this form of conflict is already here. In this threat environment, disruption and emerging threats can be expected to become as important as, or more important than, WMD (weapons of mass destruction) issues. Effective response to these threats demands a high degree of interoperability among all levels of responders – local, state, federal – between a variety of disciplines (law enforcement, fire service, public health and medical), and between civil and military agencies. Intelligence is an important element of forging an interagency response. To be effective, this intelligence must embrace network attributes and effectively fuse with networked operational forces.

In the aftermath of the 11 September attacks, recognition of the need for new approaches to combat terrorism, policing and war-fighting are beginning to emerge, albeit slowly. For example, the New York Police Department (NYPD) has placed efforts to combat terrorism and enhance intelligence capabilities at the top of its agenda. Joining crime suppression and quality-of-life enforcement, counter-terrorism and intelligence are now core NYPD missions. In order to meet the challenge of preventing and preparing for future terrorist attacks, the NYPD has established two new high-level positions: deputy commissioner for counter-terrorism and deputy commissioner for intelligence. A retired Marine Corps Lieutenant General and senior-level Central Intelligence Agency specialist in espionage, counter-terrorism and counter-proliferation will respectively spearhead these efforts which will involve training all the NYPD's 40,000 member force.[13] This change in the largest US police force signals the rapidly advancing recognition of our immersion in Fourth Generation Opspace.

Novel approaches to intelligence and intelligence-operations fusion are an essential element of a networked force structure. The new tools and approaches we craft must have the ability to sort pertinent information from noise and illuminate the mission-essential tasks necessary to counter potential adversaries. This can potentially be achieved by exploiting traditional tools and the contemporary information infrastructure through better use of OSINT, deception, and development of CyberINT.

Intelligence gathered from persons, widely known as HUMINT, is an essential element. Combining traditional tools, HUMINT, OSINT and CyberINT can assist in identifying the precursors and indicators of violence (such as group mobilization, criminal exploitation, proliferation of WMD materials, and so on) that may trigger a military (or combined military-civil) response. Adopting the concept of deep indications and warnings ('Deep I&W'), that is extending sensing to capture trends and potentials prior to recognition of an overt threat to minimize the OPFOR (opposition forces) advantage, is also essential.

The 'TEW' Model

The terrorism early warning (TEW) group model was first established in Los Angeles County in 1996 to address the challenges of post-modern terrorism. The TEW follows a networked approach, integrating law enforcement, fire, health, and emergency management agencies to address the intelligence needs for terrorism and critical infrastructure protection. The TEW integrates local-federal echelons and operates pre-, trans-, and post-incident. Significantly, the TEW model recognizes that a networked approach must be grafted upon traditional organizational hierarchies to quickly assess the situation and develop appropriate responses from a number of potential organizations – including military support to civil authorities.

The TEW essentially provides two functions: indications and warning, and operational net assessment. To do so, it is evolving the next generation of C4ISR tools and seeking to identify ways to bridge interdisciplinary gaps and build appropriate mechanisms for civil-military interoperability.

The Los Angeles TEW was designed to provide the operational intelligence development of potential courses of action necessary to quickly move through the decision cycle (OODA loop), forecast the potential event horizon, and craft meaningful course of action for interagency, interdisciplinary response.[14] It relies upon open source intelligence (OSINT) for scanning/monitoring trends and potentials that influence training and doctrinal needs. Additionally, during an actual threat period or attack, the TEW provides consequence projection (forecasting) to identify potential courses of action to the unified command structure.

TEW Net Assessment Mission and Organization

During an actual event, the TEW activates a 'net assessment group' to determine the scope of the event and its impact on the operational area. The net assessment mission follows:

> As directed, the TEW will provide unified command structure (UCS) with the impact of an actual attack on the operational area, gauge resource needs and shortfalls, continuously monitor and assess situational awareness/status, and act as the POC for inter-agency liaison in order to develop options for courses of actions (COAs) for incident resolution.

For Net Assessment functions, the TEW is organized into command/OIC (officer in charge), analysis and synthesis, consequence management, investigative liaison, and public health/epidemiological intelligence (Epi-Intel) elements. The forensic intelligence support element, which includes technical means and such external resources as virtual reachback, supports the others (see Figure 1).

The Command/OIC element is responsible for interacting with the incident command entities. The analysis and synthesis element coordinates

FIGURE 1
TEW NET ASSESSMENT ORGANIZATION

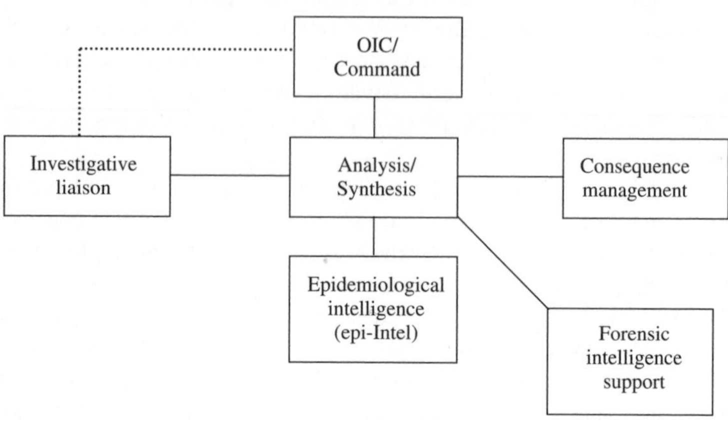

net assessment activities, tasking requests for information to the various net assessment elements and developing their results into potential courses of action which are expressed together with incident-specific information into a mission folder. The consequence management element assesses the law, fire and health (EMS-Hospital) consequences of the event. The investigative liaison element coordinates with criminal investigative entities (known as criminal intelligence groups or CIGs), and the Epi-Intel element is responsible for real-time disease surveillance and coordination with the disease investigation. The TEW model is currently expanding to other jurisdictions. There are currently TEWs in Orange, San Bernardino and Sacramento Counties, in addition to the initial Los Angeles group. These groups are evolving into a network, sharing common organization and doctrine, in order to share threat information and support each other during critical periods.

Evolving a Networked Force Structure

Law enforcement or police organizations play a key role in addressing many of the threats encountered in the Fourth Generation Opspace. Police have evolved a number of mechanisms for addressing violent terrorist networks, drugs cartels, transnational criminal organizations, militant anarchists, bandits and to a lessor degree warlords. Notable in this regard are instruments for bilateral and multilateral police cooperation through organizations such as Europol and Interpol.[15] As seen above, police are evolving their response structure and intelligence links to address the changing realities of networked conflict.

Likewise, military forces are in the process of evolving their responses to this emerging continuum of threat. Success in adjusting to threats that blur the distinctions between crime and war will require new interaction between the police, security and military services. Such efforts must at a minimum include: joint training of senior police and military officers at staff college level; discussions on the proper level of military support of civil power/authority; and co-operation in intelligence-operations fusion efforts such as those found in the Los Angeles TEW and the emerging TEW Network.

The military must reinforce its special operations focus and explore the swarming/counterswarming and pulsing/counterpulsing skills needed to effectively counter netwar. In many ways, this will require the military to go beyond the traditional special operations (spec ops) equation, where spec ops support conventional forces, to an approach where conventional forces support special operations forces.

Essential skills for counternetwar in the Fourth Generation are available in the US and allied special operations communities. In order to prevail in the now and future conflict, defense planners must draw upon this experience and recognize the value of small, light, well-trained dedicated special operations forces. Special operations will likely form the foundation of our future military responses, with conventional forces supporting the special operations forces. This reversal of conventional structures results from the post-modern return to non-trinitarian conflict.

Conclusion: Counternetwar and Societal Security

Countering netwar will increasingly require a unique confluence of military, police, and intelligence operations. The statutory and customary barriers between cooperation within the intelligence community (in particular, between the CIA and FBI), within law enforcement (between the FBI and other Federal agencies, and between Federal, state and local agencies), and between civil and military (both state and federal) authorities need to be resolved. This may require new agencies, new roles, and new relationships. These new structures should be hybrid organizations blending the benefits of networked structures with those of the existing organizational hierarchies. For example, perhaps the evolution of a new 'joint' force (such as a national gendarmerie) is warranted, or more immediately local and state agencies should take a larger role in counter-terrorism.

Improved intelligence is vital and must be a component of whichever approach is ultimately selected. This means HUMINT, and, I believe, development of new tools such as 'Deep I&W' and CyberINT. At tactical and operational levels, this must include a deeper examination of netwar and swarming and the development of counter-netwar and counter swarming tactics. These will necessarily involve 'elastic defense' rather than the fort-like approaches being advocated and adopted in response to the current phase of this crisis.

Terrorism, peace operations (such as peacekeeping, SASOs, and so on), violent militant anarchism, transnational crime and warlordism are not separate and distinct phenomena. Rather, they are different faces of Fourth Generation warfare. Tailored response involving a force mix of conventional military, special operations, intelligence and security services, police, and civil protection (fire service/medical and public health services) will be necessary. This network of operators will need to synchronize response across jurisdictional boundaries, disciplinary lines, services, and (increasingly) across borders. Domestic and international security will interact in new, increasingly interdependent ways. Homeland and expeditionary missions are likely to become intertwined with success in both spheres reliant upon actions (intelligence and operations) in the other. To address these interrelated threats which occupy the nexus between crime and war, a networked force structure, together with networked C^4ISR tools and doctrine must be developed.

NOTES

1. For a sampling of the literature of (now and) future conflict see: Martin van Creveld, *The Transformation of War* (New York, NY: The Free Press 1991); Ralph Peters, *Fighting for the Future: Will America Triumph?* (Mechanicsburg, PA: Stackpole Books 1999); Robert J. Bunker, 'Epochal Change: War Over Social and Political Organization', *Parameters* 27/2 (Summer 1997), and Steven Metz, *Armed Conflict in the 21st Century; The Information Revolution and Post-Modern Warfare* (Carlisle, PA: US Army War College, Strategic Studies Institute, April 2000).
2. See Roy Gutman and David Rieff, Eds., *Crimes of War: What the Public Should Know* (New York, NY: The Free Press 1991) for a succinct discussion of international humanitarian law.
3. One early analysis of the potential convergence of narcotics enterprises, terrorists and other networked actors was discussed in Robert J. Bunker and John P. Sullivan, 'Cartel Evolution: Potentials and Consequences', *Transnational Organized Crime* 4/2 (Summer 1998) pp.55–74.
4. See Robert J. Bunker, *Five-Dimensional (Cyber) Warfighting: Can the Army After Next be Defeated Through Complex Concepts and Technologies?* (Carlisle. PA: US Army War College, Strategic Studies Institute, March 1998) for a cogent discussion of the complexities of the evolving threat environment.
5. David Ronfeldt and John Arquilla, 'Networks, Netwars, and the Fight for the Future,' *First Monday*, http://firstmonday.org/issues/issue6_10/ronfeldt/index.html. See also David Ronfeldt and John Arquilla, Eds., *Networks and Netwars: The Future of Terror, Crime, and Militancy* (Santa Monica, CA: RAND, 2001).
6. While it is often postulated that it takes a network to combat a network, Ronfeldt, Arquilla and others note that counternetwar actually relies upon hybrids of hierarchies and networks. Either way, the side that masters networks (and their relationship with other organizational

forms) is likely to prevail in the now and future conflict.

7. Robert J. Bunker, 'Networked Organizational Structures in Future Conflict', Chapter 17 in Jasjit Singh (ed.), *Reshaping Asian Security* (New Delhi: Knowledge World/Institute of Defence Studies and Analyses, Jun. 2001). See also Robert J. Bunker, 'Networked Threats to Governments: Dynamics, Emergence, and Response', in Emil Görnerup (ed.), *Proceedings from the Conference 'Armed Conflicts'* (Stockholm, 17 Oct. 2000, FOA/Defence Research Establishment, Stockholm: Division of Defence Analysis, Dec. 2000) FOA-R-01693-201-SE.
8. See John Boyd, 'A Discourse on Winning and Losing' (28 June 1995) as depicted in Grant T. Hammond, *The Mind of War: John Boyd and American Security* (Washington DC: Smithsonian Institute Press 2001) p.190.
9. Gen. Montgomery C. Meigs, 'Operational Art in the New Century', *Parameters* 31/1 (Spring 2001) pp.4–14.
10. Ibid.
11. See especially Russell W. Glenn, *Heavy Matter: Urban Operations' Density of Challenges* (Santa Monica, CA: RAND 2000).
12. See Scott Gerwehr and Russell W. Glenn, *The Art of Darkness: Deception and Urban Operations* (Santa Monica, CA: RAND 2000) for discussion of urban clutter and its impact on deception.
13. William K. Rashbaum, 'Police Shift Focus to Terror With Spymaster and a Marine', *New York Times* (28 Jan. 2002) found at <www.nytimes.com/2002/01/28/nyregion/28KELL.html> downloaded 2 Feb. 2002.
14. See John P. Sullivan, 'Integrated Threat and Net Assessment; The L.A. Terrorism Early Warning (TEW) Group Model', *Bioterrorism: Homeland Defense Symposium: The Next Steps* (Santa Monica, CA: RAND, Feb. 2000).
15. See Paul Wilkinson, 'The Role of the Military in Combating Terrorism in a Democratic Society', *Terrorism and Political Violence* 8/3 (Aug. 1996) pp.1–11.

Part Four

Archives

The Structure of War: Early Fourth Epoch War Research

T. LINDSAY MOORE

Proposal

A few scholars educated in the post-Vietnam era of American political science and history have begun to question the adequacy of the prevailing view in providing a full and complete account of war in the twentieth century. The nature of the 'Cold War', Korea, Vietnam, low-intensity conflict, and campaigns of power projection all pose a vigorous and serious challenge to the received opinion on the meaning and significance to be accorded war and our understanding of its conduct.

These scholars have come to believe that investigations into political affairs without reference to the state and its political purposes have approached a sterile scholasticism. Accordingly, they are proceeding, at least implicitly, on the basis of a perspective that views politics, the state and war as of a piece. New questions are being addressed and new concepts are beginning to evolve.

If we accept this view, what new aspects of war might emerge? Primarily among them would be a recognition that, as currently conceived, the principles of war – initiative, agility, depth, synchronization and other such concepts – fail to provide an adequate foundation for the study of war. Employing such abstract principles, an investigator could construct any of a number of alternative actions a commander might have taken under the circumstances, all of them more or less appropriate. Why the actual decision was taken while others were rejected would, however, leave the investigator wondering about the arbitrariness of the commander's actions.

Why, for example, did the French conduct such an uncoordinated and piecemeal attack against the English archers at Crécy (1346) and why, knowing the devastating results of that previous action, did they repeat the process at Poitiers (1356) and again at Agincourt (1415)? The answer turns on knowing what it meant to the French to 'know the results' of Crécy. Without a knowledge of medieval feudal relationships and the ideology that supported them, the French actions seemed foolhardy; with that knowledge, it seems perfectly consistent with the then current ideas about fighting. What distinguishes one war from another cannot be explained solely in military terms nor by the technical characteristics of a weapons system; resort must be paid to the political context.

Power is the decisive concept in the study of politics. Aside from recognizing that power applies in the context of human action and is relational in use, the term shall remain undefined; instead, I shall examine the forms political power takes. Political power consists in the triad of resources, instruments and purposes. The resources of power are energy, matter and information in any variety of forms. Its instruments are those of force, bribery and fraud, and are interdependent in their appearance and inseparable in their operation. In the purposes to which it may be put, political power may be either creative or reproductive. A political community I shall regard as a shared collection of resources, instruments, and purpose directed in the pursuit of what the community regards as the 'good life' – that is, a political community is defined by the application and limits of its power.

The use of the terms 'force, bribery and fraud' is intended to focus attention on basic human motivation. First is force, by which is meant the destruction or threatened destruction of something of value. War, of course, is a prime example. So, too, is a system of criminal justice. Whenever an exchange of value occurs, bribery is present there. 'An honest day's work for an honest wage' is a familiar form of bribery, as is a system of welfare administered to insure order in the streets. Fraud, the third form of political power, involves action that is undertaken because of a belief in the rightness of the action itself.

The ultimate values of a political community are embraced in its ideas of right and wrong. In summary, people appear to act because they in some way feel compelled to do so (force) or because they conceive an action to be in their interest (bribery) or they believe an action to be right or wrong (fraud). These are the military (including police), economic and ideological institutions and processes used by a community to achieve its place in the sun, they exhaust, I believe, the significant institutions of a political community and comprise its political structure.

Though divergent in detail, all political structures share a common requirement in the need for a fundamental source of energy. Because an energy source has its own inherent possibilities and limitations with respect to the technology it can sustain and the power it can produce, the basic structure of all political communities employing that energy is similar; because change in a fundamental energy source is a rare event, that structure will persist for a significant period of time. I shall refer to those periods where one energy source dominates as an (epoch).

Selection of the term ('epoch') warrants further explanation. The use proposed here is meant to convey the idea that when faced with roughly the same conditions and constraints, people, being what they are, will respond in much the same way. Despite nuances in geography and weather, the physical conditions of life remain constant over long periods of time. So, too, do the technical and traditional folkways for responding to and shaping those conditions.

Accordingly, political life, though widely dispersed in space and separated in time, will nonetheless display a *shared pattern of coherent practices*. Moreover, and perhaps most telling, when for some reason conditions and constraints change, a pattern will be modified in much the same way by groups unrelated to one another. To be sure, there is imitation and the process of diffusion does occur. But recognizing that fact only forces us to reflect on why it is that the alteration of the pattern also makes good sense to the imitators. If the concept of an (epoch) suggests a shared pattern of coherent practices, the notion of (epochs) suggests a succession of patterns fundamentally different and incompatible with one another.

If we trace a political community through its history, we become aware of variations in the structure of that community. At one time its military forces may advance to battle on foot, at another on horseback, and at still another inside containers driven by internal combustion engines. The material things a community consumes may once have been produced in the countryside, later in an urban home workshop and still later in a factory. The people may believe circumstances to be the work of accident, but only after surrendering a notion that they were the workings of God's justice; and they could believe in justice only after they could no longer believe the world a result of the arbitrary, whimsical and capricious play of gods. This historical dissonance suggests that Western civilization, rather than proceeding in an unbroken line of cumulative progress, is, from time to time, disrupted by upheavals producing remarkable discontinuities.

Given this foundation, we may conveniently divide the history of Western civilization into three major (epochs); the Classical, the Medieval and the Modern. Extending from the Greek and Persian wars of the fifth century BC, the Classical (epoch) was dominated by energy derived from human beings. In keeping with this, the primary weapons system was infantry, the economic organization was that of slavery and the salient ideological concept was the virtue associated with different human natures (master, slave, etc.).

Beginning with the Barbarian raids, invasions and migrations in the fourth century AD, animal energy began to dominate life in medieval Europe. Cavalry thus came to rule the battlefield, the political economy was organized in terms of feudalism, and the cardinal ideological principles conceived the world in terms of divine providence. The Modern (epoch), commencing about the fifteenth century, is an empire of mechanical energy.

Warfare is conducted under the overarching umbrella of artillery (broadly defined), capitalism is the authoritative economic system and a notion of utility obliges all systems of ideology. Historically, war furnishes the dynamic process that transforms one (epoch) of Western civilization into another.

(Epochs) begin and end in what we shall call a 'war of destiny'. Of such wars we shall have more to say later. For the moment, it will suffice to note three immediate consequences following from a war of destiny: the demonstration of a new and viable form of energy, the rise in importance of a new geographical region, and the painful and almost universal awareness of a breakdown in the bonds uniting the military, economic and ideological life of the community.

Each of these developments emerges directly from a demonstrably successful system of military defense. Initially, attempts are made to integrate the new military system, but ultimately, integration proves impossible. The institutions and processes of the old (epoch) prove incapable of absorbing the revolutionary character of the new military. The new technology demonstrated by the military stimulates the development of new skills and practices, and a more sophisticated division of labor is fashioned. In its turn, that new division of labor creates new wealth resulting in novel economic, cultural and political relationships thus increasing the strain on ancient ways.

Occasionally, bold departures from existing political structures are undertaken as a more coherent form of political organization and administration is sought. Basic political questions are addressed. Ideological consensus, without which no political community can long survive and whose purpose is to validate new claims upon the distribution of resources and privileges within the community, is by force, bribery and fraud re-established. Though not without a history, all political life begins anew.

An (epoch) has an historical development. In its earliest stages, military forces are concerned with providing defense against external attacks and consolidating political power on a local level. Simultaneously, there is the matter of successfully demonstrating the viability of the new energy source beyond the battlefield and a 'working out' of its economic and ideological implications. In its more mature phases, there is a 'making use' of the resources generated by the (epoch's) new way of doing things. The result of this activity is the establishment of a logistical base for the purposes of expansion – commercial, military and ideological. Expansion continues until a kind of exhaustion sets in signaling the coming end of the (epoch). Demonstration, working out, making use and exhaustion comprise the phases of an (epoch). The process is one of a slow, evolutionary development.

First, there is the matter of demonstration. The viability of the new energy source must be demonstrated, and a battle is an awesome display of just that. Beyond this it must be shown that the energy is capable of a variety of applications. The stirrup harnessed the energy of the horse to war; the plow, collar, and shoe made possible its use in agriculture, hauling, and the generation of power (capstans and treadmills). Demonstrations are not limited to technological artifacts but extend to organizational structures and conceptual schemes as well. A disciplined body of men, a formation if you will, is a tool easily adapted from battle to other tasks requiring coordinated action.

In describing the division of labor, Adam Smith could just as easily have selected Marshal Maurice de Saxe's training manual of musketeers as the pin example, and without any loss of appropriateness. The flight of a cannon ball displayed curvilinear motion in defiance of Aristotle and thereby made a major conceptual contribution to the scientific revolution of the sixteenth and seventeenth centuries. In each of these instances and many others like them, a technology introduced on the battlefield was shown to have far wider application – that is, it displayed promise.

The concept of promise can be understood if we consider the decision to abandon the longbow and crossbow in favor of the arquebus. A comparison between the three would show that the longbow was a relatively easy weapon to manufacture but required extensive training in its use. The crossbow, on the other hand, was difficult to manufacture but easier to train a soldier to use. The arquebus combined the worst of both systems. It was difficult and costly to manufacture, and required a lengthy period of training in the complexities of its use. Yet the two forms of bow had exhausted their potential; the energy they employed had reached the limit of its efficient use in that form. The arquebus, primitive though it was, could be seen to have great developmental potential; no such potential could be envisioned for either longbow or crossbow.

A successful demonstration directs attention toward expanding the scope of technological applications, increasing their scale and achieving ever greater efficiencies. The process is one of extended development, a kind of 'working out' of the promise inherent in the new energy source and the technology it makes possible. Since there is much to be done, developments are sporadic, arising from a variety of sources giving the appearance of much randomness. At some point, the new foundations are taken for granted and definite structural features become apparent. Indicating a specific point in time when an (epoch) truly takes form is difficult if not impossible. But, when ancient traditions, practices, skills, and techniques are either abandoned or converted into art forms (dressage and fencing), it is a sure sign that the working-out process has taken command and is proceeding successfully.

Great effort is spent in 'piecing together' the puzzle of the new political fabric. In something resembling the rippling of a wave in a pond, change in one aspect of life eventually leads to change in all other aspects. The introduction of the stirrup into Europe provided a military solution to the invasions of the Barbarians, and that led to a new political system for allocating and holding land (the wealth of the [epoch]) called feudalism. Technologies associated with the horse (the collar, shoe and plow) led to an agricultural revolution in the tenth century that provided manpower for an industrial revolution in the eleventh.

This, in turn, provided wealth and ambition for launching the Crusades. Piece by piece, life was fitted to the technological change that was the horse. Gunpowder ushered in the (epoch) of mechanical energy. It made possible a new weapons system. When combined with the opening of new silver and gold mines, the resources for recruiting a mercenary army were present. The result was the development of standing armies and the centralization of authority in the modern state. Vassalage thus declined into obscurity and, in due course, disappeared altogether. Its disappearance necessitated radical changes in the concepts of duty, honor and obligation.

Since the meaning of these concepts had been grounded in the personal relationship between lord and vassal, either new meanings would have to be supplied, or they would go the way of that relationship. Modern nationalism has absorbed much of the content of those terms. That absorption, however, depended very much upon the development of democratic forms of political administration. The structure of an (epoch) can be said to be fully displayed when its structural features become a model for human nature. Hobbes uttered the phrase, 'Man is a machine', and provided a metaphor that has served as the intellectual foundation for innumerable philosophical treaties and research programs in the Modern (epoch). The notion that 'man is an information processor' serves in precisely the same way today and is as characteristic of this age as the machine analogy was for its age.

An industrial revolution (eleventh and nineteenth centuries) signals the beginning of the mature stages of an (epoch). Military forces have secured the lines of communication and these, together with agriculture and industrial products, bring about a reorganization of the technological foundations of commerce and trade on a global basis. The accumulation of wealth in whatever form defined by the (epoch) becomes a primary motivation and occupation. The earlier period, characterized by a trial and error process of experimentation, selection and rejection, now gives way to the processes of standardization and institutionalization. The formal codification of power relations, internal and external, allows for the centralized control and allocation of resources. Boundaries between political communities harden as the influence of an (epoch) widens and deepens.

Military action, formerly defensive in nature, now takes on an offensive character. Political expansion is the order of the day. The struggles for political supremacy among various centers of political power is the distinguishing feature of a mature (epoch). These are 'wars of efficiency'; they are global, annexation and colonial wars familiar to everyone. Their purpose is to determine which among several competing organizations of political power is the most efficient. As a result, there are constant shifts in the power relations among and between political communities.

The Peloponnesian Wars, Alexander's expedition into Persia, and the Punic Wars are examples of wars of efficiency in the Classical period. During the Medieval (epoch), Christianized Europe was, at one time or another, arrayed in various wars of efficiency against the Muslims, Magyars, and Northmen. The constant warring among feudal lords fall into this category also. There has hardly been a time in the Modern (epoch) when one or another war has not been under way. Such wars test the logistical foundations and combined arms organizations of the political communities engaged.

Eventually an (epoch) exhausts the energy source on which it is founded. This is not the same as running out of energy, though this can be a part of the process. It is that the cost of providing ever greater efficiencies becomes more than the gain from the marginal advances such efforts produce. Innovation also becomes more costly. There is a sense in which the technology made possible by the (epoch's) fundamental energy source has been extended as far as it can go.

If new innovations are to evolve, they will require a new source of energy. Military parity sets in as military systems come to resemble one another. Victory and defeat are less dependent upon technological advantage and more on the quantity and quality of the armed forces employed. Resources become harder to locate and more costly to acquire as political communities undertake to protect what resource base they possess. Thus, new wealth becomes more difficult to generate except through the manipulation of financial instruments.

The ideological foundations of the political community are subjected to searching examination and, to some degree, discredited. A mood of cynicism, despair and resignation dominate the intellectual and cultural life of the most developed political communities of the (epoch). Each war of efficiency will have brought a greater concentration of power. The exhaustion phase of an (epoch), however, is marked by a constant de-concentration of power as the largest of the extant political communities begins a phased withdrawal. Should a new weapons system arise at this point, a very unique kind of war will be waged.

Scholars, as required by their methodological and professional cannons, typically regard wars as much the same from one generation to the next.

Different weapons systems may be employed, but the principles of war are treated as independent of context and enduring in time. On this view, changes in the practice of the military art are seen as cumulative and progressive. The meaning to be accorded war, victory and defeat are well enough known and accepted among a sufficiently broad community as not to require, if not preclude, any deep or extended thought on the question. MacArthur, without fear of contradiction and never doubting that he would be understood, could proclaim, 'There is no substitute for victory.'

The collection of shared assumptions pertaining to war, which makes confidence possible, forms the authoritative core of military thought. The core makes it possible for research to address such questions as what combination of weapons systems is most likely to produce victory? How are such systems to be the most efficiently organized into a combined arms force? How are operations to be conducted so as to take effective advantage of the strength of our formations and the weaknesses of an enemy's?

Without fundamental agreement on a set of broad principles, such questions could admit of no solution for there would be no standard to evaluate the admissibility of any answer proposed. With agreement, and its relegation to 'deep background', investigation into these and other questions like them can and does proceed. During the life cycle of an (epoch), the search for solutions to these sorts of problems is the central activity of military study and planning. The cumulative mustering of solutions builds a body of knowledge and it is on the basis of such a corpus that wars of efficiency are conducted. Victory in such wars measures progress.

What, then, does defeat register? Most often it is taken to mean a failure in understanding the principles of war or misjudgment in their application. Moreover, the causes of defeat, whatever they may be, will appear obvious, and any adjustment necessary to remove deficiencies will seem a matter of routine (that is, better weapons, more rigorous training, bolder leadership). Nevertheless, times arise when matters are not so routine, the causes of defeat not so obvious. Times such as these are induced by an entirely new weapon employed in an unprecedented manner. This was the case when Roman heavy infantry met Barbarian light cavalry. So, too, the French knight when faced with English archer. The recent introduction of nuclear-tipped missiles remains an open case; but, in any event, the situation is not at all unique in the history of warfare. Confrontations of this nature provoke a crisis in the military art.

Crises are a regular part of the history of Western civilization. Though a direct challenge to core assumptions, they transform the major concerns of those who practice the military art. No longer is the supreme question how best to fight and win but, rather, what does it mean to win in the first place. Questions such as 'what is war' and 'what is victory' lay claim to an ever increasing share of the attention of those whose business it is to think about war.

The reason why is not difficult to understand. It rests upon the simple fact that the military, rather than being an institution apart, is thoroughly integrated into the life of a political community. If the close combat tactics of the Roman soldier, symbolizing the bravery, glory and virtue of Roman civilization, are constantly defeated by Barbarians on horseback employing missile weapons and hit-and-run tactics, then the very foundation of the Roman understanding of war, and with it Roman civilization, must come into serious question. If the foot soldier, who plays no role in the scheme of Medieval warfare, constantly defeats the knight, instrument of God's justice on earth, then war, justice and the feudal way of life loose all meaning.

In the instances just described, a new weapon defeated a prevailing weapons system, thus calling into question not only the traditional practice of the military art but the assumptions upon which that practice was grounded. A military crisis ensued and was not resolved until a satisfactory military solution had been found. The period during which the hunt for a solution is underway is referred to in this essay as a 'war of destiny'.

Wars of destiny are not wars between great powers, though they may take on the character of one as did the Hundred Years' War. They do not decide who among several competing political communities shall be the ruling one. Rather, they determine what shall be the fundamental nature of a political community – its military force, economic organization and ideological structure – in keeping with the new energy and technological capacity of the dawning (epoch). Determinative for the structure of all political communities within an (epoch), they are wars between very different foundations of political power arising out of a novel source of energy. They open with the defeat of the prevailing weapons system, and close with the rise of an entirely new weapons system. When a war of destiny has run its course, Western civilization will have passed through an historical discontinuity. Not only the military art, but all history begins anew.

Candidates for the two wars of destiny in Western civilization are the Barbarian raids, invasions and migrations that mark the boundary between the Classical and Medieval (epochs) and the Hundred Years' War that divides the Medieval and Modern (epochs). Adrianople (378) denotes the start of the transition from Classical to Medieval life, and Crécy (1346) the move to the Modern (epoch). Such dates are, to some extent, arbitrary; nevertheless they represent battles in which the defeat of the prevailing weapons system is clear enough for all to see the lesson.

Closing dates are more difficult to identify. They depend upon a successful demonstration of the weapons system that will come to dominate the new (epoch). While Adrianople shows the superiority of light cavalry over heavy infantry, it was heavy cavalry and the castle that prevailed in the Medieval (epoch). The reign of Charles Martel (714–741) is probably the best indicator that the times had changed. And while it was light (English longbow) and heavy (Swiss pike) infantry that defeated the armored knight, it was at the Siege of Constantinople (1453) that artillery finally defeated the castle and began its rise to prominence in the Modern (epoch).

Although lengthy and generally without decisive battles, wars of destiny come to an end. While they last, Western history is characterized by a desperate search for a military solution brought about by the defeat of dominant weapons system of the prevailing (epoch). When that solution is produced, a new primary energy source will have been demonstrated and a new (epoch) in Western civilization opens, the call to destiny answered. When events such as these transpire, Western civilization is, in very fundamental ways, irrevocably altered.

Implications

What are the implications of the perspective advanced here? The concept of an (epoch) and the distinction between wars of efficiency and wars of destiny, if taken up, would require research programs thoroughly interdisciplinary in character. The core of the program would be the complex web of political relations embracing war, the state and technology. Several key topics would provide focal points, initially for case studies and aiming, eventually, at more quantitatively oriented approaches.

In addition to standard studies of wars of efficiency (the current focus of war studies) wars of destiny, their character, how they are fought, and how they are recognized would be a primary subject. Exploring the role of the military in fostering change would emerge from an obscure specialization to one of major emphasis. Considerable modification in the principles and concepts of war would be necessary. It is not the intent of this essay to draw up a detailed blueprint; at this stage of development it would not be possible to do so anyway. Nevertheless, a broad outline can be sketched.

The life-cycle of an energy–technology matrix can be described as an 'S-curve'. Initially progress is slow; at some point advances in technological applications become quite rapid; eventually the curve flattens out as the costs of advance become large relative to the scope of advance. Not all political communities progress along the technological curve at the same rate; that is, there is uneven development. Do the domestic and foreign policies of a political community differ according to the prevailing phase of an (epoch)? Do they differ according to a community's progress along the curve? What is the impact of technology transfer, and how does it take place? What, if any, is the relationship between different phases, the relative developmental progress of different communities and types of wars?

The point of view suggested here is that wars of efficiency are fought against a backdrop of technological advance while wars of destiny are fought against a background of technological exhaustion. If wars of efficiency test the organization, administration, allocation and utilization of resources of competing political communities, then wars of destiny test the capacity of an (epoch) to adapt its military, economic, and ideological institutions and processes to a novel form of energy. In short, wars of efficiency test the capacity of a political community to mobilize existing resources; wars of destiny test the capacity of political communities to initiate and carry through fundamental change. Wars of efficiency have received considerable attention; wars of destiny remain virtually unexplored.

Research would highlight the role of the military in bringing about change. Military institutions are perceived as notoriously slow in responding to change. A simple charge of military conservatism based upon the 'conservative nature of the military mind' can hardly be regarded as an adequate explanation. Given that a weapons system has demonstrated long term success in battle, for what reasons should it be discarded and another taken up? Defeat in battle is insufficient cause.

Weapons form only one part of an armed force and defeat may be suffered for any number of reasons. Victory may be due as much to surprise brought about by the novelty of a new weapon as any inherent and long term superiority. Hannibal's elephants are a classic example of just such a case. Moreover, the principles of war promise that with sufficient cleverness a solution to a new weapon can be found. Attacking an elephant's legs proved its undoing. The relationship between uncertainty and change needs much deeper examination than it has so far received.

Not surprisingly, a successful weapons system attracts adherents; the longer that success lasts, the deeper its influence and the commitment to it. The adoption of a variant to an existing system may indeed increase the rivalry between components of the armed forces for budgetary allocations; but this is a normal sign of technological progress.

Consider the current competition between aircraft and missile, carrier and submarine, tank and helicopter. If, as this perspective has suggested, the historical development of an (epoch) is the process of various political communities adjusting to the dominant weapons system of the (epoch), then the adoption of an entirely unprecedented weapons system based on a new and unexplored source of energy would require dismantling the entire political edifice of an existing (epoch). Those who benefit from the structure of privileges (broadly defined) created during the course of (epoch) development are the ones who will rule on the adoption of any new system.

It is for this reason that the two changes in weapons systems in the history of Western civilization, from infantry to cavalry and cavalry to artillery, entered that civilization from outside its accepted borders. The Barbarians brought the horse to the West, and the Welsh contributed the longbow. We know little about the political intricacies and intercises of commitments (financial, technical, psychological) of the 'military-industrial-ideological' complex of an (epoch). Yet it is this web that is most directly challenged by a war of destiny. If a political community is to respond appropriately to a war of destiny, then we need to know far more than we do now.

View from the Wolves' Den: The Chechens and Urban Operations

DAVID P. DILEGGE and
MATTHEW VAN KONYNENBURG

In 1998, the United States Marine Corps was presented with an opportunity to conduct interviews with Chechen commanders and key staff officers who participated in combat operations against Russian forces in the 1994–96 conflict. The Corps was particularly interested in obtaining the Chechen view as it was then conducting a series of experiments (Urban Warrior) designed to improve its capability to conduct urban operations. Having studied the horrendous losses the Russians experienced during its first incursion into Groznyy, and faced with the dilemma of finding solutions to the high casualty rate inherent to the city fight, the Marines thought it prudent to gain the perspective of those who had planned and conducted an urban insurgency against a modern conventional force.

Approximately 20 interviews were conducted during June and July of 1999 in Chechnya by Dr Marie Benningsen-Broxup,[1] a Central Asia expert who had close ties with the Chechens. Dr Broxup spent time with the Marines to include one of the authors in preparation for the interviews and after the fact for translation, transcription and clarification. In February 2000, the Marines also had the opportunity to conduct an eight hour seminar Q&A with another commander, Tourpal Ali-Kaimov, who was visiting the US as part of a Chechen 'government delegation'.

While the interviews have seen wide distribution through unofficial channels, these first-hand accounts have not been officially published or presented in any professional journal. Excerpts from selected interviews are presented here and are intended to provide insights on urban operations that pit conventional against irregular forces. Though other environments and situations are included, the primary focus of this article is on urban operations.

These are the recollections of some of the key Chechen personnel and as with all first hand accounts of combat operations; the natural bias and limited perspective of the participant, the overall military and political situation at the time of occurrence and the possible agenda these participants might harbor must be taken into consideration before drawing definitive conclusions. Nevertheless, these are the words of those who participated in operations that stunned not only the Russian military establishment, but also many of the experts attempting to find solutions to conducting operations in the complex and dangerous urban environment.

The Chechen Commanders

Space constraints preclude including the interviews of each commander and staff officer. The following text contains excerpts from the interviews of the Chechens (with their 1994–96 position) listed below. Topics covered in this article include the first battle for Groznyy, the recapture of Groznyy by the Chechens, urban ambush tactics, logistics and intelligence.

Aslan Maskhadov – Chief of Staff of Chechen forces
Husein Iskhanov – Mashadov's Aide-de-Camp
Said Iskhanov – General Staff Officer and Intelligence
Tourpal Ali-Kaimov – Chechen Commander
Payzullah Nutsulkhanov – Head of Logistics

Background

On 11 December 1994, a force of approximately 40,000 Russians attacked into Chechnya against a force of no more than 5,000–7,000 Chechens. After reaching the Chechen capital of Groznyy, 6,000 Russian soldiers conducted a three-pronged mechanized attack into the city following a 10-day aerial and artillery bombardment of the city against a force of not more than 1,000 Chechens. Instead of the anticipated light resistance, Russian forces encountered a determined enemy armed with 'massive amounts'[2] of antitank weapons. The Russian attack was repulsed with shockingly high losses and it took another two months of heavy fighting and changing Russian tactics to capture Groznyy. The estimated Russian casualty count between January and May 1995 totaled 2,805 killed, 10,319 wounded, 393 missing and another 133 captured.[3]

The results of these catastrophic losses in the initial battle for Groznyy have been set as a text-book example on how a determined unconventional force can utilize the urban operational environment to defeat a technologically and numerically superior force.

The First Battle for Groznyy

Aslan Maskhadov: The Russians did not wage war properly; they were just prepared to take enormous losses and destroy everything that got in their way. While they did not value their soldiers, we counted every man. Our first problem was to avoid retreat and engage the Russians in combat. The first 'battle' was literally fought on the doorstep of the Presidential Palace in Groznyy; my headquarters (HQ) was in the basement. The 131st Motorized Brigade, the 31st Samara Tank Regiment and other units were able to enter Groznyy without opposition. We had no regular army to speak of to oppose the Russians, only some small units defending various points within the city. The Russians were able to ride into Groznyy on their armored personnel carriers (APCs) and tanks, without dismounted infantry support as if they were on parade. After my HQ was surrounded by Russian tanks (they filled the city) I decided that we must engage in battle. I gave the command to all our small units to immediately descend on the Palace. They did not know that I was surrounded but knew that once they did arrive, they would be engaging the enemy.

As the Chechens arrived they saw the Russian positions and immediately began the fight. The Russians did not know what hit them. They were sitting ducks; again, all lined up as if on parade around the Palace and on the square opposite the railway station. A majority of their tanks and APCs were burned down in less than four hours. What was left was on the run, hunted across Groznyy by our rocket-propelled grenade (RPG) launcher teams, even by boys with Molotov cocktails. This lasted for three days and in the end some 400 Russian tanks and APCs were destroyed. The city was filled with Russian corpses.

A major factor in this success was the 26 November 'rehearsal' against Chechen units under 'contract' to the Russians. As they advanced on the Presidential Palace we were able to destroy the first tank and after 3 hours we had destroyed or captured all of their vehicles to include another 10 tanks. It was then that the Chechen resistance lost all fear of Russian tanks as we realized that they were 'match-boxes'. This first success gave confidence to our men and, on 31 December, when they located a tank they considered it their duty to destroy it. In some cases it became a competition: 'leave this tank, it is mine'.

After all the Russian vehicles were destroyed on the 31st I decided to stay and defend the Palace. As volunteers arrived from every corner of Chechnya, I registered them and relayed: 'here is a house, you have so many men, defend it and do not move from there'. Thus, little by little, the defense was organized around the Palace.

We defended the Palace for 18 days and only the shell of the building was left after constant mortar fire. As additional Russian units, including a commando division, were deployed into Groznyy the battles raged for every house in every quarter of the city. Our units behaved well and repelled most of the attacks. The Russians were reluctant to use infantry and I had the impression that they were scared; all they seemed to want to do is dig into defensive positions or hide in their vehicles. This was impossible in these conditions, so the tanks and APCs burned and the Russian soldiers perished. There was no attempt to protect or camouflage the vehicles or accompany them with dismounted infantry. They would just advance *en masse* and as they did they were destroyed.

One battle raged around the Council of Ministers where we had 12 fighters. The buildings they occupied were surrounded by tanks firing relentlessly. They called for help but I could not provide it and told them so. One hour later, they destroyed one tank, then another. Our fighters gained confidence and the Russian soldiers' nerve broke and they retreated. That is how we fought.

On 18 January Russian aviation dropped 'depth' bombs on my HQ. Three bombs hit the cellar, one landed in the adjacent corridor, another in the infirmary and the other in a back room. We were left with just the sky over our heads and the decision was made to abandon the Palace and withdraw all our units across the Sunzha River which divides Groznyy in two. I planned the withdrawal at night, around 10 p.m. Those units on the outskirts or were surrounded in the city were the first to retreat. Those covering the retreat and at the Palace were the last to leave at 11 p.m. Soon, all those who could manage to withdraw were across the Sunzha where we set up another HQ. The Russians seemed unaware of this development and continued to bomb the presidential Palace for an additional three days, seemingly unwilling to advance their troops.

The next decision was to put all my available forces in a defensive position along the Sunzha. While the Russians were still bombing the Palace, we rapidly took up positions and built defenses on every bridge consisting of every man we could spare – five to ten men per bridge. I set up my HQ in Town Hospital #2.[4] As time passed we strengthened our positions with new arrivals and we managed to hold our ground there for another month with 'attacks and retreats, attacks and retreats'. On the opposite side of the Sunzha the Russians razed every building but could not drive their tanks across the bridges because of our defenses. However, the Russians did manage to break through from the direction of the tramway station, to attack us from the rear. We were virtually surrounded.

It was then that we decided, against conventional military logic, to counter-attack. We were in a dilemma, our fighters did not want to dig defensive trenches as they considered it humiliating and the buildings in this area were too small and fragile to withstand a tank attack. So we made a line between the Sunzha and Minutka, dug trenches and with approximately 40 to 50 men we advanced meter by meter digging more trenches as we crawled forward. We did this until we reached the first line of tanks and burned them. We pressed until the tanks retreated then built additional trenches and advanced even further.

Meanwhile, other developments were taking place at the Voykovo suspension bridge across the Sunzha. Russian tanks along the river were providing covering fire to infantry troops who managed to cross the bridge. They advanced within 200 meters of my HQ and though I threw all my available forces against them, we could not manage to stop the offensive. It was at this point that we decided to move our HQs and abandon our positions along the Sunzha. The withdrawal was organized in the same manner as retreat from the Presidential Palace and each unit knew in which order and at what time to conduct this operation. Soon, we had all retreated to our third line of defense along the mountain ridges that skirt Groznyy. When we held Groznyy we had a feeling of exhilaration and we also felt that if we left the city we would be vulnerable. It was easier to fight in the city, so we fought for every house. That said, because of Russian scorched-earth urban tactics we did not fight as we did in Groznyy later in Shali and Argun. We gave them up as our determined resistance would have condemned these towns to oblivion.

Husein Iskhanov: I was with Commander Maskhadov in his cellar HQs at the Palace. We knew that we did not have adequate forces to stop the Russian's initial advance. According to the journal we kept there was an initial Chechen force of 350 fighters. This was the number who registered with HQ; I estimate that we had an additional 150 who did not register – men who came to shoot for a couple of hours and then return home.

For us the numbers did not matter as much as our knowledge of the Russians and the urban terrain. Most of us had experience serving in the Soviet Armed forces and we knew their tactics, habits and language. We also had the same communications system and radios. Our head of communications at that time, Colonel Taimaskhanov, knew his job perfectly. We had a special room in the Palace for our radio operators and whenever we had a moment we would go there and 'talk' to the Russians. We listened to their transmissions and determined who was in command and who subordinate commanders were. We waited for the moment when they were giving their orders and then intervened, giving different orders in a confident manner, providing false positions and so on. We used these tactics throughout 1995 and they were very beneficial, more often then not resulting in the Russians loosing troops to friendly fire or units loosing their sense of direction in urban areas.

One of the units we faced in that first battle for Groznyy was the 131st Maiko Brigade. Practically the whole brigade was annihilated in just one night on 31 December. The Russian claim that 100 soldiers survived but I do not believe it because we captured the crew of the last remaining APC of the brigade. The brigade commander was killed, and his second-in-command was captured with that last APC.

Another unit we faced was the 81st Samarski Regiment. They attacked from the direction of the airport and were allowed to penetrate to a point near the Palace. Then we struck, destroying the first APC of the column, then the last one and then a couple in the middle. The Russians were squeezed because it was difficult to maneuver tanks and APCs in the city, visibility was bad and the buttoned-up drivers could not see where they were going. We then surrounded the remaining vehicles and destroyed almost the entire regiment.

Throughout January the Russians persisted with a determined attack against the Palace and little by little they got nearer our HQ. That success cost them dearly. Towards the middle of January, there was heavy fighting within 100–200 meters of the HQ with the Russians occupying a five-story building in front of the Palace and the National Archives across the road.

In the first two weeks of January we used mostly sniping as our main means of defense because we had an acute lack of ammunition for most of our weapons. We also had another handicap in that our men were reluctant to use tracer rounds because they feared that their positions would be revealed to the Russians. While true, especially in urban areas, we had to utilize every piece of ammunition we had. I exhorted them to imagine the fear of the Russian soldier when he could actually 'see' the bullet that would kill him. Gradually our men got used to the idea, we had little else and it indeed became true that the tracers began to create more panic among the Russians than ordinary rounds. To get back to the sniping tactic, we instructed our fighters to use single shots and no automatic fire and the Russians came to believe that we had snipers everywhere. In actuality, we had a few sniper rifles captured from the Russians and few 'trained' snipers.

Most of our re-supply of arms and ammunition came from the Russian vehicles we destroyed or captured. We even transformed the guns from Russian tanks into individual hand-held weapons. Our dire logistic situation also dictated many of the tactics we used in Groznyy. There was no point in forming large units because HQs was not in a position to feed and supply them. Our initial formations averaged 10–20 men and as a rule there would be one RPG allocated to each group of 10. Once we armed a unit with 12 RPGs and by our standard that was a very powerful force.

Conditions were not easy at the Presidential Palace. On 18 January our HQ suffered from a massive air and artillery attack. By our estimation, a rocket was hitting the palace at a rate of one per second. Our HQ was a very easy target as it stood well above the surrounding buildings. One aviation 'depth' bomb that hit the palace penetrated 11 floors and destroyed the ceiling of the camp hospital in the cellar. It was a 'precision bomb' as it hit within 20 meters of Maskhadov's HQ's area. We had made mistakes and the information on the actual location of the HQ was well known. Many people were permitted to come and go at the Palace; we let anybody in to include journalists, Duma deputies, Russian soldiers' mothers and prisoners of war. This was stupid but people were still very naïve then.

We abandoned the Palace on the night of the 18th in small groups. Journalists have since written that we escaped in tunnels. Believe me as I had explored the entire building and there were no tunnels. Our next line of defense was beyond the Sunzha River. Though we attempted to blow all the bridges as we crossed we lacked the explosives to drop the one on the main road. The front line was set along the river with us controlling the right bank and the Russian the left. This lasted for nearly a month, with no close combat and the Chechens conducting sniping operations. The Sunzha afforded good protection as the Russians were afraid to cross the river with their APCs. Incidentally, the Russians remained concentrated around the Palace, celebrating their 'victory'. They only dared to enter the building 3 or 4 days after we had left. Though they were positioned within 100 meters they had not realized we had left.

The Recapture of Groznyy

Tourpal Ali-Kaimov: On 6 August 1996 our fighters recaptured Groznyy from the Russians. Beginning on 3 August, small, light foot-mobile Chechen groups began infiltrating the city in preparation for the assault. By daylight on the 6th we had infiltrated 1,500[5] and proceeded to conduct a simultaneous offense at 05.00 hours throughout the city. We estimated that there were 15,000 Russian troops defending Groznyy at the time.

The four main Chechen objectives were the Russian command and control assets at Khankala airfield, the northern airport, The FSB (the successor to the KGB) HQ, and the GRU (military intelligence) HQ. To prevent reinforcement and/or relief of Russian forces in Groznyy, we conducted supporting attacks and manned blocking positions in four surrounding urban areas, along the three main avenues of approach into Groznyy, and to the north of the city. These operations were conducted simultaneously with the main attack in order to create maximum confusion amongst the Russian military leadership. In this, we were very successful.

The main attack in Groznyy was over in three hours with a total of 47 Chechen fighters killed in action. During the attack and immediately after we had no problem with re-supply as the Russians were so completely caught off-guard that we seized massive amounts of weapons and ammunition as well as vehicles to transport the captured material.

Aslan Maskhadov: By June 1996 we were under attack on all fronts in a last desperate attempt by the Russians to gain the upper hand. We were surrounded with our backs to the mountains and under constant fire by artillery and aviation. On 9 June after a series of harrowing escapes by many in the Chechen command structure it was clear that there was no hope for a negotiated peace. It was then that we decided to recapture Groznyy.

I had been planning this operation for six months as we always believed that the war would end with the recapture of Groznyy. I thought about it constantly, even to the point of conducting radio rehearsals to provoke Russian reaction.[6] I had studied the maps, the Russian positions, the approaches, the routes of advance; I had everything ready. We held meetings with our commanders who gave us their intelligence reports. We had reconnoitered every inch, we knew the disposition of every Russian position, the numbers, the roadblocks, everything.

On 3 August I gave the order to move into the city. At the time the Russians were everywhere so we moved between their positions from every direction. Amazingly, on 5 August the Russian media announced that the Chechens would enter that very same day. I was worried as there were certain areas where it would be easy to ambush our troops, but it was too late to stop the attack.

The attack began at 05.00 hours on 6 August. Over 820 men took part in the operations. I gave an order that every commander should lead with his men, whether he had 20 or 200, they had to be in the forefront. All our objectives were met and it was a huge success. The Russian posts, bases, all of them were hit by surprise then our forces moved on to cut the roads and not let anyone through, leaving behind a few snipers and machine gunners to cover the objectives. When Russian columns tried to move into the city it was too late. All the bases were captured or neutralized. As we could not take the government building or the Ministry of Internal Affairs we simply burned them.

Developing Chechen Tactics 1994–1996

Tourpal Ali-Kaimov: The Chechens made no illusions about the Russians. We knew we could not meet them in the conduct of conventional combat and win. However, we knew that if we met them in the urban environment we might be able to 'punish them'. This was a lesson learned as we progressed through the Russian invasion from 1994 through 1996 – we now know that the city battlefield offers us distinct advantages.

In the conduct of armor and personnel ambushes, we configured our forces into 75-man groups. These were further broken down into three 25-man groups (platoons). These platoons were further broken down into three equal-sized teams of six to seven fighters each (squads). Each squad had two RPG gunners and two PK (machinegun) gunners. The 75-man unit (company) had a mortar (82mm) crew in support with at least two tubes per crew.

Each 25-man group also included one corpsman/medic, three ammunition/supply personnel, three litter bearers and two snipers armed with SVD sniper rifles. The snipers did not operate or co-locate with the platoons, but rather set up in 'hide' positions that supported their respective platoons.

Again, our units did not move by flanking maneuvers against the Russians but instead incorporated chess-like maneuvers to hit them. They used buildings and other structures as navigation and signal points for maneuvering or initiating ambushes/assaults against the Russians.

We segregated Groznyy into quadrants for ambush purposes. Each 75-man ambush group set up in buildings along one street block, and only on one side of the street – never on both sides of a street because of the crossing fires a two-sided ambush would create. The rationale for doing so was that we set up similar ambushes along parallel-running streets. Our units would leave opposite facing buildings vacant – with no mines or booby traps either – and by doing so, they could use those buildings as escape routes, or to reinforce less successful armor ambushes on adjacent streets. This was also an incentive for the Russians to abandon their vehicles for the relative safety of the unoccupied buildings.

We only occupied the lower levels of multistory buildings to avoid casualties from rockets and air delivered munitions coming through the upper levels. One 25-man platoon comprised the 'killer team' and set up in three positions along the target avenue. They had the responsibility for destroying whatever column entered their site. The other two 25-man platoons set up in the buildings at the assumed entry-points to the ambush site. They had responsibility for sealing off the ambush entry from escape by or reinforcement of the ambushed forces.

The killer platoon established a command point (platoon HQ) with the center squad. As the intended target column entered the site, the squad occupying the building nearest the entry point would contact the other two squads occupying the center and far building positions. Primary means of communications was by Motorola radio. Each squad had one – lack of funding prevented us from providing every fighter with a radio. Once the lead vehicle into the site reached the far squad position, the far squad would contact the other two squads. The commander at the central squad (platoon HQ) would initiate or signal to initiate the ambush.

We also employed minefields along the edges of the buildings leading into the ambush site to deter Russian infantry from forcing entry into the end buildings. The task of the two 25-man platoons in those end buildings was threefold. First, they were to cover the minefields and take out any reinforcing armor and infantry. Second, they were to reinforce to relieve the killer platoon in the event the ambush got bogged down. And third, they were to reinforce ambushes on adjacent streets if necessary.

Each seven-man squad had two or more RPG-7s, 2 or more PK machine-guns, and the remainder with assault rifles. A support element with medic, litter bearers and ammunition bearers usually occupied building with the center squad (platoon HQ).

In addition to the value our fighters placed on the RPG, we found the PK machine-gun an excellent weapon for urban warfare. The single shot mode allowed for the conserving of ammunition, while the ability to go onto full automatic either slowed or quickly broke up Russian infantry assaults.

Logistics

Payzullah Nutsulkhanov: I was Maskhadov's deputy for logistics and responsible for the whole of Chechnya. I had four men working for me at HQ and we were very active and visited all the fronts during the war. Our neighbors from the other republics helped us and we had channels for humanitarian aid to include medicine.

I became logistics chief by chance as the original commander was killed in the early days of the war. After his death our logistics effort collapsed. In the beginning we had no need for logistics as each unit brought their own supplies or found them on the spot. This was especially true when we were fighting in Groznyy. After the withdrawal from the city the situation changed and we had to organize our logistics starting from nothing. Except for the regular fighters, we did not even know how many of our men required re-supply. So we made charts and required each commander to report how many men he had. We worked out what each front needed down to the smallest detail. After the retreat from Groznyy, we had 3,000 men, so I organized our logistics to support 6,000 to be on the safe side. Our logistics became professional with each battalion having a man responsible to supplies who would inform us of their needs.

Tourpal Ali-Kaimov: While the draw-down of Soviet/Russian military units in Chechnya after the break-up of the Soviet Union allowed us to 'inherit' certain amounts of military weapons and equipment it certainly was not enough to prosecute the war.

This initial supply inherited was augmented (at times greatly) by the capture of Russian arms, ammunition and other military significant equipment and supplies during combat. We could easily identify Russian supply vehicles because they were usually open-bed trucks that did not have any cover over the stacks of ammunition and provisions loaded in the back. In the conduct of a convoy ambush, our fighters would avoid hitting the supply trucks, instead keeping them intact as 'war trophies'. This became the our primary means of re-supply. Captured supplies were immediately reported to the General Staff and they decided how it would be distributed based on their knowledge of the overall logistic situation among subordinate units.

We also had a constant supply of fuel for vehicles. Chechnya sits on extensive oil reserves ('a pool of oil'). The Chechens are very adept at refining this oil into diesel through the use of 'homemade' refineries at private residences and small factories.

Food was normally procured from local farmers or brought up from Georgia. The Russians avoid moving through passes between Chechnya and Georgia. They prefer to use one main artery between the two countries, enabling the Chechens to move easily and unmolested between Georgia and Chechnya.

Intelligence

Tourpal Ali-Kaimov: Know the territory – day and night. That is what we did and we used this knowledge to our advantage. Detailed reconnaissance is a must to be successful in the conduct of urban operations and our normal routine included a map reconnaissance, followed by a foot reconnaissance and then bringing the reconnaissance asset back to headquarters with his map. Chechen scouts briefed commanders and planners personally. Whenever possible, we ordered another reconnaissance mission to confirm the results of the first.

Chechen reconnaissance personnel were not told why they were performing a particular mission in case they were captured. Traditional reconnaissance methods were augmented by human intelligence and reconnaissance performed by elders, women and children. Virtually every Chechen was an intelligence collector. Reconnaissance personnel, to include mobile patrols as well as women and children, were supplied with Motorola radios to enable timely reporting.

We learned that the scale of maps is very important – key urban terrain is at the micro level. We never relied on streets, signs, and most buildings as reference points. They can be altered in such a way during urban combat as to be deceiving. We used cultural landmarks, prominent buildings, and monuments as reference points – they usually remain intact and are easily distinguishable. If they were altered we annotated it on our maps. We had a good supply of maps and 'to scale' drawings and sketches of Groznyy. This greatly facilitated our command, control, and communications. The Russians did not possess the same quality or quantity of maps, nor did they conduct effective reconnaissance of the city to verify or validate the maps they did possess. We did use captured Russian maps – but only after confirmation and updates performed by reconnaissance personnel.

Counter-reconnaissance is also crucial. The Russians performed reconnaissance during daylight hours and subsequently either attacked during the day or employed indirect fire or air that night. Our forces performed daylight reconnaissance in support of a night attack. This counter-reconnaissance enabled our forces to conduct a night movement closer to Russian positions or other pre-planned alternate sites in anticipation of a Russian indirect fire or air attack, based on the results of the Russian daylight reconnaissance. Being well versed in Russian reconnaissance doctrine, we often let the Russians observe our daytime positions as part of a deception plan.

Our commanders placed so much value on detailed knowledge of the urban terrain that, upon receiving 40 Ukrainian volunteers with military backgrounds, they required them to perform extensive reconnaissance with attached Chechens before entering combat. Only then, were the Ukrainians deemed combat ready and as a result performed their combat missions and tasks with great effectiveness.

The importance of detailed reconnaissance and accurate intelligence cannot be understated in the conduct of urban operations.

Said Iskhanov: After Budennovsk,[7] I was sent to Groznyy by Maskhadov to set up an intelligence network. I was answerable to the General Staff and was ordered to gather information on Russian positions in preparation for the March 1996 attack against Groznyy, although I did not know what was planned at the time. I had to collect information on the Russians' exact positions, their numbers, the routes in and out of Groznyy, the possible ways of bringing weapons into the town, but I had few concrete instructions from HQ. My brief was broad – to gather information everywhere.

I began on my own. I had no team, so I started by using friends and relatives. I had no way of paying them so at first I tried to be casual and did not tell them the real purpose of my inquiries. Throughout the remainder of the war, my helpers were all volunteers. I had a map of Groznyy and its surroundings. I began by traveling to the districts where the Russians had their bases and garrisons. I checked the people I knew in the area – usually 5–6 people, and recruited them.

The first task was to find the best route to reach the Russian bases. We had no training in intelligence work – to find out the number of Russian troops and equipment was pure improvisation at first. Each one tried his own manner. I often used young women. When I traveled to report to HQ with documents, I always took a young woman with me as it was a safeguard.

To gather information around the capital, we had to walk. We explored routes through woods and forests on foot between Groznyy and Urus Martan, the piedmont and the escape routes to the southern mountains. Sometimes we walked as far as the positions of our units in the pre-Alps. After we had explored a district and verified that passage for our units was possible, we selected some local people to watch and report any changes – for example, a change in the position of a road block, any movement of troops and weaponry, any unusual movement or development. Once checked, these areas came under constant surveillance. We knew that we had to update our information all the time.

One of our best sources of information was the market. People in the market were in touch with traders who themselves were in contact with all the principal Russian garrisons. These garrisons usually had small markets nearby which provided them with goods, alcohol, narcotics and so on. The traders had their 'favorite' clients among the Russian soldiers who had plenty of money stolen during clean-up operations. They chatted with the traders who, naturally, got information. When we were organizing a special operation it was essential that we knew when a Russian column would be on the move. That was when the traders were useful.

Of course, between the time we gathered the information and the March 1996 operation, changes inevitably occurred. One commander grumbled afterwards that some of our numbers were not accurate. But we had no possibility to update information every day. Passing on information was not easy. Our radio communication was poor because priority was given to military operations. Our radio did not reach all the mountain regions. We had to get to the highest houses in Groznyy to communicate and would waste two or three hours to raise HQ. When we had finally established communications they would often be cut off. More often than not, we had to report in person, with all our notes.

Our asset was that we were able to melt into the civilian population. As a rule, we did not bother with small posts of 20–30 men. They became useless as soon as they were isolated among Chechens. But we always watched the larger garrisons, looking for Russian soldiers wandering out through the minefields surrounding them. Then we would capture and interrogate the solider often resulting in information on their bases, their numbers, weaponry, reserves of ammunitions, relations between officers and troops, and so on.

Conclusion

This has been but a sampling of the information contained in the original Chechen Commander's interviews. The authors fully intend on writing follow-on pieces that will include the impact of Chechen culture on conduct of the war, Chechen moral and leadership, command and control, communications, weapons, and psychological operations. Moreover, we hope to also drill down further into the topics covered here and to add commentary on the implications this material may have on conventional forces operating in an urban environment and facing an unconventional foe.

NOTES

1. Marie Benningsen-Broxup is the editor of the quarterly *Central Asian Survey* in London, has studied the North Caucasus for many years and has traveled there extensively.
2. Marine Corps Intelligence Activity, *Urban Warfare Study: City Case Studies Compilation* (March 1999).
3. Ibid.
4. Often the Chechens would select hospitals or schools as HQs as in many areas of the city they were the only large buildings with cellars.
5. This number differs from Maskhadov's count of 820.
6. The Chechens would broadcast in the clear that they would be conducting a certain operation and often the Russians would 'take the bait', thus tying up troops while the Chechens attacked elsewhere. Alternately, the Chechens would announce in advance an operation they intended to mount. Thus was the case with the recapture of Groznyy. The double-bluff worked, the Russians did no believe it and were unprepared.
7. The 14 June 1995 raid by Shamil Basayev and 148 other Chechens that unintentionally became a hostage situation in the town hall of Budyonnesovsk, Russia.

Selected Bibliography

John B. Alexander, *Future War: Non-Lethal Weapons in Twenty-First-Century Warfare* (New York, NY: St Martin's Press 1999).

John Arquilla and David Ronfeldt, 'Cyberwar is Coming!' *Comparative Strategy* 12/2 (Spring 1993) pp.141–65.

John Arquilla and David Ronfeldt, *The Advent of Netwar* (Santa Monica, CA: RAND 1996).

John Arquilla and David Ronfeldt (eds.) *In Athena's Camp: Preparing for Conflict in the Information Age* (Santa Monica, CA: RAND 1997).

John Arquilla and David Ronfeldt, 'Networks, Netwars, and the Fight for the Future', posted at <http://firstmonday.org/issue6_10/index.html>.

John Arquilla and David Ronfeldt (eds.) *Networks and Netwars: The Future of Terror, Crime, and Militancy* (Santa Monica, CA: RAND 2001).

John R. Boyd, *The Essence of Winning and Losing* (28 Jun. 1995). Access via<www.au.af.mil/au.awc> .

John R. Boyd, Lecture, US Naval Institute Seminar (Washington DC: Sept. 1996).

Robert J. Bunker, 'Epochal Change: War Over Social and Political Organization', *Parameters* 27/2 (Summer 1997) pp.15–24.

Robert J. Bunker, *Five-Dimensional (Cyber) Warfighting: Can the Army After Next be Defeated Through Complex Concepts and Technologies?* (Carlisle, PA: US Army War College, Strategic Studies Institute, March 1998).

Robert J. Bunker and John P. Sullivan, 'Cartel Evolution: Potentials and Consequences', *Transnational Organized Crime* 4/2 (Summer1998) pp.55–74.

Robert J. Bunker, 'Networked Threats to Governments: Dynamics, Emergence, and Response', in Emil Görnerup (ed.) *Proceedings from the*

Conference "Armed Conflicts" (Stockholm, 17 Oct. 2000, FOA/Defence Research Establishment, Stockholm: Division of Defence Analysis, Dec. 2000).

Robert J. Bunker, 'Networked Organizational Structures in Future Conflict', Chapter 17 in Jasjit Singh (ed.) *Reshaping Asian Security* (New Delhi: Knowledge World/Institute of Defence Studies and Analyses, June 2001).

CARE Canada and the University of Toronto, *Mean Times: Humanitarian Action in Complex Emergencies - Stark Choices, Cruel Dilemmas* (1999).

Carl von Clausewitz, *On War*. Edited and translated by Michel Howard and Peter Paret. (Princeton, NJ: Princeton University Press 1976).

Martin van Creveld, *Technology and War, 2000 B.C to the Present* (New York, NY: The Free Press 1989).

Martin van Creveld, *The Transformation of War* (New York, NY: The Free Press 1991).

Department of Defense, *Policy for Non-Lethal Weapons*. No. 3000.3 (Washington DC: 9 July 1996).

Field Manual 90-8, Counterguerrilla Operations (Washington DC: Headquarters, Department of the Army 1986).

Mark Galeotti, 'Crimes of the new millennium', 'Global Crime Watch' section *Jane's Intelligence Review* 12/8 (Aug. 2000).

Mark Galeotti, 'The new world of organized crime', 'Global Crime Watch' section *Jane's Intelligence Review* 12/9 (Sept. 2000).

Scott Gerwehr and Russell W. Glenn, *The Art of Darkness: Deception and Urban Operations* (Santa Monica, CA: RAND 2000).

Russell W. Glenn, *Heavy Matter: Urban Operations' Density of Challenges* (Santa Monica, CA: RAND 2000).

Ivelaw Lloyd Griffith, *Drugs and Security in the Caribbean: Sovereignty Under Siege* (University Park, PA: Pennsylvania State University Press 1997).

Grant T. Hammond, *The Mind of War: John Boyd and American Security* (Washington DC: Smithsonian Institute Press 2001).

Seth Hettena, 'Hundreds Protest Biotech Conference,' *The Cincinnati Enquirer* (25 June 2001) accessed 26 Oct. 2001 at <http://enquirer.com/editions/2001/06/25/fin_hundreds_protest.html>.

Eric Hobsbawm, *Bandits*. Revised edition (London, UK: Weidenfeld & Nicholson 2000).

Herbert Howe, 'Global Order and Security Privatization', *Strategic Forum* (Washington DC: Institute for National Strategic Studies, National Defense University, May 1998).

David Isenberg, 'Soldiers of Fortune Ltd.', Center for Defense Information Monograph (Washington DC: Center for Defense Information, Nov. 1997).

Ali A. Jalali, 'Afghanistan: The Anatomy of an Ongoing Conflict', *Parameters* 31/1 (Spring 2001) pp.85–98.

Brian Jenkins, *New Modes of Conflict* (Santa Monica, CA: RAND 1983).

Tara Kartha, *Tools of Terror* (New Delhi: Knowledge World 1999).

Michael Kenney, 'When Criminals Outsmart the State: Understanding the Learning Capacity of Colombian Drug Trafficking Organizations', *Transnational Organized Crime* 5/1 (Spring 1999) pp.97–119.

Qiao Liang and Wang Xiangsui, *Unrestricted Warfare: Assumptions on War and Tactics in the Age of Globalization* (Beijing: PLA Literature Arts Publishing House, Feb. 1999).

William S. Lind *et al.*, 'The Changing Face of War: Into the Fourth Generation', *Marine Corps Gazette* (Oct. 1989) pp.22–6.

William S. Lind, Maj. John Schmitt, USMCR, and Col. Gary I. Wilson, USMCR, 'Fourth Generation Warfare: Another Look', *Marine Corps Gazette* (Dec. 1994) pp.34–7.

Peter A. Lupsha, 'The Role of Drugs and Drug Trafficking in the Invisible Wars', in Richard Ward and Herold Smith (eds.) *International Terrorism: Operational Issues* (Chicago, IL: University of Chicago Press 1987).

Peter A. Lupsha, 'Towards an Etiology of Drug Trafficking and Insurgent Relations: The Phenomenon of Narco-Terrorism', *International Journal of Comparative and Applied Criminal Justice* (Fall 1989).

S.K. Malik, *The Quranic Concept of War* (Lahore: Wajidalis 1979).

Marine Corps Intelligence Activity, *Urban Warfare Study: City Case Studies Compilation* (March 1999).

Thomas A. Marks, *Maoist Insurgency since Vietnam* (London, UK and Portland, OR: Frank Cass Publishers 1996).

Thomas A. Marks, *Colombian Army Adaptation to FARC Insurgency* (Carlisle Barracks, PA: US Army War College, Strategic Studies Institute 2002).

J..J. Medby, and R.W. Glenn, *Street Smart: IPB for Urban Operations* (Santa Monica, CA: RAND, Sept. 2001). Draft document.

Steven Metz, *The Future of Insurgency* (Carlisle Barracks, PA: US Army War College, Strategic Studies Institute 1993).

Steven Metz, *Armed Conflict in the 21st Century; The Information Revolution and Post-Modern Warfare* (Carlisle, PA: US Army War College, Strategic Studies Institute, April 2000).

Major Thomas J. Milton, USA 'The New Mercenaries – Corporate Armies For Hire', *Journal of the Foreign Area Officer Association* (1997) <www.faoa.org/journal/newmerc3.html>.

R. G. Molander *et al.*, *Strategic Information Warfare* (Santa Monica, CA: RAND 1996).

Abdel-Fatau Musah, 'Liberia Conference on Private Military Intervention & Arms Proliferation in Conflicts in Africa' Report (London, UK: Center for Democratic Development, June 2001).

Joseph R. Nunez, *Fighting the Hobbesian Trinity in Colombia: A New Strategy for Peace* (Carlisle Barracks, PA: US Army War College, Strategic Studies Institute 2001).

William J. Olson, 'International Organized Crime; The Silent Threat to Sovereignty', *The Fletcher Forum of World Affairs* (Summer/Fall 1997).

Ralph Peters, 'The New Warrior Class', *Parameters* 24/2 (Summer 1994) pp.16–26.

Ralph Peters, *Fighting for the Future: Will America Triumph?* (Mechanicsburg, PA: Stackpole Books 1999).

Ralph Peters, 'The Plague of Ideas', *Parameters* 30/4 (Winter 2000–1) pp.4–20.

Gregory J. Rattray, 'The Cyberterrorism Threat', in James E. Smith and William C. Thomas (eds.) *The Terrorism Threat and U.S Government Response: Operational and Organizational Factors* (Colorado Springs, CO: USAF Academy 2001).

Paul B. Rich, 'Warlordism, Complex Emergencies and the Search for a Doctrine of Humanitarian Intervention', D.S. Gordon and F.H. Toase (eds.) *Aspects of Peacekeeping* (London, UK: Frank Cass 2001) pp.253–73.

James Rosenau, *Turbulence in World Politics* (Princeton, NJ: Princeton University Press, 1990).

Thomas C. Schelling, *Arms and Influence* (New Haven, CT: Yale University Press, 1967).

William Schwartau, *Cyber Terrorism: Protecting Your Personal Security in the Electronic Age* (New York, NY: Thunder's Mouth Press 1996).

James E. Smith and William C. Thomas (eds.) 'The Terrorist Threat in Strategic Context', in James E. Smith and William C. Thomas (eds.) *The Terrorism Threat and U.S Government Response: Operational and Organizational Factors* (Colorado Springs, CO: USAF Academy 2001).

David Spencer, *Colombia's Paramilitaries: Criminals or Political Force?* (Carlisle Barracks, PA: US Army War College, Strategic Studies Institute 2001).

Mark S. Steinitz, 'Insurgents, Terrorists, and the Drug Trade', *Washington Quarterly* (Fall 1985).

Jessica Stern, 'Pakistan's Jehad Culture', *Foreign Affairs* (Nov./Dec. 2000).

John P. Sullivan, 'Third Generation Street Gangs: Turf, Cartels and Net Warriors', *Transnational Organized Crime* 3/3 (Autumn 1997) pp.95–108.

John P. Sullivan, 'Urban Gangs Evolving as Criminal Netwar Actors', *Small Wars and Insurgencies* 11/1 (Spring 2000) pp.82–96.

John P. Sullivan, 'Integrated Threat and Net Assessment; The L.A. Terrorism Early Warning (TEW) Group Model', *Bioterrorism: Homeland Defense Symposium: The Next Steps* (Santa Monica, CA: RAND, Feb. 2000).

Mao Tse-Tung. *On Guerrilla Warfare.* Translated by Samuel B. Griffith (Garden City, New York, NY: Anchor 1978).

Sun Tzu, *The Art of War*. Translated by Thomas Cleary (Boston, MA: Shimbhalla Press 1988).

Paul Wilkinson, 'The Role of the Military in Combating Terrorism in a Democratic Society', *Terrorism and Political Violence* 8/3 (Autumn 1996) pp.1–11.

Phil Williams, 'Transnational criminal organizations and international security' in M. Klare and Y. Chandrani (eds.) *World Security: Challenges for a New Century.* 3rd edition (New York, NY: St Martin's Press 1998).

Brigadier Mohhamad Yousaf and Major Mark Adkin, *The Bear Trap: Afghanistan's Untold Story* (Lahore: Jang Publishers 1992).

Abstracts

The Transformation of War Revisited

Martin van Creveld

As the title indicates, the purpose of the analysis is to revisit the main theses of *The Transformation of War* a little more than decade after it was published. The first section provides a brief recapitulation of the processes which, especially in view of 9-11, have caused large scale interstate warfare to go down and 'non-trinitarian' warfare to go up. The second takes an equally brief look at the most important problem that *The Transformation of War* has not addressed, that is, information warfare. The third asks whether war in fact is what Clausewitz says it is – a continuation of politics by other means. It concludes that, from the point of view of the vast majority of those who have to fight and die, the answer to that question is very often in the negative; and ends by serving a warning that those who ignore this fact do so at their peril.

The New Warrior Class Revisited

Ralph Peters

The warrior, whether a terrorist, guerrilla, mercenary, pirate or international criminal, will continue to be the most frequent violent opponent of rule-of-law states. After a decade in which the United States failed to respond adequately to the proliferation of warrior-driven conflicts, the events of September 11th, 2001, triggered a profound change in America's willingness to employ military power against asymmetric opponents. Confounding the expectations of the terrorists, the attacks on New York City and Washington unified the American people, galvanized the US government, and unleashed a furious response that will continue, in a variety of forms and locations, for years, even decades, to come. While this long struggle will not be easy – or bloodless – the United States and like-minded nations can defeat warriors in every encounter … but only if our strength of will remains stronger than that of our enemies. Requiring military ferocity, fighting warriors is ultimately a very human struggle.

Transnational Organized Crime: Law Enforcement as a Global Battlespace

Mark Galeotti

As society becomes more complex, organized, transnational and interconnected, so too do criminals, and we are witnessing the globalization and inter-penetration of organized crime. As 'old', and 'new', security worlds merge, transnational organized crime will represent a threat to the state on a variety of levels: as force multiplier, to terrorists and insurgents; as covert weapon in inter-state conflicts; degrading security assets; and subverting national morale, identity and financial and political structures. One of the defining security issues of the 21st century will be the struggle between an 'upperworld', defined by increasingly open economic systems and democratic politics and an underworld willing and able to use and distort these trends for its own ends. This struggle will be played out within a battlespace as indefinite as it is ubiquitous, ranging from cyberspace, through the campaign to shape the ideals and habits of generations, to the overt struggles between states and criminals.

Drug Cartels, Street Gangs, and Warlords

John P. Sullivan and Robert J. Bunker

The nature of crime and conflict has changed and continues to evolve. The now and future war is and will be influenced by irregular combatants – non-state soldiers – that utilize technology and networked doctrine to spread their influence across traditional geographic boundaries. This era shift in political and social organization, fueled by rapid developments of technology and exploitation of network organizational forms, blurs the distinctions between crime, terrorism and warfare. The resulting transitional period – a Dark Renaissance – benefits a range of non-state actors: drugs cartels, street gangs, terrorists, and warlords. Criminal organizations appear among the first to adapt to the new operational context resulting from this shift. This paper examines the journey of street gangs, one type of transnational criminal organization – the drug cartel – and warlords through this evolution. Respectively, these entities provide direct and indirect challenges to the solvency of nation-state institutions, potentially emerging as new war-making entities.

Private Military Companies: Mercenaries for the 21st Century

Thomas Adams

The last decades of the twentieth century saw the rise of private military companies, organized as international corporations and providing military services for hire. This development has been greeted with something close to loathing by various political entities and international actors, notably some elements of the United Nations. These entities and actors regard the rise of business-like military service providers as an aberration and a danger to peace and stability. Some commentators regard them as possible threats to the dominance of nation-states. This article contends that such corporations are an accommodation to the reality of the Post-Cold War world, generally act in the interests of states, present little danger to even weak states and, for the most part, contribute to stability rather than threaten it.

Non-State Actors in Colombia: Threats to the State and to the Hemisphere

Max G. Manwaring

This study seeks to explain the Colombian crisis in terms of non-state threats to the state and to the region. The problem in Colombia is that that country, and its potential, is deteriorating because of three ongoing, simultaneous, and interrelated wars involving the illegal drug industry, various insurgent organizations (primarily the Revolutionary Armed Forces of Colombia, FARC), and 'vigilante' paramilitary groups (the United Self-Defense Groups of Colombia, AUC). This unholy trinity of non-state actors is perpetrating a level of corruption, criminality, human horror, and internal (and external) instability that, if left unchecked at the strategic level, can ultimately threaten Colombia's survival as an organized democratic state, and undermine the political stability and sovereignty of its neighbors.

In that connection, there is now explicit recognition that Colombia's current situation has reached crisis proportions. The critical point of this argument is that the substance, or essence, of the Colombian crisis centers on the general organization, activities, and threats of the major violent stateless actors at work in that country today. Each of the three armed non-state players in Colombia generates formidable problems, challenges, and threats to the state and the region in its own right. What, then, of an alliance of the willing – even if that alliance represents a complicated mosaic of mutual and conflicting interests?

Kashmir, Pakistan and the War by Terror

Jasjit Singh

The war in Kashmir for the past 14 years represents the rise of sub-conventional war as a means of pursuing ideologically driven nationalism. It also represents the exploitation of religious extremism to pursue territorial objectives in the name of a 'holy war'. This would not have been easily achieved but for the growing alienation of the youth in the valley of Kashmir consequent to maladministration and a degree of rising prosperity which was accompanied by growing sense of relative deprivation. Pakistan's Kashmir war was also linked to its search for 'strategic depth' westward through installation of the Taliban in Kabul. In a late 20th-century transformation of the Clausewitzean concept, terror, legitimized in the name of religion, has been employed as the instrument of policy in prosecuting the sub-conventional war. The terror war finally turned inwards into an ethnosectarian conflict until 11 September, and the consequent global war against international terrorism started to reverse the processes.

Battlespace Dynamics, Information Warfare to Netwar, and Bond-Relationship Targeting

Robert J. Bunker

In the coming wars between nation-states and non-state entities, both traditional and advanced forms of weaponry and concepts will be employed. Increasingly, however, advanced forms of war-fighting will play a dominant role in counter-OPFOR (opposing force) strategies because of the new capabilities which they offer. Battlespace dynamics, information warfare to netwar, and bond-relationship targeting all represent viable strategies which can be utilized by nation-states against non-state entities. They are not stand alone solutions to combating networked OPFORs but rather can be combined with each other and with additional strategies based on developing urban CONOPS, nonlethal and hyperlethal weaponry, with better use of intelligence and planning prior to the engagement of hostilities, and with friendly C4I networks for operational support and direct operational impact in 'not crime-not war' operational environments.

Cleansing Polluted Seas: Non-state Threats and the Urban Environment

Russell W. Glenn

Non-state organizations often require support from their environments to a greater extent than do regular military forces. Mao addressed this need in his depiction of the relationship between members of a population and guerrillas; he likened the former to water and the latter to the fish that inhabit it. Most attempts to categorize urban non-state actor threats do so by focusing on the nature of the groups themselves. It is perhaps more constructive to consider an alternative perspective. This brief offering describes urban non-state actors in terms of five categories, each drawing its defining elements from the nature of the support provided by the population that constitutes the urban 'sea' rather than the actors themselves. The article concludes with a consideration of how to purge an urban area of unwanted elements via treatment of the waters on which they rely. While the focus of the consideration is urban, the model has considerable potential for application to other environments.

Non-Lethal and Hyper-Lethal Weaponry

John B. Alexander and Charles 'Sid' Heal

The future of conflict: it's small, smart, fast, precise, unconventional, and death is optional. The main danger facing today's military leaders is preparing to fight the war they want to fight versus the war they are going to fight. While the technology advantage will belong to US and its allies, decisions about when and where engagements will occur are likely to be relinquished to the adversaries. That is the nature of asymmetric warfare.

September 11, 2001 was a defining day in American history. In a period of a few minutes, the world changed forever. It also portended the necessity for a unique juxtaposition of complimentary weapons systems, non-lethal and hyper-lethal. Now more than ever there is a need to be able separate combatants from noncombatants. Requirements exist to deliver punishing devastation to intended targets wherever they may be and yet control the level of effects on demand.

Intelligence Preparation for Operations

Matt Begert and Dan Lindsay

Intelligence preparation for operations (IPO) is described as a countermeasure to an asymmetrical enemy or opposing force (OPFOR) that does not use the modern nation-state model of use-of-force. It is intended to be a post-modern concept for the threat of 4th-generation warfare and the criminal-soldier of the present and the near future. It is designed to be of use in combating terrorism as a way of supporting an active defense of an operational area and to facilitate the connectivity of multiple networked operational areas. IPO is intended to be an asymmetric response to an asymmetric operational force. The ability to collect, process and analyze information to create useful intelligence, the ability to operate as a network and thereby leverage speed of information, dissemination and decision making are key capabilities and functional goals. The concept is described using two classic views of war and conflict, an entrepreneurial method of operation and a straightforward but complex explanation of decision making and action.

Networked Force Structure and C^4I

John P. Sullivan

The face of terrorism and warfare appears to be changing. This paper describes ways to develop a networked force structure and C4I (command, control, communications, computers, intelligence) apparatus based upon improved intelligence and operations fusion capabilities to enhance the way we wage war and protect the public in the now and future battlefield of global and transnational, homeland, cyberspace conflict. This operational space and the adversaries that exploit it ignore proscriptions against attacks on civilians. Urban operations, the blurring of war, crime and terrorism – all issues which the US and Western military and civilian policy communities at all levels of government sought to avoid – are now part of the operational environment. This paper examines the profound nature of the new conflict we are currently immersed in and suggests a path forward: one which builds upon evolving efforts to enhance the interface among military, public and private entities involved in intelligence and information gathering and response activities.

The Structure of War: Early Fourth Epoch War Research

T. Lindsay Moore

This is an excerpt from an unpublished document written in late 1987. The document had been lost for years and rediscovered by the editor in the back of one of his old files. Dr Moore, the advisor for the independent study which resulted in the emergence of Fourth Epoch War theory, has given his permission for this archival document, which he wrote, to be published for the first time. Our initial working term for this theory was 'ICAB Epics'. ICAB meant 'Infantry-Cavalry-Artillery-Beam'. This represented the dominant weapons system each Western historical era developed or was projected to develop, as in the case of the post-Modern era. The term 'epoch' eventually replaced the term 'epic' as the standard term for each historical era. In this excerpt, the term 'epic' will be replaced with 'epoch' (in brackets) to keep this essay in line with other published Fourth Epoch War documents.

View from the Wolves' Den: The Chechens and Urban Operations

David P. Dilegge and Matthew Van Konynenburg

In 1998, the United States Marine Corps was presented with an opportunity to conduct interviews with Chechen commanders and key staff officers who participated in combat operations against Russian forces in the 1994–96 conflict. While the interviews have seen wide distribution through unofficial channels, these first-hand accounts have not been officially published or presented in any professional journal. Excerpts from selected interviews are presented here and are intended to provide insights on urban operations that pit conventional against irregular forces. Topics covered in this study include the first battle for Groznyy, the recapture of Groznyy by the Chechens, urban ambush tactics, logistics and intelligence. These are the recollections of some of the key Chechen personnel and as with all first hand accounts of combat operations; the natural bias and limited perspective of the participant, the overall military and political situation at the time of occurrence and the possible agenda these participants might harbor must be taken into consideration before drawing definitive conclusions.

About the Contributors

Dr **Thomas K. Adams** is a Senior Analyst, Research Planning Inc., on contract to US Army Special Operations Command, Fort Bragg NC for unconventional warfare analysis. He is a retired Lt. Colonel of US Army Special Operations where he specialized in military intelligence. He held various command and staff positions during a period of service that extended from Vietnam to Bosnia. As a special operations officer his assignments ranged from counter-insurgency through humanitarian assistance to counter-drug missions. His experience in contingency operations includes Somalia, El Salvador, Rwanda and Haiti. He holds a PhD in political science (conflict theory) from Syracuse University and is a graduate of the US Army Command and General Staff College. Dr Adams is the author of *US Special Operations Forces in Action* and the forthcoming *Post-Industrial Warfare*. He has also written for *Parameters*, *Military Review* and *Special Warfare* and is the author of numerous articles on military futures and related subjects.

Dr **John B. Alexander** works with a private research institute, serves as a consultant to the National Intelligence Council, CINC US Special Operations Command and is a member of the National Research Council Committee for Assessment of Non-Lethal Weapons Science and Technology. He is a retired US Army Colonel from the infantry branch. From 1966 through early 1969 he commanded Special Forces 'A' Teams in Vietnam and Thailand. His late military assignment was as Director, Advanced Systems Concepts Office, US Army Laboratory Command. After retiring from the Army, he joined Los Alamos National Laboratory, where he was instrumental in developing the concept of Non-Lethal Defense. He also holds a PhD from Walden University and later attended Harvard National and International Security Program. Dr Alexander has organized and chaired the first four major conferences on non-lethal warfare and served as a US delegate to four NATO studies on the topic. As a member of the Council on Foreign Relations non-lethal warfare study, he was instrumental in influencing the report that is credited with causing the Department of Defense to create a formal Non-Lethal Weapons Policy in July 1996. His publications include articles in *Harvard International Review*, *Jane's International Defense Review*, *The Washington Post*, and *The Boston Globe*. His current book, with a foreword by Tom Clancy, is *Future War: Non-Lethal Weapons in Twenty-First-Century Warfare*.

Matt Begert is a project leader at the National Law Enforcement and Corrections Technology Center-West. Duties include the exploration, operational evaluation and implementation of technology for policing, law enforcement and public safety. His focus of effort is less-than-lethal technology, public order and complex incident management. He is a Lt. Colonel United States Marine Corps (Retired) with 25 years of operational experience with joint, combined, and special operations units, and has been assigned as military liaison to Department of Defense research, development and field testing projects involving the integration of technology in support of concepts of advanced war-fighting. Operational experience includes assignments with the Royal Thai Marine Corps, the 5th Brigade Special Forces of the Republic of Korea Army, the Republic of Korea Marine Corps and the Japanese Ground Self-Defense Force. Combat experience includes a flying assignment during the Persian Gulf war. He is involved in domestic counter-terrorism planning and is a member of the volunteer forces of the San Bernardino County (CA) Sheriff's Department. He is a graduate of the Naval War College Senior Officers' course in Strategic Decision Making and holds a BA in Anthropology from the University of Kansas and a BS from the William Allen White School of Journalism and Mass Communications, University of Kansas. He has written for *The Police Chief*, is a contributor to *Jane's Unconventional Weapons Handbook*; *Non-Lethal Weapons: Terms and References*; and various booklets for law enforcement use.

Prof. **Robert J. Bunker** is a counter-terrorism and less-than-lethal weapons consultant to the National Law Enforcement and Corrections Technology Center-West. He is also an Adjunct Professor, National Security Studies program, California State University, San Bernardino and past Fellow, Institute of Land Warfare, Association of the United States Army. He holds a PhD in political science from the Claremont Graduate University and has counter-terrorism operational planning experience. His research focus is on non-state threats, emerging forms of warfare, advanced weaponry and CONOPS (concept of operations), and counter-OPFOR (opposition forces) strategies. Dr Bunker has written over 100 works and essays for policy, military, and law enforcement publications including *Parameters*, *Terrorism and Political Violence*, *Special Warfare*, and *The Tactical Edge*. He is the editor and author of a series of booklets for law enforcement use, and has spoken throughout the US and overseas. His most recent works are book chapters focusing on networked threats and their operational advantages in Swedish and Indian publications, and an International Association of Chiefs of Police *Training Key* on laser threats to law enforcement.

Prof. **Martin van Creveld** is Professor of History at the Hebrew University, Jerusalem, and one of the most influential military theorists of our age. Educated in Israel and in London, England, he has held visiting professorships at the National Defense University (1986–87) and the Marine Corps University (1991–92). He has also consulted to US Department of Defense, the US Air Force, and several other defense establishments world-wide. Professor van Creveld is the author of 14 books. The best known are *Supplying War* (1978), *Command in War* (1985), and *The Transformation of War* (1991); to date, these books have been translated into ten languages. His latest book, *Men, Women and War*, was published in September 2001.

David P. Dilegge is a retired US Marine Corps Reserve Intelligence and Counter intelligence officer and former civilian Senior Urban Operations intelligence Analyst for the Corps. He was the primary author of the *Urban Generic Information Requirements Handbook* and provided instructional and operational support to the Marine Corps' Urban Warrior and Project Metropolis urban experiences. Mr Dilegge has served in intelligence billets ranging from S-2/Scout Sniper Platoon Commander at the battalion level through assignments with the Joint Staff and the Office of the Secretary of Defense. His combat service was with the 1st Marine Division during Operation 'Desert Storm'. He is currently a Senior Urban Operations Analyst with Adroit Systems Incorporated and is a charter member of the Department of Defense Adaptive Red Team (DART).

Dr **Mark Galeotti** is Director of the Organised Russian and Eurasian Crime Research Unit at Keele University, UK, the first such specialist centre in Europe. He holds an MA in history from Cambridge University and a PhD in political science from the London School of Economics. An acknowledged expert on post-Soviet security, crime and policing, he writes a monthly column for *Jane's Intelligence Review* and is the European Editor of the journal *Low Intensity Conflict & Law Enforcement*. He has worked with many commercial, government, law-enforcement and security agencies, including NATO, the US Department of Defense and the British National Criminal Intelligence Service and in 1996–97, he was seconded to the British Foreign Office in an advisory capacity. His published works include *Afghanistan: the Soviet Union's Last War* (1995), *The Age of Anxiety* (1995) and *Russian and Post-Soviet Organized Crime* (2002).

Dr **Russell W. Glenn** is a Senior Defense and Political Analyst who joined RAND in 1997 and Acting Director of Public Safety Research. His current research includes work on current and future military urban operations, non-lethal capabilities, and US Army force structure. He is a retired US Army Officer with 22 years of service. His military service included peacetime and combat tours with the US Army's 1st Infantry Division, 3rd Armored Division, and other units and organizations in Europe, Asia, and the Middle East. He was an award winning educator at the US Army Command and General Staff College's School of Advanced Military Studies (SAMS) and an author of the army's primary operational doctrine, FM 3.0, *Operations*. Dr Glenn holds a PhD in American History from the University of Kansas and is a graduate of the School of Advanced Military Studies. His publications include numerous RAND reports and articles in US and international journals. He is the author of *Reading Athena's Dance Card: Men Against Fire in Vietnam*; *Heavy Matter*; *Marching Under Darkening Skies*; *Combat in Hell*; and co-author of *Lightning Over Water: Sharpening America's Light Forces for Rapid-Reaction Missions*.

Charles 'Sid' Heal is a Captain with the Special Enforcement Bureau, Los Angeles Sheriff's Department. He has worked in law enforcement for 26 years and is a court recognized expert in law enforcement special operations and emergency management and has lectured throughout the United States and several other countries. His experience with riot and civil disorder situations includes serving as platoon and local incident commander for the 1992 Los Angeles Riots. He holds an MS in management from California State Polytechnic University, Pomona and a MPA from the University of Southern California. As a Chief Warrant Officer-5 he has over 32 combined years in the US Marines Corps (& Reserve) and has served in a variety of capacities in 20 countries. He was the principal advisor for non-lethal options during Operation 'United Shield' in Mogadishu, Somalia, 1995. He is regularly called to active duty and assigned to the Joint Non-Lethal Weapons Directorate, Operational Concepts Cell. Captain Heal is the author of *Sound Doctrine: A Tactical Primer* and *The Diversionary Device Reference Manual* and has written over 70 articles in such publications as *The Tactical Edge*, *Marine Corps Gazette*, and *Military Review*.

Dan Lindsay is a Chief Airport Safety Officer with the Los Angeles Department of Airports assigned to their Ontario International Airport. He has over 20 years of law enforcement, fire, and emergency services experience. His activities include operational-level response to terrorism involving weapons of mass destruction, emerging threat identification, and infrastructure protection. Past duties have taken him to Sweden and

Ghana. He holds a degree in social ecology from University of California Irvine. Chief Lindsay is a contributor to *Jane's Unconventional Weapons Handbook* and *Airport and Aviation Terrorism: Reference Guidebook* and has been published in *Air Beat* and *The Journal of California Law Enforcement*.

Dr **Max G. Manwaring** is a Research Professor of Military Strategy, US Army War College Strategic Studies Institute and Adjunct Professor of Political Science at Dickinson College. He is a retired US Army Colonel and has served in various civilian and military positions, including the US Army War College, the United States Southern Command, and the Defense Intelligence Agency. He holds a PhD in political science from the University of Illinois and is a graduate of the US Army War College. His focus of research is in theory of grand strategy; US national security policy and strategy; military strategy; military and non-military operations other than war; political-military affairs; and Latin America. Dr Manwaring is the author and co-author of several articles, chapters, and reports dealing with political-military affairs. He is also the editor or coeditor of *El Salvador at War*; *United States Security Policy in the Western Hemisphere: Why Colombia, Why Now, and What is to be Done?*; *Gray Area Phenomena: Confronting the New World Disorder*; *Managing Contemporary Conflict: Pillars of Success*; *Beyond Declaring Victory and Coming Home: The Challenges of Peace and Stability Operations*, and *Deterrence in the Twenty-First Century*.

Dr **T. Lindsay Moore** is employed with CORNERSTONE INDUSTRY and is currently designing and writing a series of Joint Professional Military Education courses for Senior NCOs serving on the US Joint Staffs. He also teaches for the Naval War College, College of Continuing Education. He holds a PhD in International Relations/Government from Claremont Graduate University and an LLB from the University of Miami, School of Law. Past courses taught include National Security Decision Making, Theory and Nature of War, Military History, Strategic Thought, and Operational Level of War. Dr Moore has taught at the US Marine Corps, Command and Staff College; Marine Corps University, College of Continuing Education; West Point; Claremont Graduate University; and a number of public universities. He has spoken at the Association of the US Army (AUSA) Annual Meeting, Institute of Land Warfare Program, and at other defense conferences. Dr Moore served in the enlisted ranks from 1956 through 1959. He was commissioned in the infantry through ROTC in 1961 and returned to active duty from 1966 through 1970.

Ralph Peters is a retired US Army officer, an essayist, a failed musician, and an endlessly-amused observer of the human condition. He has published widely on military affairs and security matters, and is the author of two books on strategy, *Beyond Terror: Strategy in a Changing World*, and *Fighting for the Future: Will America Triumph?* He is also the author of 12 published novels, several novellas and a collection of historical tales, published either under his own name or under a pseudonym. He contributes to a range of domestic and international newspapers and journals, and has put in more media appearances than a sensible man ever would have done.

Dr **David F. Ronfeldt** is a senior social scientist in the International and Security Policy Group at RAND. He holds a PhD in Political Science from Stanford University. He has worked at RAND for 30-plus years, initially on US-Latin American security relations, and for the past ten years on social, political, and military implications of the information revolution. He is a co-author (mainly with John Arquilla) of the following RAND publications: *In Athena's Camp: Preparing for Conflict in the Information Age* (1997), *The Zapatista Social Netwar in Mexico* (1998), *Countering the New Terrorism* (1998), *The Emergence of Noopolitik: Toward an American Information Strategy* (1999), *Swarming and the Future of Conflict* (2000), and *Networks and Netwars: The Future of Terror, Crime, and Militancy* (2001). While he continues to be interested in the implications of the information revolution for future modes of conflict and cooperation, he is turning his attention in two other directions: (1) the development of a framework about the long-range evolution of societies, based on their capacity to use and combine four major forms of organization (tribes, hierarchies, markets, and networks); and (2) the development of a framework for analyzing people's mindsets and cultural cosmologies in terms of their basic assumptions, beliefs, and other orientations about the nature of social space, social time, and social action.

Air Commodore **Jasjit Singh**, AVSM, VrC, VM, IAF (retd.) is Director of the New Delhi-based Centre for Strategic and International Studies. He headed India's prestigious think tank, Institute for Defence Studies and Analyses, New Delhi for 14 years (1987–2001). He has published extensively on strategic and security issues including *Air Power in Modern Warfare* (1985); *Non-Provocative Defence* (1989); *Nuclear India* (1998); *Kargil 1999: Pakistan's Fourth War for Kashmir* (1999); and *India's Defence Spending* (2000). He is a retired Air Commodore in the Indian Air Force and has been a visiting lecturer at defense and war colleges in India and abroad.

John P. Sullivan is a Sergeant with a major southern California law enforcement agency. His responsibilities include interagency co-ordination and tactical planning for terrorism involving weapons of mass destruction and emerging threats, as well as implementation of counter-terrorist doctrine and technologies. He is also a researcher specializing in terrorism, conflict disaster, urban operations and police studies. He holds a BA in Government from the College of William and Mary and a MA in Urban Affairs and Policy Analysis from the New School for Social Research, and is a member of the board of advisors for the Terrorism Research Center. He is editor of *Transit Policing*: a journal for the transit police service, and is co-author and editor of *Policing Transportation Facilities*; *Policing a Multicultural Community*; *Emergency Preparedness for Transit Terrorism*; *Jane's Unconventional Weapons Handbook*; and *Jane's Facility Security Handbook*.

Matthew Van Konynenburg is a former US Marine Corps civilian analyst who specializes in global trends, asymmetric threats and complex cultural issues. He was the primary author of the Marine Corps' definitive urban estimate that outlined the cultural challenges of urban operations. He went on to do his Master's degree at the University of Washington which concentrated on NGO/Military integration. He is currently working on concepts to incorporate better use of cultural knowledge by intervening forces and organizations in situations that require a humanitarian and democracy building response. He is also a Senior Analyst with Adroit Systems.

Prof. **Phil Williams** is Professor of International Security in the Graduate School of Public and International Affairs at the University of Pittsburgh. From 1992 until April 2001, Professor Williams was the Director of the University's Matthew B. Ridgway Center for International Security Studies. Professor Williams has published extensively in the field of international security including *Crisis Management* (1976), *The Senate and US Troops in Europe* (1986) and (with Mike Bowker) *Superpower Detente: A Reappraisal* (1987). He has edited or co-edited books on the Carter, Reagan, and Bush Presidencies, as well as on Classic Readings in International Relations. During the last eight years his research has focused primarily on transnational organized crime and he has written articles on various aspects of this subject in *Survival*, *Washington Quarterly*, *The Bulletin on Narcotics*, *Temps Strategiqus*, *Scientific American*, *Criminal Organizations*, and *Cross Border Control*. In addition, Professor Williams is editor of a journal entitled *Transnational Organized Crime*. He has been a consultant to both the United Nations and United States government agencies on organized crime and has also given congressional testimony on the subject. Most recently he has focused on alliances among criminal organization, global and national efforts to combat money laundering, and trends and development in cyber-crime. Professor Williams has edited a volume on *Russian Organized Crime* and a book on *Illegal Immigration and Commercial Sex: The New Slave Trade*. He is also co-editor of a recent volume on Combating Transnational Crime. In 2001–2002 he is on Sabbatical from the University of Pittsburgh and is a Visiting Scientist at CERT/CC Carnegie Mellon University, where he is working on computer crime and organized crime.

Index